Sugar Ray Leonard

Sugar Ray Leonard &

OTHER NOBLE WARRIORS

Sam Toperoff

SPORTS PAGES

SIMON & SCHUSTER

A SPORTSPAGES BOOK

First published in Great Britain by
Simon & Schuster Ltd in 1987

© 1987 Sam Toperoff

SPORTSPAGES
The Specialist Sports Bookshop
Cambridge Circus Shopping Centre
Charing Cross Road
London WC2H OJG

Simon & Schuster Ltd
West Garden Place
Kendal Street
London W2 2AQ

Simon & Schuster of Australia Pty Ltd
Sydney

British Library Cataloguing-in-Publication Data available

ISBN 0-671-65515-9

Printed and bound in Great Britain by
Richard Clay Ltd, Bungay

To Faith Potter,
who owns a heart as big as Ali's

Contents

Introduction

To think we actually choose the athletes, the teams, even the sports that still somehow matter to us in our adult years is like thinking we really choose our passions. It is, of course, a delusion. Our passions and our sports choose us. Personal history and individual temperament seem to make each of us susceptible to the lure of a particular sport, or just as surely to reject it out of hand.

Then there are those all-important class distinctions. Baseball and football are undoubtedly the most popular American pastimes partly because on every social level it is perfectly respectable to be a fan. Other sports are not so widely acceptable. Polo remains the private passion of the set that gives the Concorde a whirl even when it's not on the expense account. Americas Cup racing appeals to rungs slightly further down the social ladder. But even tennis hasn't quite stepped down into the barrios yet. And nowhere has cockfighting replaced a trip to the Super Bowl as a corporate perk.

So it is always interesting for me when the conversation at a cocktail party comes around to favorite sports and I, twenty-five years a university professor and considered highly civilized and reasonably cultivated by most acquaintances, announce that nothing thrills me more than a really good fight. The reactions are pretty much what I'd get if I'd said I adored wrestling or roller derby. I particularly love that combination frozen smile and inhalation of rotten eggs. What can I say? Boxing chose me at an early age and at a lower class. Thank heavens it stuck. The passion came slowly, with time, attendance at some very good matches, and the acquaintance of some wonderful fighters. With education came not the desire to distance myself from an early love but to understand it better, perhaps even to justify the passion I felt.

I'm not at all certain that any passion can ever be explained —especially by words arranged in lines on a sheet of paper. But that's what I've tried to do here. That's what most writers try to do about one subject or another most of the time. And most of the time we fail. There is really no other choice but to struggle on, trying, like most boxers, to make an impact, to show the world, and our friends, we have the heart and the technical mastery to be ranked in the top ten, maybe even to be considered for a title shot someday.

In two respects, above all, the writer's professional life and the fighter's are the same. Both work essentially alone. Advisers advise; family and friends encourage, sure, but in the final analysis it's You Alone vs. Kid White Page, and he's always undefeated. Both lives are full of personal risk. Submitting a manuscript leaves a writer as vulnerable as stepping into a ring, where everyone can see whether you've got it or not.

A book about any passion is about all passions, precisely as any turbulent love affair throws its purple light on all complex emotions. I was in love with boxing from the moment my father popped me in the nose with overstuffed gloves and justified his own pleasure by saying he was trying to make a man of me. I didn't know it was love at the time. I stayed in love with boxing even when I should have broken it off, when I came to know first hand how fighters got cheated, how some of them lost their eyesight and others their lives because the system made them such easy victims of corrupt men. Believe me, a love affair with boxing becomes a very complicated matter indeed.

*   *   *

This book is also, naturally enough, about the men who box, particularly those who have boxed bravely or unusually well during my lifetime. Their ring lives are for me the intensification and distillation of the essential human condition. Whereas most of us live in a protective bubble of anonymity, fighters must risk everything before public scrutiny: Their defeats are open matters and they take their blows on their nakedness (not on pads or helmets); their triumphs are always temporal, and bittersweet for that. Somewhere out in the darkness there is the kid waiting, as they had waited years earlier, for the champion to have that one tough fight too many and take that first step over the hill. When the time comes, youth must be served, age will be served up.

Fighters' lives speak to me in a double way: In the end, of course, we all lose; it's built into our mortality. That's the tragedy of it. But it matters terribly how we face the showdown; go down fighting well and there's nobility even in the face of certain defeat. Tragedy. Nobility. Delude ourselves as we may, there just can't be one without the other. Fighters never delude themselves about these things. They can't afford to.

In selecting a single fighter's career to parallel the story of my developing passion for the sport, I chose the finest fighter of the late 1970s and early 1980s, surely its most successful. Ray Charles Leonard, the fighter who grew to deserve his famous nickname, "Sugar Ray."

The irony here is that I didn't particularly like Ray Leonard when I first saw him box. He had too much flash and brass to suit my taste; I'd seen too many like him zoom through the night sky and burn themselves out when they hit some decent resistance. I also disliked the fact that he seemed to be a media creation: I was told more about him than I wanted to know or believed. In time, though, I discovered I was dead wrong in evaluating the two things that matter most in a fighter—the extent of his talent and the quality of his heart. Ray Leonard, for the relatively short time he dominated the boxing scene, became one of the giants of the sport and notched himself a sure place in its history.

In his talent, in his incredible financial success, in his personal growth, and especially in how little the fight game took from him compared to other fighters, indeed in almost every important respect, Sugar Ray Leonard represents the best that can be thought and said about boxing. As such, I let him stand for the remarkable exception that proves the commonplace rule about the lives and careers of most fighters. There are enough other fighters' lives captured in these pages to ensure that the dark and down sides are sufficiently and honestly reflected.

I discovered also that by examining boxing's best and brightest, the fight game's corruption takes on a new and frustrating meanness: I could see how easily its glaring abuses might be remedied; I became surer than ever no such thing was going to happen. Sugar Ray's brilliance, in other words, also showed how dingy the rest of the arena was and would remain.

The long-shot dream is what makes a Golden Gloves novice fantasize a title shot at Caesars Palace. Or for that matter, a former college professor think he can transmit the complex passion of a lifetime and do it with class and heart. Dreams are fine for starters, but you'd better be ready to deliver the goods when things get down to the nitty-gritty. Only in my fantasy life (an extremely rich and vivid one, as a reader will discover) is Sam Toperoff a respected and recognized boxing writer. This book was written to help make me a contender.

Huntington, New York

CHAPTER 1

Refining Pure Sugar

Amateur rules require that an amateur boxer be seventeen to fight in international competition. So, technically speaking, the boy was underage. But there was an easy, direct solution to his problem—he lied. And Dave Jacobs, his trainer, lied too. As did everyone around him who knew the true story. As you might have in that situation; as I'm sure I would have. They simply tacked a year onto his true age, told them he was born May 17, 1955, instead of '56.

It wasn't that lying came easily to Ray Leonard back in 1972; he simply believed himself to be the best lightweight amateur fighter in the country. Maybe in the world, especially after knocking out two more experienced Russians in his first international matches in Las Vegas earlier that year. He was fifteen at the time. He just wanted the chance to show everybody how good he really was.

When Ray Charles Leonard lied, it was as though sugar wouldn't melt in his mouth—although that's not how he got his nickname. And back in '72, with his hair in a modified Afro, his innocence a good deal fresher (he hadn't yet been asked to be sincere for the cameras), and those intense eyes radiating total honesty, it would have been impossible not to believe him, or at least not to want to.

Hard as it may be to believe, since Ray's adult looks still remain adolescent, at sixteen he seemed at least two years older. A photo showing him lined up with that U.S. team in Vegas indicates a fully developed lightweight, as well-muscled as any of his teammates and better than most. The expression on his face is serious but not joyless.

Afterward, some of the people connected with the U.S. Olympic team in 1972 said that Ray hadn't made the team because they really knew he wasn't old enough. That they'd kept him around to give him experience, to prepare him for '76. Since that information surfaced only *after* the Munich Games, it can be easily dismissed, especially since our boxers were abysmal, winning only one gold that year.

So for a variety of reasons 1972 was not going to be Ray Leonard's year, even though he had arrived in Cincinnati for the Eastern Olympic Trials very highly touted after his big showing against the Russians. To put it bluntly, Ray would have to wait four more years because the amateur boxing establishment was a corrupt buddy system, boxing's equivalent of Cook County politics. People owed people; debts had to be paid, turns taken. Occasionally the best man won.

Ray Leonard, Dave Jacobs, and the Palmer Park (Maryland) program they represented didn't have any buddies, so they were on the outside looking in. They weren't the first to be made to pay their dues; they wouldn't be the last.

If you didn't know any better, you'd think that discovering the most competitive prizefighter would be a good deal less subjective than, say, evaluating schnauzers at a dog show. And you'd be wrong. Because unless a fighter leaves his opponent on his pants or at least works him over pretty good, a reasonably close decision can be bent and justified in a variety of ways.

Ray Charles Leonard was a prodigy, and no one in boxing really likes a prodigy. For most old-timers, who were made to pay their dues by even older-timers, approval for young fighters is bestowed reluctantly and in inverse proportion to the amount of punishment they've taken. In this ultimate school of hard knocks, all natural talent is very suspect. It would throw the whole system out of whack, cast all self-sacrifice into the area of doubt.

Leonard had won the National Golden Gloves lightweight championship less than two years after he committed himself to Dave Jacobs' boxing program at the Palmer Park Recreation Center. His progress was extraordinary.

During an earlier rite of passage in Washington, when Ray was seven, at a time when the family members were living six to a tiny apartment in D.C.'s inner city, Ray took the blows of another seven-year-old at the L Street Boys Club. Those punches prompted the first of his many retirements from the ring.

Ray came out of retirement at fourteen, after the family had moved to Palmer Park, a black Maryland suburb looped by the nonstop traffic on the Capital Beltway, and almost immediately rediscovered the medium in which he expressed himself best. Ray didn't know he was one of the Gifted Ones, those rare individuals who discover early not what they should or could do with their lives but what they were born to do. At fourteen he threw himself into boxing completely and passionately.

Of course the Gifted Ones are not entirely fortunate. The world of nongifted, ordinary men, operating out of narrower possibilities and who are easily threatened by something different, makes the gifted pay a high price. In the presence of genuine talent, died-in-the-wool boxing people, who tend toward extreme conservatism, feel very uncomfortable.

Training for young boxers is in many important respects like preparation for classical ballet. There are prescribed maneuvers, attacks and counters, for every conceivable situation. All have been time-tested; when properly executed, they work. There are, as well, a limited number of punches—jab, hook, cross, uppercut— to be mastered by repetition in very precise fashion and then thrown in effective and pleasing combinations. Economy of movement and balance that increases force are the telltale signs that a boxer has been well trained.

Sometimes—in dancing masters as well as with boxing coaches—an appreciation for good form produces a classicist. More often, it produces a martinet, an unimaginative second-rater who uses drillmaster authority to cover a multitude of inadequacies. Many of the men judging Ray Leonard in 1972 were such types.

Ironically, the basics were already there in the kid for those with eyes to see. His sense of balance was remarkable, as were his instincts; he moved as he should, when he should; he punched with form and economy much of the time. Too many of the men who mattered on the U.S. Olympic Boxing Team chose to notice the sometimes flashy style and not the solid substance.

There were moments back then when Ray did get carried away with his own possibilities in the ring, when the artist in him thrilled to the chance once again of transcending his limitations. During those moments no one outside his head could possibly understand what he was doing, why, or feel what he felt while moving and dodging and risking. There were times when he felt he could do whatever he wanted. He could circle by gliding in either direction; he could cut off the ring and corner an opponent or avoid being cornered. He could step in behind his lightning jab, throw a swift orthodox combination, and then do a variation on the same theme, knowing instinctively where the target would be even before it got there, and then slide back out of harm's way—Ray could do it all literally before you had time to check your watch. Even he —or he most of all—so enjoyed the rapture of the proper moves perfectly timed that he let his exuberance show.

Why not show the crowd just how quick he really was? That's when he might wheel his right glove around bolo style as a distraction and wing in the left. Or, like the young Ali, put himself purposely in danger and escape without the opponent landing a blow. Like every really fast black kid, Ray did a mimicking version of the Ali "shuffle" to put a little spice in the combat and a flourish in the dance.

See, see all the stuff I can do. Enjoy me as much as I do. That's the message he thought he was sending.

But that wasn't what was coming across. Dave Jacobs, the trainer who had set up the boxing program at the Palmer Park Rec, told him the judges didn't cotton to that stuff. Looked too smart-ass. Made the other fighter look bad. Bad strategy all the way around. And using Ali as a model was the worst part of it.

The boxing establishment, which was overwhelmingly white on both the amateur and professional levels, despised Muhammad Ali. They had stripped him of his heavyweight title for his conscientious objection to the Vietnam War in 1967, and even in '72 were still calling him Cassius Clay with great relish.

But even earlier in his career Ali's tendency to use the ring as a backdrop and boxing as a medium of personal expression offended the so-called purists, the boys who remembered better, whiter days. The real irony in Ray's mimicry of Ali was that for years afterward the style, the shuffle, the double and triple feints, would mask an artist every bit as original and of comparable quality.

Still, no one could legitimately deny the talent, and even less the results. The kid had never been beaten. Nevertheless, here's the sort of thing you heard them saying about Leonard: Sure, the kid was good, real good. Genuine prospect. But at least Clay was eighteen when he won the light-heavyweight gold medal at Rome in 1960, and he'd already been boxing five years. There were other fighters and, more important, trainers who'd been standing in line much longer. Wouldn't it really be better for the kid to shoot for Montreal in '76? Such was the justification already being prepared for why 1972 wasn't going to be his year.

It'a funny how, when they're not going to give you your due, they take perverse pleasure in showing you how it's really for your own good. Precisely the sort of rationale a threatened Antonio Salieri could have constructed for another wondrous teenager who hadn't paid his dues, Wolfgang Amadeus Mozart.

Although there may have been some unpleasant aromas spreading in Cincinnati, Ray and Dave weren't sniffing. They believed the champion would ultimately have to select himself in the ring, as he should. In this most individualistic of sports, Ray could control his own destiny, or believed he could.

He sliced through his early opponents as though they were his mother's apple pies—fast and with pleasure. What surprised some of the experts—and would continue to do so throughout his career—was Ray's punching power. It is often assumed in boxing circles that a fighter who has excellent hand speed, who moves and slips punches well, can't really hit. And certainly hasn't got the taste for being hit. And it is a reasonable assumption, based on the unlikelihood that a flashy boxer would also be a complete fighter. Or, put another way, that virtuosity could come in a tough package.

In the fight game it takes years to change first impressions, if you're fortunate enough to change them at all. Early on, Ali had that problem too. Because he was so brash and so talented, word spread that he didn't have "heart," couldn't take punishment. The criticism bothered Ali so much that in some of his early championship defenses—the Chuvalo fight comes to mind—he allowed himself to be hit just to show he could take it. Later, with his rope-a-dope strategy, he used taking an opponent's punches as a tactic—one very costly to his health, it turns out.

Most trainers, when they talk about heart, the *sine qua non* of professional boxing, usually bend courage into machismo and that into masochism. "Only way to tell if a fighter has heart," says New York trainer Rocky Davis, in an irreducible definition, "is if the other guy is beating the shit out of a guy and he fights back." And that's where classical ballet and boxing part company.

Ray Leonard, with only one notable exception in his career—the first Duran fight in 1980—neither relished nor saw tactical advantage in being hit. For him, boxing could be reduced to the same mystically simple objective as for the sixth-century martial Zen master Bodhidharma: "To strike without being struck as cruel repayment."

When a very fast young fighter, a boxer type, as opposed to a puncher or a counterpuncher—fight people sometimes call them "movers" or "stickers"—steps inside the danger zone to hit, he doesn't ordinarily stay close enough, long enough, to deliver many heavy blows. In addition, because movement is uppermost in the hit-and-run fighter's value system, it is rare indeed to see a mover who has the balance and the leverage to throw knockout punches.

But Ray had been putting opponents down consistently, and at a greater rate as the level of competition rose. One reason very few observers appreciated his punching power was that hardly anyone could see his best combinations. His hands were so quick—among the quickest ever—his movement so easy, the shifting of weights so natural that there would be a glide, a flurry, a blur, a whirl, and the other guy would go down awkwardly, almost as though he'd stumbled or been tripped. Faced with the contradiction of floored opponents and the abstract judgment that the kid was quick but not a puncher, boxing people stayed with the label. Why? Because in a business where fighters were typed early and the label stuck no matter what, Ray was strictly a boxer and that was that. Besides, Ray was a pretty boy, and everyone knew pretty boys didn't like to pay the price. It was as though "heart" rested only in ugly chests.

In Cincinnati there was a notable, if private and low-key, exception to the judgments being made about the teenager from Palmer Park. Tom Johnson, a middle-aged black man everyone at the trials seemed to know and respect, thought Ray Leonard was something very special. That mattered. "Sarge" Johnson was perhaps the best trainer of amateur fighters in the United States. He was also an assistant coach on our Olympic Boxing Team.

Men like Sarge Johnson are the backbone of boxing and one of the best things about the sport. Extremely knowledgeable and kindly, they find poor kids who like to fight and teach them how to fight. A few kids become good fighters; more of them learn to live a little better. In the usual scenario, unfortunately, these first, local trainers are usually dumped when a promising fighter turns pro. That's also generally the first step a fighter takes toward misfortune.

There's a story in the fact that until his death in 1980, when a plane crash in Poland took his life as well as the lives of some of our best amateurs, Sarge never became head coach of a U.S. Olympic Boxing Team. After the crash Ray would say what most of the fighters already knew: "Sarge was the guy who pulled our Olympic team together for Montreal in '76." The recognition was belated and not widely enough appreciated.

Back in '72, Sarge would watch Ray working out, tip his pork-pie back on his head, smile, and hum as though he were tasting something delicious. Versions vary as to exactly where and when Sarge Johnson anointed the boy as the new "Sugar" Ray—it was either there in Cincinnati or after the finalists were selected in Fort Worth—but there's no doubt it was Sarge. "That kid you got," he told Dave Jacobs, "is sweet as sugar." The nickname stuck, but it wouldn't be well or widely known until Ray became a media star at the '76 Olympics in Montreal.

Given his style and the *Ray*, the "Sugar" was probably only a matter of time, just as a chubby pool shooter is automatically called "Fats," or a mean, black lineman becomes "Bubba." To boxing people, though, there was only one legitimate "Sugar"—Walker Smith, who fought under the name Ray Robinson. But Sarge Johnson was boxing people too; and he knew precisely what was at stake when he offered the name. It was more than an evaluation—it was a legacy.

Dozens of fighters since Robinson's salad days in the 1950s called themselves "Sugar," and even the best of them were about half as sweet. In the narrow, mean-spirited passages of boxing, to call yourself "Sugar" was at best foolish, at worst sacrilege. For Ray Leonard, the nickname gave boxing insiders yet another reason to dislike the kid.

It was funny, but names always seemed to hold unfulfilled possibilities for him. His mother, Getha, christened him Ray Charles, hoping that the talent of the black soul singer she adored would be transferred to her youngest as though by sympathetic magic. And could her sweet boy sing! Not in the rough-throated, bluesy style of his namesake, but in a smoother, cleaner manner that other members of the church choir envied.

He quit the choir about the same time he got serious about boxing. It isn't fair to say he broke his mother's heart, but it was close. A new name, a new destiny were waiting to be fulfilled.

No one, least of all Ray, could have known back then that he was destined to be one of those rare fighters, indeed almost unique among non-heavyweights, to bring boxing to a much wider audience, to people who hadn't heard of an earlier "Sugar." To them, *he* was the original. And it was just the right name for just the right fighter and personality, coming along at just the right time.

If you believe that some people are simply luckier than others, that fate, or chance, or destiny, or whatever, has singled them out for preferential treatment, Ray Leonard's career supports that belief. Not that all the luck was good—it wasn't. But Ray even had a way of slipping misfortune a combination and copping the decision when all the cards were finally tallied. In a game that's known for breaking people, even champions, this is a notable talent. No doubt about it, Ray was not only among the Gifted, he was one of the Lucky Ones too.

Even the name was an example of good luck out of bad. Sarge offered it partially as a consolation when it became clear to him that Ray wasn't going to make the team. As a matter of fact, Johnson had his own kid from Indianapolis, lightweight Norman Goins, who he was pushing for the same spot. Johnson had a special affection for Goins, a kid he'd known and brought along for years. Kindly as Johnson was toward Leonard, he, like most Olympic boxing coaches, had conflicting interests—Cook County politics again.

Because they were in different brackets, the likelihood was that Leonard and Goins would meet in the finals. Johnson was hoping the better fighter would emerge clearly in the ring, eliminating a difficult and perhaps unfair decision. That's what he was hoping, even though he knew the two kids were very close, mostly because Goins was much more experienced.

The fight never happened.

Ray stepped into the ring for his semifinal against Greg Whaley knowing everything was on the line. Occasionally in the past he had taken an opponent lightly; no chance of that happening with Whaley. Nine minutes—three three-minute rounds—to prove again he was the best amateur lightweight boxer on earth.

Can't take anything for granted with Whaley, Dave Jacobs explained. He's sneaky fast. Lots of experience. Got heart too. Don't count on putting him down. The strategy: Box him. Score points. Hurt him if you can, but mostly try to outbox him. Don't let up a minute.

Amateur boxing, especially in tournaments, is much chancier than the pros, where an opponent's style, tendencies, his strengths and weaknesses are well known, often captured on tape and viewed repeatedly. More often than not, if you're an outsider in the amateurs, you draw a kid you've never seen, or not seen often. Watching Whaley fight earlier in the week, Dave and Ray couldn't tell very much. Best approach, then, is to take the first few minutes to see what he's got. In three-round fights, though, there isn't much margin for error. Figuring an opponent quickly was one of Ray's instinctive talents, fortunately: He had speed enough to experiment and get away with some dangerous stuff.

Whaley caught Ray early with some clean shots that impressed the judges. From the punches, Ray deduced that Whaley wasn't a big enough hitter to hurt him, so he did more counterpunching than usual. Whaley took a good deal of punishment in the fight. To his credit, he never stopped throwing punches himself.

It was, by all accounts, the best fight of the tournament. As he stood in the center of the ring with the referee, waiting for his hand to be raised, Ray was thinking about what a good fight Whaley had put up. You couldn't deny the guy's courage. When the ring announcer's mike echoed, "Winner . . ." Ray's arm twitched reflexively upward. ". . . Whaley."

Ray Leonard had never been beaten before, and he had never been as confused in a boxing ring as he was during those next few seconds. From the darkness beyond the ropes he heard the boos and catcalls. He saw Whaley smiling and waving into the darkness; he saw Whaley's people leaping gleefully around the ring. He saw Jacobs yelling and pleading at the judges. Whaley came over and said something Ray didn't understand. Ray kept muttering, "Good fight, good fight." He walked around the ring in circles waiting for Jacobs. Still it hadn't hit him completely.

Dave Jacobs threw an arm over his shoulder. He was talking about lodging a protest. The fans crowding the aisle on the way to the dressing room continued to boo the decision and told Ray as he passed that he'd been robbed. Ray was numb. Didn't quite know how to react. Didn't know how to explain it.

Whaley was from Cincinnnati. That explained it. Hometown boy, hometown decision. As much a part of the fight game as the ring ropes. But even in the realm of bad decisions, this one was terrible. All night and into the next morning, other fighters and trainers, reporters and fans who came by told Ray he'd gotten a raw deal. He smiled and shrugged.

When you're sixteen it takes a while to understand all the implications of a specific defeat, especially when it's your first. In this case it meant no Goins fight in the finals; in fact, no finals. No Olympic Boxing Team, no Munich for Ray that July. He was invited to Fort Worth for one last look before the team was chosen, but that was just to keep him interested; he never fought in that tournament.

Years later, when time and events had transformed bitter disappointment into nostalgic recollection, Sugar said, "That first loss in the trials was a real bummer. I gave that kid Whaley an awful beating." It wasn't an overstatement. Greg Whaley was unable to show for the finals against Goins. In fact, his taste for competitive boxing had been quenched; Greg Whaley never fought again.

The Olympic coaches knew that Leonard was too good a prospect to lose; they also knew that four years are an eternity for a kid and that many things could intrude and cause him to lose interest. Tom Johnson knew that too and made sure to stop by with some encouraging words before Ray left Fort Worth for home.

A lot of things can happen to a young fighter in four years, most of them bad. Family problems, job problems, girl problems; he could get caught up with the wrong crowd; drinking or drugs; most commonly, though, he could lose his taste for the rigors of training, which is as continually unnerving to most boxers as perpetual diet is for most jockeys. Every trainer has a heartbreaking story about a superb prospect who lost his way out there, all of them ending as poignantly as Marlon Brando's soliloquy in *On The Waterfront* when ex-fighter Terry Malloy says to his brother, Charley, "You don't *understand*. I could've had class. I could've been a contender. I could've been somebody."

Ray Leonard somehow avoided the pitfalls. And the temptations: He even turned down some attractive offers to turn professional. Ray's life back in Palmer Park had a single obsessive long-range goal—to win the Olympic championship in 1976.

Talent and luck hardly ever hook up in life; in boxing, they're as rare in combination as the classy boxer who has heart. Sugar Ray was that double rarity. He was so lucky, in fact, that even adversity had a way of reshaping itself and working to his advantage. Although it was a major blow, not making the '72 team was in retrospect the best thing that could have happened to Ray.

First of all, the Munich Games were remembered for nothing so much as the terrorist attack that left among the Israeli athletes dead. If Sugar Ray were destined to burst on the scene, Munich could not have been the launching pad.

Secondly, it is not at all certain that Ray would have taken the gold in '72. The overall level of competition in his class was higher that year, and the Pole who won the lightweight division was a much cleverer boxer than the Cuban Ray put on the canvas in Montreal to win the light-welterweight gold medal four years later.

The U.S. team in Munich was an unmitigated disaster. Only Ray Seales won a gold. James Busceme, the fighter who had decisioned Norman Goins in Fort Worth after Ray had been withdrawn from consideration, was easily defeated in the third round of Olympic competition. With the exception of Seales and a West German middleweight, all the other titles were taken by boxers from Soviet Bloc countries. The showing was so disgraceful, U.S. team coaches knew they had better produce in '76 or face a house cleaning. It was no longer a matter of owing Ray Leonard—they needed Ray Leonard.

In many ways '72 was the dark cloud that provided the backdrop to the golden lining four years later for Sugar. The fame and the wealth that were to arrive with television exposure were unsuspected by everyone, especially by Ray. So you could argue that the most important thing about the year Ray *didn't* make the Olympic team was how much he'd learned and how his appetite for success had been whetted. Call it "refining Sugar."

In deeper retrospect, however, something even more important happened as a result of the painful lesson Sugar was taught in 1972. It was the last time the boxing establishment—*any* boxing establishment, amateur or professional—ever got a piece of Sugar Ray. And there are very few fighters, including some of the greatest of champions, about whom that can be said.

CHAPTER 2

A Good Little Man

Although I'd never have called him that within earshot, in the streets and schoolyards of the old neighborhood a kid was expected to call his father "my old man." Well, my old man, who ran a depressingly dark and failing candy store in Brooklyn, required of his son two skills above all: to be able to make change of big bills accurately and to defend himself with his fists. He was my first, last, and only trainer.

During those times when the store was empty—and there were plenty—he'd put on the gloves with me near the public telephone in the back of the store. I was seven when we started. After weeks of working on the stance, and months on the proper form and order of punches, we began to spar. My old man's been dead for thirty years, but it's remarkable how clearly and lovingly I now recall those punishing lessons in self-defense.

Specific phrases stick indelibly in my mind. "The object," he'd explain at the start of every session, "is to hit and not be hit. Repeat that." And I would. "For every problem, there's a solution. Everything is completely up to you. Your fate is in your own hands," said the candy-store individualist. Since my first lessons came during the tail end of the Depression, it's clear to me now that some matters are not in your own hands. They surely weren't in his.

My father died poor and unsuccessful in the world's eyes in his mid-fifties. He never saw Ali or Ray Leonard box, but he'd have loved them, particularly Sugar Ray. He wasn't partial to heavyweights; he loved the little men. If he didn't quite give me the skills to keep myself from getting whipped half a dozen times in the schoolyard, he gave me an eye and an appreciation for superb boxers.

Like most trainers I've seen at work since, my old man kept up a crisp chatter while we sparred. "Jab—jab—step in—hook—back away." It was never clear, though, if those were instructions to me or if it was what he was doing to me as he spoke. All I know is that there wasn't a hell of a lot to hit every time I waded in. His belt buckle was my only reasonable target. I still see it, the brass unpolished, his initials barely distinguishable. He had such a tactical height and reach advantage then—not to mention experience—that every time I went for that target, punches rained down on my head from every angle. My old man, I realize now, must have been working out a lot of his own frustrations during *my* boxing lesson.

I hated those sessions. And I loved them. The plum-colored gloves were soft, the cheap ones you'd get at a department-store toy section. They stung and rubbed rather than popped you hard even when you got hit flush. I swear I can smell them now, especially after they'd been moistened with my sweat and tears; I can taste the cheap leather, like acidic cardboard on my lips, as his glove lingered on my mouth like a taunt after he'd stuck a jab in my face.

My eyes got watery early in the lesson, after his first few jabs got in on me. My best defense was my version of the peek-a-boo style that Cus D'Amato, the boxing strategist, designed for Floyd Patterson more than a decade later. My old man, a purist about such things, would not abide such unorthodoxy. "Proper stance," he'd say. "Tuck in that chin," he'd say. "Bob 'n' weave, bob 'n' weave." Then, biff—biff—bam, he'd find me with two jabs and a left hook.

Between rounds, which were of arbitrary duration, he'd provide the philosophical underpinning for why I was learning to box the hard way. Back then I didn't think I was even listening. Who pays attention to a lecturing father? Now I can recall every phrase, or think I can. "There are times when there's no one to protect you in this world, so you have to learn to take care of yourself. A kid calls you 'Dirty Jew,' what're you gonna do? Run away? Make believe you didn't hear it? And if it's not that, it'll be something else. That's the way this world is. It stinks. Of course we"—his eyes indicated the apartment above the store where my mother was cooking—"will protect you, but there will come a time when you'll have to be able to take care of yourself in all ways. If you can use your fists, there's a limit to how much guff someone will try to give you." *Guff* was a word back then.

His version of Polonius's speech reduced not to "This above all—to thine own self be true," but to what he always said when he pulled my ear to indicate we were ready to go again—"It's all a matter of self-respect."

The thing that bothered him most was my tendency to close my eyes when I threw a punch in close. It was a natural reaction that he assured me could be overcome by willpower and training. I didn't believe him. (Recently I discovered that Ray Leonard had the same tendency and didn't overcome it until well into his amateur career. The discovery pleased me.)

It's funny, but I remember these workouts occurring only on rainy or overcast days; the lighting in the rear of the store was particularly gloomy. It was a melancholy activity in fact as well as in memory. The best part of my training came after we went a few rounds and a customer finally came in to break the mood. Rarely did we go back to my training after a customer stayed for a few minutes. When we were alone again the hard little man would usually soften. "Want a malted?" he'd say by way of offering a reward. I always nodded yes.

I'd sit on the ice-cream case and he'd tell me about fighters he'd seen, always starting and ending with the man he called "the greatest fighter ever to lace on a pair of gloves": Benny Leonard.

Before TV changed the world, fathers and sons talked about important things. And you saw boxers only if you went to fights or, as in my case, if your imagination recreated them from spoken words. Thinking back to what my old man told me about Leonard and his fights, I perceive the same elemental and even mythic qualities that have been part of boxing's mystique for thousands of years.

We're talking about men participating in an activity that is to a very great extent ritualistic and which stretches back even beyond Homer's description of a title fight in Book Twenty-three of *The Iliad*. That's where the first classic match is described in great detail, a contest between "the wily, compact, clever-with-his fists Epeius," and the puncher Euryalos. Even a blind man like Homer knew a sucker bet when he saw one. Although the "huge, well-built Euryalos" was a superior warrior, Epeius, the boxer, the sticker and mover, was the smart money.

It ended early when Epeius—who was the guy who thought up the Trojan horse, naturally enough—slipped a punch, moved in close underneath, and "leapt out with a long left hook and smashed the other's cheek as he peered out through puffed eyes." My old man would have backed the winner because Epeius, like his idol Benny Leonard, could "hit and not be hit." The boxer would win every time, or just about. It was almost as though he was telling me that a good little man could beat a good big man if he knew what he was doing. My father was one for going against the conventional wisdom. He was also five feet six, 135 pounds.

Leonard, he told me once, wasn't Leonard at all but Benny Leinert, a Jew. That was a surprise to me because I thought Jews were supposed to shun fights if they possibly could in favor of violin lessons and solving math problems. His nickname was "The Ghetto Wizard," a combination of magic power and perverse pride. [Fighters' nicknames, by the way, convey a great deal about the ritual warrior nature of the activity. "The Manassa Mauler" (Jack Dempsey) and "The Michigan Assassin" (Stanley Ketchel) are fairly well known, but consider if you will the fright created by "Easy Dynamite" and "Super Human Power," a pair of misnamed Nigerian middleweights of the 1950s. Both were beaten by a fighter who was to become a particular favorite of mine, Richard Ihetu, who won two world's championships under the wondrous name Dick Tiger.]

My old man described and demonstrated the Wizard's toughest fights round by round, recreating in detail Benny's remarkable hand and foot speed, but better than that, his ability to double and triple feint. Terrific. Unfortunately, I was cast as the out-classed and vulnerable opponent. "That's why," his voice slowed dramatically to indicate a very important moment, "he was known as the world's first scientific fighter." Just as I'd suspected, math problems, the stereotype after all.

Leonard, it turned out, was also a great talker (my old man wouldn't say braggart) both in and outside the ring. And since he held the lightweight title for over seven years, the non-Jewish public must surely have had quite a dose of this tiny proto-Ali. I sensed, as my father talked, the tribal element in boxing—namely, an ethnic people investing in their representative, their "champion" in the chivalric sense, their aspirations and their desire for esteem. It was precisely what Negroes were feeling at that time for Joe Louis. And Jews as well, but to a lesser extent, after "The Brown Bomber's" one-round knockout of Max Schmeling, the German champion, in 1938.

Even though he had me hooked, my old man was saving the best for last. Almost as an aside, he said, "I can personally attest to how great Leonard was. When we fought I couldn't even touch the man with my jab."

"Fought! You fought Benny Leonard!"

"Sure. Didn't I tell you?"

"No. Where? When?"

I sat on the ice-cream case. He leaned against the shelf that held the glasses. "We were in the Army together in the war." He didn't have to say which war, for it was the only other subject of his that truly interested me. "Benny and I. And he was supposed to put on exhibitions at the Governor's Island barracks, where we were both stationed. No one would even step into the ring with the man. So finally I volunteered. What could he do, break my nose?" The humorous allusion to his own flattened nose, which could not have been disfigured more by man's hand than by nature's carelessness, caused my old man to break into a rare smile.

He and the soon-to-be lightweight champion of the world fought a series of exhibitions, according to my old man. Although he could rarely even touch Leonard, Benny didn't exactly have his own way either, to hear my old man tell it. I guess I believed his history. Clearly this was far and away the highlight in the otherwise uneventful life of an unsuccessful candy-store man. Then, in the most magical of moments, his eyes flashed and he said, "Keep your eye on the place for a minute." I heard rummaging in the storeroom.

I could make out a glossy photo in his hand. He let my antic-ipation build before handing it over. A picture of a boxer. My first true reaction was a wave of disappointment. The fighter, or rather the pose and the garb, looked archaic. For openers, the dark hair was slicked down and parted dead in the middle. In 1940 no one would have been seen dead looking like that. Or *only* seen dead. He wore a shirt that had shoulder straps and was ribbed, for God's sake, a lot like my old man's underwear. The shorts were thigh-length and skintight; they looked like cutoff long johns. It was a downer all the way around.

There was script in ink across the fighter's spindly legs. The handwriting had the same rounded generosity as my father's. It read "To Murray and that *very* quick jab. Best, Benny."

My old man told the story and brought out the photo three or four times a year thereafter until I was fourteen, the year I retired from the ring. Unlike most aging fighters, I have stayed retired. I realize now, as I sensed then, there were always little discrepancies in my old man's Benny Leonard stories. One time a particular round would be fought on Governor's Island, another time it was at Fort Hamilton, another Fort Jay. In one version they went three rounds, in another four. In one they didn't wear headgear, in all the others they did. Same with mouthpieces. The sizes of the crowds and who they were rooting for varied too. No matter. It was my old man's reality, the highlight film of memory.

Three times in my life I saw my old man fight. Two of those three times, he was really egged on; I saw him try to resolve matters peacefully but he could not. The first two were with cus-tomers, and we were living above the store where I got the boxing lessons. The third was in Manhattan.

The first was with a boozy Irishman who said my father had shortchanged him on a carton of cigarettes. The second was with a big Swede who claimed my old man had sold his son a defective hockey stick. In both instances he managed to get them outside the store so the cases and the merchandise wouldn't be damaged. Crowds gathered on the street. The opponents struck first, or attempted to, with amateurish roundhouses like you see in the movies. The Swede, I recall, grazed the top of my old man's ducking head. Then in a flash he was inside their swings, and his fists moved upward almost imperceptibly, his elbows like pistons. They each "ooof-ed" comically and crumpled at the little man's feet as though deflated. He reddened, looked around embarrassed, and sent me back inside the store ahead of him.

"Didn't want to hurt my hands on them," he explained. "And I didn't want to break their bones. They're the kind that sue. Soon as I saw they were brawlers, I knew I could get them scientifically." Both Leonards—Benny and Ray—would have loved my old man in action in front of the candy store. I did.

Then he went on to explain the science of delivering the solar-plexus punch, which was the great mystery blow of his youth, a tactic used by Bob Fitzsimmons, another scientific "little" man. Fitzsimmons was the English middleweight who moved to Australia and won the heavyweight title in 1897, the year my old man was born, by bringing Jim Corbett to his knees with the solar-plexus punch. The Englishman weighed 167, Corbett 183. In a career that spanned thirty-five years, Fitzsimmons terrorized much bigger men. His last match, at the age of fifty-two, was declared no decision, the equivalent then of a draw.

It seems that the vulnerable area just below the chest and above the stomach, when struck properly with force, simply knocks the wind out of an opponent, causing him to deflate like Corbett, the Swede, and the boozy Irishman. Every time we sparred thereafter, I shot for that spot with all my might and never hit it once, taking plenty of cuffs on the ears for my trouble. Finally I came not to believe in the solar-plexus punch, at least until a few years later when I got hit with a beauty in a schoolyard fight with Jackie Perpulski. I never told my old man about the fight or the punch because I was actually the one who picked the fight, egged on by some of the bigger kids who didn't like Jackie. It was humiliating as hell down there on my knees, not being able to breathe or to get up. All the kids that had rooted for me till I got hit disappeared as though they owed me money. There was an important lesson in that too.

My old man showed me the defense for the solar-plexus punch, as he did for every situation. "It can work only when the other guy steps straight in. That's what Fitzsimmons saw in Corbett's style—he walked straight in, especially when he got tired. So you always turn sideways when you advance, that way his blows will always glance. And bend, too, never stay straight up."

I recall saying, "There's so much to remember."

And his saying, "That's what makes it so scientific."

I don't know why precisely—it wasn't my birthday, nor had I reached a plateau of distinction as a candy-store boxer—but my old man did something very rare and, it turned out later, important in my life. He announced he was taking me to my first fight. Not only that, but we were also going to watch the fighters working out in Stillman's Gym in the afternoon. What was remarkable about the proposal was his agreeing to leave the candy store completely in my mother's hands for the better part of a day.

The year was 1947. I was thirteen and already as tall as my father. I remember it exactly because later that year Joe Louis beat Jersey Joe Walcott on a split decision in the first TV fight I ever saw. Boxing fans earmark time by important fights they've seen, as more respectable people do with movies, songs, or the car they were driving. Actually, I thought Walcott had won the fight; it was a judgment my old man saw as sacrilege.

About that day with my old man, some of the most important things that happened are impressions, made fuzzy in the mind with unsure brush strokes; others are etched now as sharply focused photographs. For example, I know where we ate dinner—Child's Restaurant on Broadway and Fifty-seventh. I know what I ate—I can see my roast beef under steaming thick gravy against mashed potatoes and peas on a blue-bordered plate. But I can't for the life of me remember who was supposed to fight the feature bout that night at St. Nicholas Arena.

Similarly, if there weren't some old-timers around who remember working in Stillman's when it was *the* fight gym in New York, I wouldn't know precisely where to place it. All I remember my old man saying was that "it's over on the West Side." It was actually on Eighth Avenue between Fifty-fourth and Fifty-fifth streets, not far from the old Madison Square Garden. In 1959 it became a garage. When Stillman's was torn down, the *Times* obituary quoted Damon Runyon on the gym's best days: "Stillman's is an open sesame to low society in any part of the world." I sensed that even at thirteen, and it was thrilling.

We got there by taking an elevated train and walking to a trolley and then walking some more. The afternoon sun was pale, the air still held a winter's crispness. My old man, who rarely went anywhere, imprisoned as he was by his profession, walked very briskly. The entrance to Stillman's had a heavy metal door, rusted over and partially painted green. Inside that door an old man in a newsboy cap pointed to a sign—"25¢." My old man gave him a half dollar. The old guy motioned at me with his chin and shrugged; he handed back a quarter.

The sounds amazed me. Rattling speedbags, the grunts of fighters, the thud of fists on the heavy bags, jump ropes smacking the floor. I was particularly taken with the crossovers the rope skippers could do, and I vowed to begin mastering the technique first thing in the morning. What I never expected was that many of the fighters sparring in the various rings made threatening noises timed to their punches, growls and whooshes and snorts. Also, the smell of the place had hit me like a poisonous atmosphere. It was as though every foul male odor that my mother warded off over a lifetime with ammonia and scrub brushes had been welcomed here, encouraged to root and fume.

Men in blue and brown suits, most of them with cigars in their mouths, lined one wall and watched the scores of sweatshirted boxers, many of whom were black. I hadn't ever seen so many black men in one place in my life, except in *Gone With the Wind*. My father walked me along the far wall until we found an out-of-the-way vantage point beyond a distant ring but before a wall of mirrors, where two tiny fighters were shadowboxing and admiring themselves like showgirls.

"That's Lou Stillman over there," my old man whispered, pointing to a gray-suited, owl-faced man who reminded me of a mean-spirited Ed Wynn. He walked about with an air of proprietorship, his thumbs in his vest, a smirk on his face. Sometimes he sidled up to a guy with a cigar, leaned alongside against the wall, and spoke out of the side of his mouth.

We watched and listened for a very long while. I discovered that the odor, in time, had a satisfying underscent. Bells rang automatically at three- and one-minute intervals, the exact periods of rounds and rests. There was something to see everywhere. In one of the rings two black fighters sparred; only the lighter one wore headgear. In other rings trainers wearing pads on their hands like catchers' mitts were bobbing around taking punches instead of baseballs on the moving targets. Arriving fighters were being gauzed and taped; others were having their midriffs peppered with medicine balls; a few were getting rubdowns. I'd never imagined a place like this existed in the world. Open sesame!

Every time my old man saw a boxer in the lighter weights doing something he'd already shown me, he'd touch my shoulder and nod in the direction of the lesson being properly demonstrated. I acknowledged. Whenever a heavy fighter lurched forward off balance or threw punches with a brawler's wasted effort, he indicated the sin with a superior smile on his face. We watched in a timeless void of bells and cracking leather.

The spell was broken by a flurry of activity near the door. Much of the motion in the place slowed; sounds diminished and heads turned. A large brown man in a sandy rich camel-hair coat, surrounded by smaller brown men, was shaking hands, smiling shyly, nodding to some of the distant fighters. I recognized him before my father did, but he looked so much like his photos I refused to believe it was really him.

Slowly Joe Louis worked his way back through Stillman's. Serene welcomes of "Hi ya, Champ" preceded his advance like genuflections before the Pope. He acknowledged them with a little wave. He was almost upon us when my old man whispered, "Ask him for his autograph." I didn't have a pencil, nothing to write on. I said, "Nah," as though I had chosen not to pester him.

Joe seemed to be bathed in an aura as he passed. I remember distinctly how perfectly set were the glistening, skull-tight waves and how immaculate was the wide part in his dark brown hair. His jaw was smooth and immense; his darker lips did not part when he smiled; he smiled mostly with his eyes. A white silk aviator's scarf lay casually across his shoulders.

He was very close now and my old man prodded me forward. Fortunately, Joe was looking away as I almost brushed his arm. I can still recall the way he smelled: a combination of ripe fruit—

a pear perhaps—and a nut-flavored sherry. The moment has never faded.

I met Joe again, at a San Antonio motel, in 1977. It was as brief an encounter as at Stillman's. I was in San Antonio doing an investigative article for a national sports magazine on a very spurious boxing tournament that Don King, the promoter, was packaging in various cities for ABC television. King's tournament contained just about everything that stunk in boxing: falsified fighters' records, shoddy medical examinations, mismatches, kickbacks, some very questionable decisions. Joe Louis was part of King's traveling circus, his presence at ringside an attempt to lend the promotion a touch of class, if not credibility. He was asked only to sit prominently at ringside and sign autographed photos, not too different from the sort of thing he'd been doing as a greeter at Las Vegas casinos for a few years already. Not exactly *Requiem for a Heavyweight*, but for the greatest heavyweight of his era, close enough.

I stepped out of my motel room into glaring sunlight on my way to the restaurant for breakfast. It was too early for the fight crowd to be up and around. Not for Joe. Although he'd put on a good deal of flabby weight in the thirty years since Stillman's, he looked smaller to me. The hair was sparse and dull, his familiar face puffed to the limit of recognition. Joe was having great trouble trying to extract the local newspaper from a coin-operated machine. I moved closer. Joe, who wore a loose, short-sleeved gray shirt and corduroys, was muttering. He said to me, in a broken stutter like an untutored child, "Help . . . with . . . this . . . darn . . . thing. . . ."

Truth was that for a few seconds I couldn't figure it out either, and the coin release wouldn't give back his change. That's when I noticed the double slots, one for weekdays, the other for Sunday. It was a Sunday morning. I put two quarters in the proper slot and the machine gave up a paper wrapped in comic strips. Joe picked it out and mumbled his thanks. Time and boxing had diminished him in almost every way; only time had been working on me. I watched him trundle away. Sentimental as I knew it was, I whispered, "You're welcome, Champ."

But my singular day with my father was far from over when

Joe left Stillman's, entourage trailing. We stayed till dark, had our fancy dinner, and walked farther uptown through the crisp night air. We hardly spoke, content to watch our vaporous breaths and to think private thoughts of having crossed paths with a demigod.

St. Nicholas Arena, up past Columbus Circle just off Central Park, struck me as a weird cross between an old concert hall and an abandoned warehouse. My old man bought us seventy-five-cent tickets, and because we were among the first to arrive, there was a small sea of empty folding chairs between us and the brilliantly lighted ring. He said, "Up high gives the best perspective." If that was true, we were in the catbird seat.

My old man's eyes glowed with a curious pleasure I knew was intended to pique my interest. He had a secret. I refused to go for the bait. As four-round preliminaries of no distinction but plenty of knockdowns tumbled by us, the arena filled to about half. I sensed my old man's secret straining to come out. At last he said, "That referee, you know him?"

Of all the things I'd been taken with at my first boxing match, the referee was not one of them, even though he'd handled a great deal of action—stepping into lots of clinches, backing crude fighters into neutral corners, warning for hitting on the break and low blows, counting over knockdowns. I began to pay more attention. Gray shirt, darker pants, blue bow tie, black leather sneakers; short, about the same height as my old man, a bit thicker through the mid-section, though. Dark hair plastered in place. Aging movie-star face, George Raft maybe. I waited an appropriate time before I said, "Who?"

"Who? Who? Greatest fighter ever to lace on a pair of gloves. The Ghetto Wizard himself."

"Wow!"

"Maybe we'll go back to see him after."

I immediately began to pay much more attention to the referee walking in brisk circles around two plodding light-heavyweights. Benny Leonard, my independent research had convinced me, really was one of the greatest fighters of all time; he'd held the lightweight championship for seven years, seven months, a record for any champion. No wonder he'd left his mark on a generation of working-class boys. Nevertheless, it was unthinkable for me that he could have been any better than Joe, or Willie Pep, or Ray Robinson, the best of the active fighters then. The fighters of your youth, like the movie stars, the ball players, and the popular songs, are and always remain the best. So I tried hard to be tolerant of my old man's memories.

In the semifinal, two boxers, their names and weight divisions long lapsed into oblivion, answered the opening bell and touched gloves in the center of the ring. I do recall that the darker man wore white trunks, the lighter one black. I watched Leonard's footwork. This was his fifth or sixth bout of the evening, and he no longer even attempted to take those mincing toe-steps that indicate a referee is on top of things. Before any serious punches were thrown, I saw Benny stumble slightly and he toppled off balance toward a neutral corner. There he grabbed the top ring rope and fell to his knees. Neither boxer noticed, and they worked into and out of a clinch by themselves. Black trunks noticed first and got struck for his inattention.

Leonard released the rope and fell sideways; then he rolled over onto his back. A handler with a towel rushed in from one of the corners. Both fighters were watching now. The bell was rung twice and twice more. All the spectators were on their feet.

Other handlers, a doctor, some officials and friends surrounded the fallen man. At first the boxers huddled around too, but they eventually retreated to their corners. For a while they did some suggestions of shadowboxing, but as minutes stretched into a quarter of an hour, they sat on stools, getting up periodically and shaking out arms and legs, windmilling heads and shoulders.

Many minutes later, a stretcher was carried down the aisle. Leonard was slid gently under the ropes and from the ring apron on to the stretcher. He disappeared in the darkness beyond the aisle opposite us. The ring announcer told the buzzing crowd that the fight was canceled. The disappointed boxers left the ring.

"He'll be okay," my perspiring old man said. "Just overcome. The heat. The lights."

Benny Leonard was already dead, had died almost the moment he tumbled. The radio the following morning established the time as 10:55 P.M., the cause as cerebral hemorrhage.

"It's late already," my old man said. "The main event won't be much. Your mother will worry."

The last time I saw my old man in action was just before he died. It was on West Forty-third Street just across from *The New York Times* building. He had a small soda stand there that catered mostly to the newspaper's pressmen on their breaks and cab drivers who worked the Times Square area. One particularly warm afternoon, an immense, swarthy cabbie ordered my old man's coldest soda, flavor didn't matter. When he got it he said it was warm as piss, refused to pay for it, and poured it contemptuously on the sidewalk. My old man came through his cubbyhole in no time flat and didn't even bother to set up his famous solar-plexus punch. He went to the jab exclusively.

The cabbie had his fists clenched and up in front of him, chest high. But my old man's jab found parts of his face anyway. And with each punch he shouted, "Not cold, eh?" When the cabbie raised his hands higher my old man jabbed under the defense into the chest. When the hands dropped slightly—"Not cold, eh?"—he struck the cheek. Hunting and pecking in this manner, and using only the lightning-quick jab that had perhaps impressed the Ghetto Wizard, my old man began to back the big guy up. A crowd of pressmen and other cabbies formed around them and the movable fight glided toward Seventh Avenue, past the rear doors of movie houses, past the dance school, toward Bickford's restaurant. I stayed to guard the soda stand and witnessed the retreat. A few times the cabbie tried to make a stand, but my old man's intent, his staccato rhythm, his maneuvering were too much for the outclassed buffoon. It ended somewhere near the sandwich shop. The cabbie was bleeding slightly.

When my old man got back to the stand he looked ashen and it took him a very long while to get his breath. He sat out of sight on a soda crate sucking for air. Before he recovered fully he explained to me that he didn't really want to hurt the guy, only to humiliate him, the way he'd been humiliated. That explained the single-punch strategy. "Everyone knows," he wheezed, "my sodas are the coldest in town."

That was his last fight. It had been five years since I'd sparred with him—we didn't have the room either in the stand or at our tiny apartment. I didn't think I'd miss that jab in my face as much as I do now.

My father died the following year. A combination got him—a sudden heart attack and a profound sense of failure. But he'd demonstrated to his son in a variety of ways how a good little man, scientific and courageous, could beat a good big man.

CHAPTER 3

No, I'm Finished

Looking backward, it's very easy to squeeze time into tight accordion pleats. But when you're sixteen and it's 1972 and you're only living for two weeks in July of 1976, time has a way of unfolding before you like an endless, slow-tempo chord. For Ray Charles Leonard the first few months after the debacle of the U.S. Olympic Boxing Team were so charged with commitment, they flew by. Although he was a bit disappointed by the team's terrible showing in Munich, Ray knew it meant a major improvement in his own fortunes. He trained so hard, so quickly there was a real risk of burnout before '73 was over.

Once again, in uncanny fashion, the fulfillment of his destiny came in the form of setbacks, which, viewed individually and out of context, would seem like the worst possible luck. In fact, they almost turned him away from his consuming quest for Olympic boxing gold. But if any boxing career is testimony to the ultimate power of destiny, as well as commitment, it is Sugar Ray Leonard's.

The first major problem began to develop early in the year in the form of increasingly severe pain in his hands, particularly across and between the knuckles. The discomfort had begun in

1972, but it was just that, discomfort. Now Ray's feverish activity had aggravated the condition, one that many if not *most* fighters face as an occupational hazard. Tendonitis or, worse, calcium deposits around the knuckles have ended a good many careers and made lots of others sheer agony.

If, as the poet says, the eyes are the windows to the soul, to a fighter, the hands are the front and back doors. Without useful hands a fighter is nothing, not soul, not heart, not bread or butter. The legs take you in position to do some damage; the eyes and brain see and select the punching combinations, but only the hands can complete the assault and win the fight. Yet even eight- or ten-ounce gloves tend to flatten or "pack" during a fight, making them more lethal as weapons but less protective to hands, especially if those hands are tender and belong to an amateur, who must use only prescribed wrapping techniques.

In a tortured simile about fighters' hands, Paddy Flood, a cynically sweet (he'd have bristled at the adjective) New York fight manager, now deceased, once told me, "They're like the pearls [he actually said *poils*] that are made by an oyster [*erster*]. They come from impurities, but the oyster wraps them and wraps them until they're smooth as pearls. Believe me, I know how to wrap poils."

Somewhere along the way, though, either from the continual use of his fists in unnatural fashion, maybe from an unlucky mispunch (usually against the skull, the hardest part of human anatomy), or a conformational vulnerability, a boxer will probably run into hand problems. To hear my old man tell it, back around the turn of the century, as a carry-over from bare-knuckle days, toughening the hands was a normal part of a fighter's training. Long soaks in pickle brine were standard, but he also recalled a bizarre variation—horse manure that was allowed to dry over the fists. Its curative power was a lot less potent than its stench, he thought.

The modern approach is to lay off for a while, to cushion the knuckles as much as possible in training so the more intense pain can be limited to the the match itself, when the flow of adrenaline might be able to mask much of it. The danger in such an approach, of course, is that a fighter so psychologically anesthetized could, and probably would, do himself even more serious damage.

Ray recalls having hurt the right hand seriously in the 1973 National Golden Gloves tournament, but doesn't remember the specific punch that did the real damage. His hands had long been tender and subject to lingering discomfort, even after a workout on the heavy bag. It was clear that this might be a problem for him during his entire career. If he wanted to reach his goal in '76, he'd have to finesse the situation, ease off a little from time to time, and get used to living with pain the rest of the time.

Medically, the condition was diagnosed as an inflamed synovial membrane, a calcium buildup in the tissue around the middle knuckle of the right hand, that causes tremendous swelling and numbing pain when the hand makes contact in a punch. It leaves many fighters with an arthritic condition, but that's usually the least of an old fighter's troubles. Conventional treatment while active: ice packs, Epsom salts baths, willpower.

Ray Leonard's hands, now that his career may be over, are not the blunt instruments you'd imagine as weapons necessary for a successful ring career, although rough use has distorted and marked them a little. The most surprising thing about them is their finely boned delicacy. The fingers are long and tapered, and Ray uses his hands in an expressive, Mediterranean manner when he speaks.

If a chiromancer, one of those rare practitioners who believe you can read character from the shape and lines of a hand, had examined Ray's mitts, she'd have seen the side of him that Getha Leonard had hoped would be the dominant one—the sensitive, the soulful, the artistic side. And that element of creative temperament was undoubtedly there, but in Ray's case it was used to find ways to win prizefights. Yes, all there in those hands, precisely where Ray was most vulnerable, an aspect of his character that made him special as a boxer, capable at certain times of being moody and unpredictable, but also of being able to rise to unparalleled heights of brilliance and inventiveness. In 1973, though, the most significant thing about those wonderful hands was that they hurt like hell all the time.

If hand problems cause promising fighters to quit, there was a problem trainers feared even more. So frightening is this destroyer of boxers that most managers and trainers won't even discuss it in their fighters' presence. The word itself may stigmatize their boys as if by a voodoo spell. O, fatal enemy of pugilistic dedication, thy name is Woman.

With boxing, as with most of the oriental martial arts, deprivation and an almost monastic commitment to purity have been the main method of training fighters. But it's a relatively recent approach in boxing. History tells us that boxers up until the turn of the century tended to be crude louts who could down their booze and broads as effectively as they could their opponents. That image began to change with the defeat of the beer-guzzling "Boston Strong Boy," John L. Sullivan, in 1892 by "Gentleman" Jim Corbett, a fighter who would show the world the superiority of speed and conditioning over boasting and brawn. Corbett also gave away thirty-four pounds.

That championship match happened to have ushered in the modern era since it was the first to have been contested by what were called "big" gloves. The win by Corbett reawakened a dormant classical tradition in which the boxer was not merely a bully but a virtuous and brave young man whose sacrifice and cleverness would be rewarded by positive results. The Golden Boy tradition was carried along through the century by many of the boxers my old man admired. Sugar Ray Leonard would surely have been among them. But there was many a Golden Boy who turned base by yielding to temptation.

"Don't tell me about dames," Paddy Flood moaned one day, pushing the air away from his face with beefy hands as though it were contaminated. "I could give you a list of fighters ruined, completely buried by dames, that would break your heart." These fighters had obviously broken his heart, and he shuddered at the thought. "There's two ways. First, they come between a fighter and his manager, and nothin' should do that. But they do. They say they won't and that they don't want to, but they always do. Then there's all that screwin'. I don't care what they say, it can't help. You've been laid, right? When it was over did you want to jump out of bed and do road work?" Paddy Flood rested his case, glowing with irrefutable logic. But it wasn't completely rested: "A fighter with woman trouble is like a guy fighting with one hand tied behind his back. Only it ain't his hand that's tied up, if you get my drift." He winked obscenely, if you get my drift.

You couldn't honestly say Juanita Wilkinson was a woman. She was a girl, the kid who lived down the block, the teenager who went to Parksdale High School with Ray, and she was pretty and fun and bright. It took a while for him to get up the nerve to ask her out, but when he did she said sure and they got on easily. Juanita came to the gym after school to watch Ray work out; they'd go to the movies occasionally, but more often they went to her house or his to eat and watch TV. Only a fight guy as cynical as Flood could possibly have anticipated trouble.

Dave Jacobs, a former professional fighter himself, knew about the traditional pitfalls outside the ring and early on determined that Ray would avoid all the major ones. Said Jacobs, "When he started I told him he had to train hard, and I never had to worry about him running around every night."

Juanita Wilkinson told Ray Charles Leonard she was pregnant early in the summer of 1973.

Abortion was quickly ruled out. The most common scenario then, for teenagers like Ray and Juanita, was to marry quickly. Then they move in with the folks until they can save a little money. Ray, of course, quits school, finds a job, maybe at the gas station, maybe at the supermarket where his father, Cicero, works. Maybe he'd even try to turn pro, but then, good as he was, he could end up just another fighter, having to take matches for the money, go into fights over his head, find himself at thirty poor and exploited, maybe damaged. It's happened to plenty of very good fighters.

And what about the Olympic dream? How much resentment or downright bitterness would build if the dream were taken away? And how in the world could such a marriage ever survive? But there were also genuine responsibilities: This was his woman; this would be his child, not an impediment to his own fulfillment. Maybe he'd keep working out in the evenings, trying to get enough time off from work to compete in important amateur tournaments, keeping that Olympic hope alive. There were some tough decisions to be made.

Juanita and Ray's decision was courageous—and very unconventional. They'd have their baby and Ray would be the legal father, but marriage would be postponed until after the Olympics in July '76. Juanita Wilkinson was wise enough to know that a Ray Leonard without a chance at his dream wouldn't be much of a husband, not the sort of man you could grow old with. In an extraordinary act of unselfishness and intelligence, she allowed Ray the chance to live out the dream. She dropped out of school. Ray, Jr. was born in late November.

It was probably foolish for Ray to think that life could go on pretty much as before, without guilt pangs, mood swings, depressions. Ray was not at all himself through much of '74 and '75. It would have been impossible for him to have maintained his intensity under the best of conditions for so long a period, and probably unwise anyway. But his state of mind, even more than the condition of his fists, took much of the pleasure out of his boxing activities. He didn't relish training as he used to; he seemed distracted a lot of the time.

In the 1973 National AAU finals in Boston, Ray was upset, cleanly beaten by Randy Shields for the junior welterweight championship. The decision was incontestable. Now Ray had still another worry: He had a potential rival for the Olympic berth he believed he had a lock on, a rival who took some of Ray's best punches and came back with punches of his own that connected solidly.

Later that same year Ray lost twice more, to the Russian champion, Anatole Kamnev, in Moscow, and to Kazimier Szczerba in Poland. These losses didn't cloud his Olympic dream as much as the one to Shields because in each instance the local hero was beaten but awarded the decision. Kamnev, in fact, acknowledged as much by walking across the ring, bowing, and generously presenting Ray the winner's trophy he had been given. There were reasons to worry about the losses, though. First of all, they were on his record, a reality that depressed Ray; more important, they were reminders of how tenuous his goal was. An off night, a lucky punch, another lousy political decision, and everything he and Juanita, their families, and Dave Jacobs were risking would all be lost, stolen. Ray Charles Leonard second-guessed himself a thousand times during those slow-moving, introspective months.

During some tournaments there were too many matches for his tender hands, sometimes as many as three in a single day. So Ray saved himself, punching in flurries, sometimes trying to look impressive rather than being impressive, scoring points rather than taking out opponents. There was no denying the fact that the intensity wasn't always there; fortunately, it wasn't absolutely gone either. Ray could usually turn it on for national tournaments like the Golden Gloves, the AAU championships, and when friends from home were there or TV was covering. The natural "hot dog" in him could make him scintillate for an important match; the Shields fight could be dismissed as an aberration.

Eventually, that long, unfolding accordion note of time played itself out, and the tempo turned upbeat. Suddenly, and at the same time not so suddenly at all, Ray's activity began to have a focus, a foreseeable destination—Montreal in mid-July—and there was real work, not just busy work, immediately ahead. Summer '75 offered the Pan-American Games; Ray had to do well there if he hoped to come up to the U.S. Olympic Trials (again scheduled for, ugh, Cincinnati) as the dominant fighter in the 139-pound class. After the June trials there would be another month of intensive Olympic Boxing Team competition at the University of Vermont in Burlington. Then, finally, what Ray had fantasized since the rebuff in '72, the end of the long journey to prove he was the finest amateur junior welterweight boxer in the world—the ring in the Olympic Stadium, Montreal, Canada.

With the end at last in clear sight, the goal seemed achievable again. The personal sacrifices, the sacrifices of the people who loved him, made a lot more sense, so Sugar Ray rededicated himself to the final assault. Juanita Wilkinson, who too often in the years since Ray, Jr. was born had felt isolated, hung in there too.

The Pan-American Games were a little scary because they proved to be so incredibly easy. The Cuban fighters were, as always, expected to be very tough; that was precisely what Ray was looking for in order to prepare himself for the world's best. The Cubans were clever. They didn't want to show their best fighters in certain weight classes with the Olympics coming up, so Ray never had a chance to meet Andres Aldama, the big puncher who figured to be his opponent and a force at Montreal. Ray won the championship of his division effortlessly.

In Cincinnati, at the trials, only one fighter was believed to be in Ray's class. That was Bruce Curry. Form held up, and they met in the finals. Good thing Curry wasn't a local boy. Ray won a unanimous decision. One other piece of good luck: Randy Shields, almost immediately after beating Ray in the AAU's, had turned professional and removed himself as an obstacle to the Olympic gold medal.

The *Sports Illustrated* article on the trials finally gave Ray the national attention he'd deserved for a while. It described Leonard as "nearly a cinch for the gold" and quoted Rollie Schwartz, AAU boxing chairman and Olympic team manager, at length. "Ray Leonard is the greatest amateur I've seen in my thirty-eight years of amateur boxing. He has the fastest reflexes and the greatest balance. Reflexes like Muhammad Ali, balance like Sugar Ray Robinson. . . . Right now he could beat any lightweight or welter-weight in the world, amateur or professional." That last statement, of course, wasn't true, but it wasn't all that preposterous either. The only distortion was the "right now."

Ray Leonard fought, the article also noted, "with a picture of his girlfriend and his son taped to his right sock." On the face of it, the detail had nothing to do with Ray's skill as a boxer. Why, then, was it there? Try this as a possibility: The magazine had tabbed Ray as a comer, not merely another fighter with a chance, but as something special. So it was important to make the readers—middle class and white for the most part—understand the kid's predicament and do it in a sympathetic fashion. Even though Ray's wasn't the family situation the magazine would have preferred, the photos in the piece showed Ray's love and fidelity for Juanita and Ray, Jr. The editor had opted to leave the infor-mation in because the year was 1976 and sexual attitudes had changed dramatically. In addition, the kid was a potential star, very bright and articulate, not your typical ghetto fighter at all.

Here's the point. One of the benefits of winning an Olympic gold in this media age was to cash in on the exposure. Ray was aware of that; it was one of the things that drove him on during the tough times. It was hard enough being a black amateur athlete; what corporate entity, as the expression goes, would willingly iden-tify itself with the father of an illegitimate kid on top of that? It is very significant that *S.I.* didn't have any major problems with these unique "human interest" touches. With an athlete who lacked Ray's talent and "sugar," it wouldn't have been worth the effort. In 1972 it probably wouldn't have been possible. By 1976, though, there was something admirable in a young man not only accepting responsibility for but openly adoring that cute kid and his "girl-friend."

When the media descended on Burlington, Vermont, in June to dig for angles on our Olympic boxing team, Ray Charles was a remarkable story just waiting to be discovered and exploited. Precisely because he never tried to "hide" Juanita and Ray, Jr., the information was passed along with surprising matter-of-factness. When ABC Television, which was going to televise the Olympics that year, arrived on the scene, it was not merely to report on the team's preparations and chances but to look for potential stars with that special flat-tube charisma. That task was the personal province of Howard Cosell, who would handle ABC's Olympic boxing coverage.

Jimmy Cannon, the crusty old New York columnist, used to summarize Cosell sarcastically in the following manner: "His name is Cohen. He wears a rug. And he tells it like it is."

On occasion he actually does.

In certain limited respects ABC Sports and Cosell have been good for the boxing business. They were very good for Ray Leonard. They, more than the other networks, managed to make boxing attractive to fans other than the hard-core boxing types. Boxing's general appeal can, of course, be traced to Ali and the eruption of the great social forces of the sixties and seventies that he came to symbolize. By identifying so closely with Ali early on, Cosell insinuated himself and, by extension, ABC into the Ali phenomenon.

Additionally, by introducing their regular boxing shows with a feature billed as "Up Close and Personal," ABC made fighters seem like members of the human race. They were shown informally, with their families, in the gym, sometimes at their regular or part-time jobs, talking about their backgrounds and aspirations. Viewers could then develop a human interest and a rooting interest in fighters they might never have heard of before, people they would never have met. An articulate young man with talent and an attractive camera personality, one whose promising career was just shaping up, was exactly what ABC was looking for.

To give Cosell his due, he had known instinctively and from long experience that you couldn't "manufacture" a media star. The boxing talent simply had to be there. So did that magic on camera. Ray Charles Leonard, the one they were calling "Sugar" and who looked like a cuddly puppy as well as a sure thing for the light-welterweight gold, was Cosell's pick. Cosell had picked right.

Ray, Jr. and Juanita were neither avoided nor overplayed as part of the Sugar Ray story. Rather, they constituted just the sort of "indiscretion" that, at a distance, a viewer could be sympathetic with and forgive, thereby creating an even stronger identification. As a potential media star, Leonard was handled by the normally caustic Cosell in a manner extremely sympatico. Cosell and Leonard quickly learned to use one another lovingly and effectively.

After all those years of sharpening his skills and plying his craft excellently but in relative obscurity, Ray Leonard was really ready for the fuss everyone was making. To hold up his end of the bargain, Ray was more than willing to tell and show the world how good a fighter he really was, all within the bounds of an acceptable modesty. So what if it put even more pressure on him to win. It was a good, invigoratiag pressure as opposed to the wearying kind of late '73, '74, and early '75, when he simply had to win to put himself in position for this potential pot of gold, even though no one out there was paying particular attention.

What better example that Ray was one of the Lucky Ones than the fact that his time came in '76 rather than in '72. The national fervor loosed by the bicentennial celebration peaked in July to coincide with the Olympics. In addition, the easy access to Montreal by American fans was a very different matter from a flight to Munich. This time Ray Leonard was in the right place at the right time. And he was the right sort of kid to become a star. All he had to do was be charming—and win.

Ray was expected to win the the light-welterweight championship in Montreal. Cosell told millions of Americans he'd win. Pat Nappi, head coach of the U.S. team, said for publication, "This Leonard kid . . . throws better combinations than Ali, he has a professional left hook, a sharp jab, and throws the right from a dozen different angles. Then, of course, he also has the great legs. And remember, he's just twenty, but already a tremendously poised fighter as an amateur. If he ever chooses to turn pro, there's no telling how far he might go."

Nappi meant what he said, naturally, but he'd gone on record with it just before what promised to be some of the toughest matches of the Olympic tournament, the three fights leading up to the finals. Nappi had judged Ray as the sort of kid who got better the more pressure you put on him; the greater the expectations, the deeper Leonard would have to dig. Nappi was dead right.

Because the quest to be an Olympic champion had been not merely weeks or months but years, his entire adolescence, in fact, Ray was likely to fall apart after he got to the mountaintop, *if* he got to the mountaintop. His hands were killing him, but as he approached his final goal there was a strangely satisfying, bittersweet quality to the constant ache, which the ice packs and Epsom salts baths soothed only slightly.

When Ray easily decisioned Kazimier Szczerba, the Pole who'd beaten him in Warsaw two years earlier, the last fighter to defeat him, it was Sugar Ray's fifth decision in the tournament. In each case the five international judges were unanimous in choosing Leonard. So clear was his dominance that even where political pressure and national pride usually influenced objective judgment, it was simply not possible for them to justify any choice but Leonard. He was pitching an Olympic shutout, fulfilling all expectations.

Form was holding up elsewhere in the division: Andres Aldama, the Cuban puncher who also figured to be there at the end along with Ray, had knocked out all of his opponents in the first or second round, usually with a deadly left hook.

Ray had beaten all his opponents in the manner that my old man's idol, Benny Leonard, would have, by punching in classic, flashing combinations and moving out of danger fast—in other words, by hitting and not being hit, the elementary principles of boxing. He was so sharp, he took perhaps three solid punches in his five matches. For Aldama, however, Sarge Johnson, the assistant coach, proposed a different strategy, one that absolutely defied the safer go-with-what-got-you-here mentality so common with unimaginative coaches in every sport. Because it was a change, it was risky. Had it failed, Ray's career would surely have taken a different course.

Johnson noticed that Aldama needed punching room to be effective. Like all the Cubans, he was well conditioned and technically quite skillful. His hook was so powerful that if it caught Ray coming in or backing away, it might drop him, and one knockdown, or even a standing eight count, which is a discretionary call in amateur boxing imposed if the referee thinks a fighter has been hurt, could tip the decision to the Cuban. If the fight were longer than three rounds, staying away from a dangerous opponent until you have an idea of what he can and can't do and then going after him later makes some sense. A three-rounder calls for something else.

Sarge Johnson believed the way to beat Aldama was to stay right on top of him, smothering him so he had neither the distance nor the leverage to connect with his big punch. He also thought Aldama was vulnerable to the body but couldn't be sure because no one had stayed with him long enough to try him there. Head coach Nappi supported the theory, and Ray, whose active mind and naturally adventurous spirit loved the element of surprise in the strategy, was grateful for the opportunity to show still another dimension of his talent. Because he was obviously very quick and skillful—the boxer type—few fight people were aware of his strength or willingness to mix it up inside. Ray Leonard went to sleep dreaming of the unusual tactics that would make him the Olympic gold medalist with his 145th victory in 150 amateur fights. And his final one.

The plan to drive from Palmer Park to Montreal in his van if Ray made it to the finals had been in trainer Dave Jacobs's mind for a while. He hadn't liked relinquishing his tutelage to the Olympic coaches, but he had no choice. After thinking things over, he knew he wanted to be there for the triumph in which he'd played such an important part. Showing up with Ray's folks and Juanita at the eleventh hour might be just the emotional boost Ray needed.

What Jacobs hadn't counted on were Ray's older brother, his younger sisters, and friends—finally, ten in a van that was already crowded with six. Cicero Leonard's boss at the supermarket wasn't enthusiastic about allowing him to see his son's big moment, he thought the father ought to be content watching the fight on TV. He vowed to dock Cicero's pay for any time he missed.

Taking turns at the wheel, they drove all day and all night; sandwiches, thermoses, unscheduled roadside stops; missed turns and wrong turns; the music that got on people's nerves, the conversation that was sometimes even worse. But they finally made it in time for the big fight. Ray was surprised and certainly appreciated the effort. But he didn't really need it to get himself up for the fight.

Aldama never had a chance. Ray Leonard fought the perfect fight before an encouraging international crowd, but mostly Canadians, that had come to appreciate him almost as much as Cosell had, and for purer reasons. By getting off first repeatedly and pressing the dangerous Cuban from the opening bell, Leonard upset Aldama's composure, threw off his timing, and took away his punching room.

But although Ray was consistently beating Aldama to the punch and landing more punches, the Cuban never backed off. The two came together hard and often in the center of the ring with Ray smothering Aldama's punches usually before they were properly launched. Slowly, Aldama began to come apart, revealing his frustration first by lunging forward before they closed and then by using his left more as a roundhouse than an economical hook. In the second round, somehow thinking the Iranian referee had indicated "step back," Aldama dropped his hands and drew away. Ray caught him with a clean left, and Aldama, stunned but not hurt, was knocked off balance to the canvas, where he was forced to take an eight count on one knee.

If that single punch had determined the outcome, Ray's victory would have been tarnished. Fortunately, it didn't. The referee also had to give Aldama a standing eight after Ray threw a barrage for which the Cuban had no adequate defense. So with the crowd chanting "Su-gar-Ray," and with the small Palmer Park contingent stamping and crying and cheering right along, Ray Charles Leonard was awarded a unanimous 5-0 decision for the sixth and final time in the tournament.

In the ring Ray was confounding most ABC viewers by parading triumphantly with a banner no one could quite identify. An American flag of sorts, but not quite. The orange, white and blue banner bore the insignia of Saint Georges County, Maryland, of all things, and was a too subtle hint of what he was about to tell the television audience and, later, the press. Ray Leonard intended to go home and stay home.

What he had to say to an international TV audience seemed very emotional, the relief of a man who had made an extreme, extended effort and had somehow finally achieved an impossibly distant goal. His impulse was to turn away quickly, almost in disbelief, before the immensity of what he had accomplished became unreal, a dream only. Even as Cosell was telling the English-speaking world of the golden future that beckoned before this young boxer, Ray was shaking his head slightly.

There was neither doubt nor regret in Ray's voice, only weariness, when he said, "No, I'm finished. . . . I've fought my last fight. My journey has ended. My dream is fulfilled." The poetic temperament had revealed itself at the peak of success. Ray Charles Leonard had retired himself from professional boxing before he'd begun. The following day there were eleven in the van back to Palmer Park.

It was our most successful boxing team in Olympic history. Leo Randolph (flyweight), Howard Davis (lightweight), Michael Spinks (middleweight), and his brother Leon (light-heavyweight) also took gold medals. They all intended to use their Olympic successes to vault themselves into promising professional careers. Not Ray Leonard.

In light of the relatively fast unretirement that followed, some cynics believed Leonard's actions were part of a calculated plan to create even more public interest in himself and his career. That tells you more about the cynics' conspiratorial view of life than about Ray Leonard. Sure, he was a kid who had learned to use the media, and loved doing so, but he wasn't Machiavelli.

Ray had announced his retirement for a variety of very understandable reasons. First, he had aimed for that single goal so arduously and purposefully for so long that when he had attained it his body and his mind simply cried, "Enough!" And his hands hurt like hell.

But he also had a very practical plan: he intended to use his success and public exposure as other prominent Olympic athletes had, to do endorsements and television commercials. Mark Spitz seemed to do all right, and Bruce Jenner was going to give it a shot, so Ray, with a scholarship to the University of Maryland, a gift from the grateful citizens of Glenarden, Maryland, planned to study business administration and communications, marry Juanita, and make a comfortable, nonviolent, middle-sized niche for himself in the world.

There were those who thought such a plan naive. It might be an option for certain white amateurs, but it had never really worked for black Olympians. Not for Jesse Owens, not Wilma Rudolph, not Rafer Johnson. Ray was aware of that, but he believed that just as sexual attitudes had changed, so had racial ideas. He thought America was ready for the change; he also believed he had that certain magic on camera to pull it off; that his youthful exuberance, his good looks and ingratiating style, if they could not eliminate racial resistance, might at least be able to circumvent it.

Because his plan never really got off the ground, we can't know whether or not it would have been successful. I'm inclined to think that, with experience, Ray would have been able to jump the color line because it is less skin tone that matters on the tube than the degree of menace a black man projects. And Sugar Ray has always come across as the kid down the street, the kid you don't mind integrating the neighborhood.

The media scenario became totally academic when, a few days after Ray returned from Montreal, the Washington *Star* hit the street with some stunning news: "Sugar Ray Leonard Named in Welfare Dept. Paternity Suit."

Yes, Juanita had indeed filed an application to receive $156-a-month child-support payments from Saint Georges County. No, Juanita hadn't told Ray about the application. Too ashamed, she claimed later. Yes, Ray was indeed the child's father, but he'd never tried to hide the fact—why did the newspaper story make it seem as though he did? No, it was not the sort of news with which a would-be All-American boy launches an ad campaign for any major product in the United States of America. So much for the dream of resting forever on Olympic laurels.

It would be a while before this bad news could be undone. A while before pure chance stepped in once again and turned Olympic gold to bankable green.

CHAPTER 4

Learning with Losers

My love affair with boxing's losers happened by chance. A close college friend became a reporter for United Press International in 1963, and although most of his time was spent sending minor sports stories out on the national wire during his night shift, he also quickly became the guy who covered the weekly fight beat in New York. Not the "senior" boxing man, the "regular" boxing man. That meant Brooklyn, Queens, and the Bronx as well as the bonus of Madison Square Garden just about every Friday night.

The senior man covered the big fights—title shots at Yankee Stadium. Only if the main event at the Garden had some special interest to the sporting world, or if he wanted to impress some dame, did the senior man claim one of the two press passes set aside for UPI at ringside. That's why most Friday nights I was the "other" UPI man at the Garden. I got bumped from my ringside seat maybe half a dozen times over the next three years. That created no particular hardship for me, boxing being in such general decline then that free seats in the first few rows were easy to come by once you were a familiar face at ringside to the Madison Square Garden boxing department.

My friend and I were usually joined by two or three thousand others, on a generous count, only about half of whom were likely to have parted with any cash. My friend usually banged out 150 to 300 words, depending on the reputations of the main-event fighters, on an old Royal portable. His copy was purely factual, the content and form tightly prescribed by UPI policy. It was who fought, who won, where, when, how, how many people attended, how the winner won, what he said afterward, names and weights and results of any significant prelims. Not exactly the sort of stuff you win Pulitzers with.

In those moribund days for boxing the people who made fights found themselves in the same predicament as the people who made hats: A few were being sold to the older folks who were used to them but most just sat on the shelves. Those were the dark post-Marciano, pre-Ali days of the early sixties. Never do I recall the old Garden feeling anything but cavernous for a nontitle fight, and that was what we had most Fridays, except when we were kicked aside for the circus, the rodeo, the horse show, or the Ice Capades. Usually the crowd was so sparse the management arranged it in the sections on the Forty-ninth Street side of the ring so the TV camera opposite created the illusion of a reasonably full house. In bars and living rooms in Akron and Bakersfield— good fight towns out there—it must have seemed that boxing was still alive and well back in New York.

All of those Forty-ninth Street "customers" were included in the attendance figures. So were numerous empty seats. You see, it was more important that professional boxing in New York appear to be breathing than that the receipts appear respectable. In fact, just after the main event began at ten o'clock, a runner would circle ringside with handouts purporting to be the official attendance. My friend agreeably stuck the preposterous numbers in his story so those folks in Akron and Bakersfield would know their eyes hadn't deceived them. "They bus in claques for tenors at the Met, don't they?" he explained, using artistic license. The Madison Square Garden boxing department was grateful.

"Papering the house" is what the cognoscente called the practice. Actually, the house was doubly papered if you regarded the placement of the crowd as a theater backdrop. Where the people line ended, just beyond camera range, no one sat, absolutely no one. It was as though nine tenths of the seats in the place had been quarantined. Most of the paying customers were in the ultra-cheap seats in the side balconies, barely visible in the darkness, and present only as staccato voices, especially on those nights when a promising kid from Spanish Harlem was on the card.

Boxing historians tend to blame the decline of the sport on the overexposure it suddenly had on TV in the early sixties. And for a simple, straightforward explanation, that does nicely. Along with other major sports, boxing matches had become more available and rendered more intimately on the tube than in person. "What do you expect when you're giving it away for nothing?" my friend was saying to someone from the boxing department when a card of promising heavyweights brought out less than five hundred real paying customers one night in November. That TV was killing boxing was taken as axiomatic.

But there were some other important reasons why boxing in the TV era, at least before Ali, was taking repeated shots in the gut, and they had more to do with what was wrong with boxing than with television. Baseball was selling its wholesome, "apple pie" tradition; football, the vicarious thrill of modern warfare; but boxing presented itself with brutal and self-defeating honesty: two ruffians drawing blood before a broad slice of "low society" types—gamblers, hustlers, and con men, as well as the women who attached themselves to these types. Except for the razor-blade commercials, the matches could just as well be taking place on a barge out in the Hudson with police lookouts scattered about. Not at all the sort of sporting activity or ambience to draw members of the more respectable classes. To make matters worse, boxing was even losing some of the hard-core types that had always been its backbone.

I came to understand its severe marketing problems the night I offered the doorman of my apartment building a second-row ticket to a very good welterweight match between Luis Rodriguez, the former title holder, and Holly Mims, an exceedingly good journeyman. Not wanting to seem a piker, I had actually bought the ticket; the guy who sold it to me was as surprised as I was by the impetuous decision. The doorman, a gaunt Irishman I knew only as Tim-O, with pale freckles on pale skin and pale stubble to match, claimed to have worked the corner of "Baby Face" Jimmy

McLarnin when the fighter was the welterweight champ in the 1930s.

Many was the hour we'd wiled away under a dripping canopy as Tim-O picked up the history my old man had let fall away. "When Jimmy knocked out Benny Leonard in t'six round, we didn't even celebrate," he told me one morning. The sixth round KO by McLarnin was the Ghetto Wizard's last fight. One fight too late, as it was with most old boxers.

But Tim-O brought other histories to match names I'd always wanted to know more about, fighters he claimed to have seen sitting on stools in the opposite corner: Billy Petrelle, Barney Ross, Tony Canzoneri. Tim-O's stories never disappointed me; he had the novelist's and the Irishman's eye for almost irrelevant but usually the most telling details. "Ross? He graduated high school, don't y' know. An' at all t'weigh-ins he'd tell t'doctor to spell stet-o-scope jus' t' prove he was educated." Naturally, Tim-O became my rainy day Thucydides. For Christmas '63 he gave me his 1955 *Ring Record Book*, claiming he had two. I was surprised, then, when he turned down my gift, and by how he turned it down.

"Oh my. T'isn't possible. Livin' way out on Long Island as I am, I'd be missin' t'late train. Me old lady'd have me bony ass for soup."

That was something I hadn't considered about the decline of the crowds at the Garden. More than a few of the hard-core boxing fans had gotten caught up in the 1950s move to the suburbs. Now the urban core was harder and *leaner* than ever. And blacker and more Hispanic. No accident, then, that they'd put up a commuters' garage where Stillman's used to stand. No wonder the new Madison Square Garden would be built atop Pennsylvania Station. Signs of the times.

Tim-O wasn't finished. "Trut'fully, fighters t'ese days aren't to me taste, either. After ten, fifteen fights, t'ey're already main eventers. Don't know t'ey're skills yet like in t'old days." That I understood as solid reasoning, not the same as my old man's bias for the fighters of one's youth as always being the best. And also a reflection of the new pressures to create new faces and rush them along that come with television. But he meant even more and said it with a wink. "An' even t'ones wit' t'Irish names have t'wrong complexions." It was the wink more than anything else that saddened me.

That's when I decided to employ a scam I'd filed away a year or so earlier for just such an occasion. I'd noticed a potentially profitable detail about fights scheduled for TV in the old Garden that seemed to have gone generally unnoticed. So I proposed a standing $10 bet with Tim-O on every main event that was televised.

Usually we both liked the same fighter. A problem. So I suggested that to avoid haggling and adjusting the odds, we simplify matters considerably. I said to Tim-O, "Tell you what. I'll take whichever fighter wears the white trunks in every fight. You can have the black. It'll probably even out over the year."

Tim-O's blue eyes narrowed and he considered the proposal with furrowed brow. Seemed to be a random enough way to solve the problem of duplicating choice. "Sounds fair," he said. We shook on it.

It may have sounded fair. It wasn't. I'd been noticing for a while that whenever a black boxer fought a white one on TV, the black fighter always wore white trunks and vice versa. It made sharpening the contrast on the viewers' TV sets unnecessary, I guess. Since the post-Marciano era was a time when dark-skinned (hence, white-trunked) fighters were just a little hungrier on average than their white counterparts, I'd given myself a nice edge. Of course when a white fighter fought another white fighter, or a black a black, the law of random probability really did apply.

Naturally, I didn't win every time it was black against white, but for a run of almost six months I was a winner about 75 percent of the time. I didn't for a moment mind taking Tim-O's money, especially when it was the black fighter who made him dig into his uniform pocket. "Don't know how ya do it," he told me more than once. Tim-O went to his death never having figured the mysterious superiority of those white trunks.

The big-name fighters of the early and mid-sixties were, among the heavyweights, the class that usually carries the entire sport, Floyd Patterson and Sonny Liston. The first was a polite young man of some skill but modest talent; at 182 pounds, he was a lightish heavyweight in more than avoirdupoir. Liston was a brutish ex-con, whose earlier employment was as a goon who cracked the skulls of union members to help them reconsider their anti-management positions. Both were black, and neither had a personality that made him a likely candidate for media stardom. In the early years of the decade, in fact, the phenomenon hadn't quite been discovered yet. (Cassius Clay, who ascended to the championship in 1964, was still generally considered an obnoxious braggart by the public at large, when he was considered at all. He would not fully resuscitate boxing until he took it with him from the sports page to the front page later in the decade.)

José Torres, Dick Tiger, Emile Griffith, Carlos Ortiz—good fighters all—were champions in various other divisions, but they lacked the charisma (not to mention the complexion) to lead boxing out of the wilderness. "T'Irish, t'Jews, and t'I-talians it were in t'old days gave boxing its spice. Now, t'spice is gone."

"Must've moved out to the suburbs," I said sarcastically.

Skin tone wasn't the only thing keeping boxing from general acceptance as a major sport; as a matter of fact, its popularity in the seventies and eighties was led precisely by fighters with high percentages of melanin in their pigment. In the sixties, however, it provided a convenient working hypothesis.

A deeper problem was the sleazy business practices in the sport. The real "low society" that had taken control of boxing in the fifties still held sway, and they had no Runyonesque charm. These guys broke kneecaps. When mobsters like Frankie Carbo and Blinkie Palermo moved in on a promising or an already prominent fighter, their offers were, by definition, irrefusable. All the worst characters and plots of a Warner Brothers' boxing flick were present in real life. Every boxing corruption—kickbacks, woeful mismatches, druggings, fixed fights, money stolen from honest but ignorant fighters, fighters taken away from the small-timers who had discovered them—from every movie from *Golden Boy* and *Body and Soul* to *The Harder They Fall* was being played out by mob guys with real fighters as the victims.

There was even a real "Mr. Big" who ruled his boxing empire absolutely, and for years no one could touch him. James D. Norris was a millionaire Midwesterner who headed the International Boxing Club, which was known inside the trade as "Octopus, Inc." Unlike Tex Rickard and Mike Jacobs before him, who had controlled the sport by commanding the heavyweight champs, Dempsey and Louis respectively, Norris monopolized the sport, quite literally, by controlling major boxing outlets—Chicago Stadium and Madison Square Garden—and television access. If you wanted your fighter to get seen, you signed with Norris and his IBC boys, and you did it on their terms.

After the "Octopus" got control of enough attractive fighters —and it used methods beyond mere temptation—TV sponsors had to do business with the IBC if they wanted to reach a national audience with the biggest name fighters. Naturally, IBC fighters got the best fights, for a fee, and held most of the major championships. An independent fighter like Archie Moore, for example, had to go to Australia to get matches that paid a living wage. Other very good fighters, like Charley Burley and Holman Williams, never got the title shots they deserved and had to ply their trade in relative obscurity. At least that's how it was until the government finally began to step in and threaten antitrust action.

The crummy atmosphere of the fight game in those days was nailed to memory forever in the rear seat of a taxicab by the Budd Schulberg screenplay of *On the Waterfront*. Remember? Charlie Malloy (Rod Steiger) is well-connected, the middleman in the mob's waterfront operations. His younger brother, Terry (Marlon Brando), once a promising light-heavyweight, has become a labor goon on the docks. In the scene Charlie is on his way to the Garden for the fights, but he's overcome with sudden nostalgia for Terry: "Gee, when you tipped one seventy-five you were beautiful. You should've been another Billy Conn. That skunk I got to manage you brought you along too fast."

Schulberg's stage direction for Terry Malloy reads, "Years of abuse crying out in him." And Brando plays the scene for all it's worth. Terry explodes. "It wasn't him! It was you, Charley. You and Johnny. Like the night the two of youse came in the dressing room and says, 'Kid, this ain't your night—we're going for the price on Wilson.' It *ain't my night*. I'd of taken Wilson apart that night! I was ready—remember the early rounds throwing them combinations. So what happens—this bum Wilson gets the title shot—outdoors in the ball park!—and what do I get—a couple of bucks and a one-way ticket to Palookaville."

Maybe Terry Malloy really could have been a contender; at

the very least, he and all the other real fighters who were bought and sold and then discarded deserved an honest shot. But corruption's been a part of this business ever since it's been a business.

It was a major paradox, then, that for me those worst of boxing times were the very best of times. By day I appeared to the world as a young, mild-mannered English literature professor at a respected suburban university. Most Friday nights, however, I assumed my true identity—fake UPI boxing reporter. The New York fighters of the mid-1960s were my fighters in precisely the way Benny Leonard and, to a lesser extent, Bob Fitzsimmons belonged to my old man. The way Jimmy McLarnin was Tim-O's. And I got to see them closer than I ever would have dreamed.

The first night I accompanied my friend to our ringside seats I carried his typewriter and a couple of my own spiral notebooks. I had a pencil stuck behind my ear, my tie loosened, top button open. A press pass dangled conspicuously from the top button on my suit jacket; in an earlier day, I'd have stuffed it in my hatband. A four-rounder, memorable only because both fighters were redheaded and freckled white kids, was already in progress. We found "UPI" scrawled on a piece of tape at the board that constituted a working press desk. As I set up the typewriter I believed for a fleeting moment I was the regular boxing man, my friend, the imposter.

In order not to appear too much the novitiate, I affected a bored, casual expression, checking the sparse crowd, the few other reporters and photographers already in place. I flipped open the notebook to write the date. I had no idea where the drops came from or what they were. My first thought was "sweat." Then "soda." But it couldn't have been. The blood ran across my hand, my notebook, the shoulder of my suit jacket in a dotted line, exactly as if a painter had flicked vermilion off a brush. I looked up. The redhead in white trunks was awash in the other redhead's blood. First ringside lesson: Don't wear your good suit jacket.

The so-called feature was the second of two eight-rounders: light-heavyweights Willie Pastrano and Wayne Thornton. The light-heavyweight division (175-pound limit) suffers most from being neither fish nor fowl. Heavyweights, big men who can usually demolish one another with a single blow, easily capture a fan's interest by invoking dread. Most lighter-weight boxers can be more appreciated for their skills. But light-heavies are usually too large to be loved for their virtuosity and not large enough to be truly feared. It's a tough division to make big money in, and a true light-heavyweight who can punch usually tries to eat himself into a heavyweight, where his punches are rarely successful against bigger, tougher jaws but at least he is better paid for his efforts.

The bout, as I remember it, was a lifeless exercise between an elusive boxer who didn't seem to want to be there (Pastrano) and a fighter without the skills to corner him (Thornton). When the ring announcer proclaimed the match a draw, the entire crowd, in which everyone seemed to have a bet, pressed around the ring. For a gambler, betting a draw has about the same ambiguous satisfaction as postponing your tax audit. One boisterous aficionado with a single eyebrow chided, "You think we're dumb or something? You'll have these pussies back here in three weeks." Actually, the rematch was five weeks later.

Before that fight had started, word swept the press section that Davey Moore, the featherweight champion, who had been in a coma in an L.A. hospital, had died. Moore had been knocked out in Dodger Stadium a few days earlier by Ultimo "Sugar" Ramos in a title defense he was heavily favored to win, was winning, in fact, when he was tagged and went down. At the Garden ringside the talk turned to Benny Paret, who one year earlier had been beaten to death in this very ring by Emile Griffith. The two men had hated each other personally, a rare thing in a boxing match. I could reach out and touch the canvas by coming only slightly out of my seat.

As the nondecisive Pastrano-Thornton decision was being rendered, my friend turned to me and said, "What do you think I should do? I'm supposed to get a quote from the winner." But there was no winner, and their dressing rooms were on opposite sides of the building.

I was on it in a moment. "I'll take Pastrano. You get Thornton. Meet you back here."

A small knot of reporters were in the gray hallway, which could have been a perfect location for any fight movie—drab walls, caged lights hanging from the ceiling, ominous shadows cast along the concrete floor. Holding forth in front of the dressing room door was Pastrano's trainer, a swarthy little man with owl eyes and nose to match. He was interrogating himself. "Why didn't we get it?" He thought. "Bunch a reasons. You guys interested?" It seemed to me incredible that the regular fight guys were more interested in listening to the trainer than the fighter.

"Who is he?" I whispered to an old-timer, realizing I risked blowing my cover.

"Angelo Dundee. Better copy than any fighter. Listen."

In my notes I miswrote *Dundi*, but I got the following: "I heard something about Davey Moore. What's the latest?" A scholarly-looking guy said there was a rumor but he'd checked and Moore was still hanging on. Dundee said, "Good. You guys know I worked Ramos's corner that night? I think Moore'll make it. You know he was on his feet after the count. He even told me he wanted a rematch. Can you believe that?" Dundee explained that it wasn't the punch that did the damage. Moore's head snapped against the bottom strand of the ring ropes when he went down.

Finally, and reluctantly for Dundee, talk turned back to the unsatisfying draw we'd all just witnessed. "It's bad times in the game when they penalize finesse. They're giving points for swinging your arms nowadays, not for hitting. Willie never got hit." And: "The judges was sitting too low. From their angle they miss all the good stuff my fighter was doing on top. They ought to be up higher like at a diving meet." My notes read at that point: *Dundi demonstrates Pastrano slipping move. Bends reporter over and hits him mock blow as he moves around behind.*

"And they ain't wild about an out-of-towner coming in here without them getting a piece of him." A while later: "Frankly, we stunk out there. Still, we did enough to win. Just enough. It's hard to believe, gents, but you just saw the next light-heavyweight champion of the world tonight."

Reporter: "Yeah, which one was he?"

Dundee: "We're just setting them up. Making people think Willie ain't nothing to worry about."

Reporter: "That, you sure as hell did."

Somehow the subject of terminology for evaluating fighters came up, probably when someone asked Dundee to rank Pastrano. The scholarly guy suggested awarding stars, like the Michelin Guide. "Nah," said Dundee, "what we already got in the business is fine." He classified from the bottom up. "Everyone knows a 'Tomato Can,' a guy who's garbage but still can get a fight. A true 'Bum' ain't much better, but he's at least a cut higher. Then there's the 'Opponent,' someone who you should beat but still looks good on the record, but he's no absolute sure thing. A 'Journeyman' has some skills, modest ones, but he's hardworking and stays in shape most of the time; he could be hard to beat. Next comes a 'Fighter' and a 'Real Fighter'—a combination of heart and skill, the difference between the two is maybe one has more talent. These can be dangerous guys if you're making a match, but you're going to have to meet them somewhere along the line if you're ever going to get anywhere." Dundee took a breath and considered for a moment. "Then there's a 'Hell of a Fighter.' " It seems that in a business that prides itself in withholding superlatives, this is the best you are going to get from Dundee. But no. "That's about all you can say about a good one while he's active. You wait a while, compare him to other fighters who've gone and who've been seen by the old-timers and then maybe you can say 'Great.' "

I understood in that dark hallway that the boxing business was as much talk as it was action, and the talk could be terrific even when the action wasn't. So colorful and convincing was this Dundee that I left thinking Pastrano really had won the fight—no, not beyond a shadow of a doubt, but sufficiently. Because it was late I never stayed to see Pastrano, who did indeed win the light-heavyweight title later that year and managed to hang on as a particularly lackluster champion for a while.

To a great extent his success accrued to the clever little man who was his trainer. The world would come to know how good Dundee was at what he did as corner man to Muhammad Ali. Perhaps his finest work was done as master ring strategist for Sugar Ray Leonard after that brilliant amateur decided to turn pro. As a subject for a writer, Angie Dundee was pure Liebling spiced with more than a soupçon of Runyon, and if I'd had a flirtation with boxing up until then, I fell helplessly in love in that hallway.

Davey Moore died two days later.

For almost every fight thereafter—and frankly I don't recall seeing another main-event draw—when my friend went off to get a quote from the winning fighter, I headed for the dressing room of the other guy. That's how I became a specialist in interviewing losers.

Most of the time the scene was woefully similar. Forlorn women in the hallway dabbing Kleenex at mascaraed eyes or biting ruby lips. Inside the dressing room, silence, a swollen and bloodied fighter sitting on a table or a metal folding char, his head in taped hands, or maybe he's lying facedown on the rubbing table. A few relatives and hometown friends, all men, leaning against the wall. A manager pacing the floor. Trainer poised to be of some aid when the fighter indicates he's ready.

Managers usually made excuses, and after about three years worth, I'd heard most variations on three basic alibis—"rotten decision," "dirty fighter," "lucky punch." Don Elbaum, now a fast-talking Atlantic City fight promoter but then a fast-talking manager of mediocre fighters, once gave me a virtuoso performance after his best fighter, Johnny Bizarro, a game kid from Erie, Pennsylvania, lost a close decision to a Puerto Rican fighter in a very gritty fight.

"First of all, they always screw me when I come into this building. Understand that and we'll be all right. Now, after all the trouble they've been having, it's worse. They're afraid if they don't give it to the Puerto Rican, the goddamn balcony'll come down on their heads. So if you don't knock the son of a bitch out, forget about the decision. Added to which, this guy [the referee] lets everything go for the other guy, and when we start banging back, he steps in and pulls us out. It don't bother him a bit that he's using his head in close like maracas on Johnny's chin, his thumbs like he's digging for oil, and low-balling us all the time. Besides of which, he was absolutely numb out there. Never fight that good again in a million years. And still I thought we beat him." If Casey Stengel had been a fight manager, he'd have been just another talker. In baseball he was considered phenomenal copy.

Johnny Bizarro, a good enough fighter to have gotten a couple of title shots, looked up from his hands and said softly, "Don, don't bullshit this guy. He beat me tonight. Maybe another night I take him, but he beat me tonight." Class act.

If my pose as a hard-boiled reporter hadn't forbade it, I would have hugged Bizarro. As a matter of fact, I discovered during my love affair with losers that fighters, probably because they risk so damned much in so frightening, dangerous, and lonely an activity, generally have extremely well-developed bullshit rejectors and a tremendous sense of personal integrity. Those are qualities that can sometimes compensate for a lack of formal education. The bitterest irony in the fight game is that professional fighters tend to be good men in a very un-good business.

Although I was already in my late twenties, old enough to know better, I was still too inexperienced to realize that losing is the ultimate test for every one of us. No, not in the hopeful, power-of-positive-thinking sense of forging character or of teaching us how to win eventually. But we don't win eventually. Even if everything goes our way, we all lose the big one in the end. The Fix is in. The only intimations we have for the ultimate defeat are the knockdowns and bad decisions we suffer along the way. Positive thinking be damned, I loved the losers.

Two other losers stand out from the scores of others. One was Rubin "Hurricane" Carter, who was later to be immortalized in song by Bob Dylan as a great fighter who had been unjustly imprisoned as an armed robber and murderer. Dylan may have been wrong on both counts. Using Dundee's evaluative scale, Carter was a "Fighter." Big hitter that he was, tough as he was, Carter lacked the developed skills to be kicked up to "Real Fighter." After a public outcry at the injustice of his imprisonment, Carter won a retrial. He was again convicted on the evidence. Last year Carter was released once more.

His power to intimidate was frightening, pound for pound even greater than Sonny Liston's. Just his face in a newspaper photo scowling out from behind a Fu Manchu mustache scared the hell out of me. The buildup for his match with Dick Tiger, the former world middleweight champion from Nigeria, was a bad guy–good guy thing.

Although I believed Tiger to be a "Hell of a Fighter," I was a little worried for him. I'd never shaken Plato's notion that, all things being equal, a bad man would always beat a good man. Fortunately, things weren't equal, and Tiger tamed the Hurricane decisively, knocking him down three times in winning a unanimous decision.

Then came the test of *my* courage. I had to go and ask the Hurricane precisely how and why he got beat so badly.

No women mourned in the hallway. No other reporters were present because Tiger was not only the winner but one of the most popular fighters with the writers. I knocked. No answer. So I opened the door slowly on a scene of conventional loser gloom. A few dour men sat in chairs. But there was no fighter. "He's in the shower," one of them said absently, and I waited, trying to exude business as usual. I had my pad and pencil poised.

Carter stepped out and stood before me naked, the water beading on his bitter-chocolate skin. I didn't allow my eyes to examine the body, but I sensed a metallic hardness about it that went beyond flesh. I didn't comprehend how anyone could beat this man. He was virtually unmarked by the fight. "Well, Rubin, how do you feel?"

His eyes looked around the room as though in serious thought. Finally he said, "Ree-jected."

The worst beating I ever saw close up at the old Garden was on December 10, 1965, in a rematch between two heavyweights named James J.—surnamed Beattie and Woody.

Jim Beattie was the sacrificial lamb, seemingly chosen for his role by destiny. A huge six-foot-nine, 235-pound, raw-boned Minnesota farm boy with a deceptively successful amateur career behind him—his sheer size had defeated most of his opponents—Beattie had gotten his job as a professional fighter through *The New York Times*. He had answered an ad promising up to $150,000 a year for the right sort of young man willing to try to become heavyweight champion of the world.

The idea of advertising for a big white galoot who could be retooled into a heavyweight champ, thereby making everyone involved in the project rich, was the brainstorm of a New York restaurateur and some friends with disposable cash. The "white" made success more likely, since in the heavyweight class the word attached itself naturally to "Hope," and the combination often produced significant revenue. Rarely a champion.

For an on-the-job trainee, Beattie started well enough as a pro. He'd lost just once in thirteen tries; then Woody beat him by a decision in the Garden. Beattie then strung together five consec-

utive knockouts—they were mostly tomato cans—and came back
to the Garden for the rematch with Woody. There was a point
midway through the third round when I still had Beattie ahead
on my card and thought he might beat his shorter, well-muscled
black opponent. Perhaps it was weariness that reached him first,
or the hooks Woody was digging into the big blond's exposed ribs.
Or both. However it was, the beating became monstrous.

A number of things conspired to make it so. First of all, Woody
put his head on big Jim's chest and stayed so close that Beattie
had absolutely no punching room, all the while digging to the
long, exposed flanks. When the big man dropped his hands and
doubled over, Woody whipped lacerating punches to the pink
face. The blood that spattered was all Beattie's. I'd worn a red
sweater.

Because Beattie was so incredibly game and Woody was punishing but not powerful enough to put him away, the equipoise
of damage shifted by slim degrees, making the accumulation seem
less terrible than it was. In addition, Beattie was so huge, it might
have appeared to the referee he had more of himself to offer up
than a normal-sized heavyweight. I could never prove it, but I
had the distinct feeling that the crowd wanted to see Beattie punished precisely because he was so big. Lilliputian revenge.

Frankly, I didn't see the specific blow that put him down and
out in the seventh round, but I felt the boards beneath the ring
rattle when he spun helplessly and fell face forward to the canvas.
After they got him up and into his robe—white with green trim,
if memory serves—he came down the ring steps right alongside
me. I looked up into the blinding kliegs above the ring and saw
a blood-smeared face haloed in light; his eyes were dazed, the
mouth hung open. I thought he'd topple over onto me and was
glad when he went past.

But Beattie walked up the aisle past the turn to the dressing-
room area. Alone, James J. Beattie staggered up the aisle right
toward the end arena. Patrons were hooting at him and pointing
comically. I ran after him, caught him by the arm, and turned
him toward his dressing room. James J. Beattie was senseless.

Later, as I stood in his dressing room, his eye was not merely
swollen, it looked as though it might drop off. A gaping slash
lined the brow. There was hardly a square inch of face that was

not rubbed raw or cut. Had Jim Beattie stayed around New York, he'd have given Chuck Wepner, the celebrated "Bayonne Bleeder" and real-life model for Rocky Balboa, a run for his money as bloodletting champ. I broke my long tradition of asking losers foolish questions that night with Beattie. "What in the world," I said, "are you doing in this business?"

James J. Beattie didn't bat a bloody eye: "I'm still sharpening my skills." Three minutes earlier he hadn't been sharp enough to find his dressing room.

In 1970, the year after he quit boxing the first time, Beattie landed a role in the movie version of *The Great White Hope*. Beattie played the white hope. He was first-rate.

I'd forgotten that White Hopes hadn't always been a part of heavyweight boxing. Seeing Beattie on the movie screen reminded me that a day or so after my old man and I had spent that fateful day in Manhattan, my father had told me something important. He'd been reminiscing about Benny Leonard; he'd clipped the *Times* obituary. Without a transition, he said, "It seemed as natural as could be, Joe Louis walking through that gym. But it wasn't always like that."

His face clouded over and he squinted, as though trying to see something distant more clearly. "I remember my father picking up the newspaper one morning. It was in 1908. I must have been about your age at the time. He looked like he was almost in shock. All he said was, 'The *Schwartze*, the *Schwartze*.' Over and over as he read."

My old man knew he had me hooked, so he let me dangle a moment before explaining. "It was after Jack Johnson knocked out Jim Jeffries in 1908. He just couldn't believe it was possible that a black man could ever beat a white man. No one could. I remember that whole day, everyone was in a state of shock. It was real big stuff."

That was the day White Hope was invented. Jim Beattie was part of a long and pitiful boxing tradition.

During my ringside apprenticeship I visited only one winner's dressing room after a fight, and that happened completely by accident. There was a riot in the Garden, and I ran to the closest safe place I could find, the dressing-room tunnel on the Forty-ninth Street side. Wiser, more experienced heads just went to their knees and crawled under the ring. I ran through a barrage of bottles.

The first one came flying out of the darkness of the side balcony before the ring announcer finished his last sentence. It had proclaimed "Flash" Elorde a split-decision winner over Frankie Narvaez.

Much as I had liked Narvaez, a young Puerto Rican lightweight of excellent character and potential, I'd given the fight 5–4–1 even to the Filipino, Gabriel "Flash" Elorde, the world's junior lightweight (130 pounds) champion. At thirty, the Flash was acknowledged to be a Hell of a Fighter, but in this nontitle bout he had been far from brilliant but had done enough to win according to my scorecard.

Elorde had mastered every technique that had been classically honed since Epeius. He was one of the handful of fighters around in any era who could do it all. During the fight you could see some of the skills transferring themselves to the kid, Narvaez, the hard way, in precisely the manner lessons are taught by master boxers to those who would be—drop your hands, BAM, a jab gets your nose; come forward off balance, you get pushed ahead from the side and, BANG, hit again as you stumble by. Major mistakes in boxing don't just show up in the newspapers and in the record books. They are permanently recorded on your face. Hopefully, learning how to avoid the mistake and to practice it on someone else is etched in the mind as well.

Narvaez had reached a plateau of low-level excellence against his punishing tutor. Next time or the time after that he might take Elorde, if he ever got another chance. He would be a better fighter for this loss, as Elorde was for having been taken out by the inimitable Sandy Saddler in the thirteenth round ten years earlier fighting for the featherweight championship of the world. Narvaez's supporters were not in the least interested in their fighter's self-improvement. They saw yet another insult, a robbery by gringo judges who refused to give them what they'd earned. Their whiskey-self-respect had been affronted.

Waves of Puerto Ricans wielding fragments of broken chairs rolled from the end arena, chasing frightened fans before them, tearing up more seats as they swarmed. The bottles never stopped sailing out from the balcony and shattering near the ring. I tasted the fear that overcomes you when your car skids out of control on an icy road.

I ran from the entrance of the tunnel to the Madison Square Garden press office on shaky legs. Security guards and then New York cops scurried down the hallway. After about three or four minutes the sounds of riot became more distant. Police reinforcements had the rioters in retreat toward the Eighth Avenue lobby.

Because I was displaced, I thought I was near Narvaez's dressing room. When it felt reasonably safe I made my way down the hall and knocked on what I believed to be the loser's door. There was absolute silence inside, and I thought it likely that Narvaez hadn't gotten there yet. I was sure that was the explanation when on cracking the door I saw the room darkened. Except for candlelight. I let the door close of its own weight. Candlelight?

Then I entered and took my position against the wall with the half dozen other silent journalists. On the floor stood a hinged wooden altarpiece, its tiny painted religious figures reflecting the primitive iconography of a simple belief. The five tiny candles that lighted the room reflected the burnished gold of the small portable triptych. Kneeling on the floor, Flash Elorde, wearing only his boxing shorts, his fight shoes and socks, his moist black hair spiking up from his skull like stigmata, mouthed melodic, mystical words. He bent forward and crossed himself rhythmically with his taped right hand.

I recognized the guy next to me as the regular *Daily News* man. His warm breath tickled my ear: "Forgive 'em, Father, they don't know what they're doin'."

CHAPTER 5

Sugar Ray Leonard, Inc.

The horrendous welfare-paternity publicity chased away any big-time commercial possibilities, at least in the short run. But it took the star-struck Leonard a while to realize the fact. Fortunately, he had too much pride and enough good advice to take some of the crummy local TV spots that were being offered—used-car dealers, hardware stores, discotheques. They would have put him in a tacky media milieu it was usually impossible to extricate yourself from.

During those difficult days his father was having trouble recovering from what everyone assumed to be the strain of the immense excitement at Montreal. It wasn't strain; it was meningitis. Cicero Leonard was hospitalized. About the same time, Getha Leonard suffered a heart attack. She'd displayed symptoms earlier, palpitations and constrictions, but this was the thing itself.

With neither parent able to work, with his child and the mother of his child to support, without any legitimate job offers coming in, Ray Leonard really had no other choice but to become a professional boxer. That was the simple economic reality of his situation, but one he refused to accept as crucial days and then weeks slipped by.

One delusion under which Ray was laboring was that the impact he had made on the American consciousness at the Olympics still ran deep. Hadn't he been a national hero? A full-fledged media star? Wasn't there still some way to convert that value into a nonviolent livelihood? How could a few weeks have changed everything?

An old friend, Janks Morton, a fellow who had encouraged Ray early on at the Palmer Park Recreation Center and been there to help and advise him throughout his amateur career, painfully disabused Ray of his delusion and put him on the right track. Morton, a promising football player who couldn't quite cut it as a pro but who saw up close and understood the economic realities of professional sports, was a friend indeed during this time of confusion for Ray. He helped the fighter sort out fact from fiction. Morton asked Leonard to stand with him for a while at a busy intersection of downtown Washington, just to see how many people still recognized the fighter. Almost nobody. And that clinched it. Sugar Ray Leonard, toast of the North American continent weeks earlier, was now just another forgotten TV face. Ray was damned lucky to have a friend like Janks.

The decision to turn pro was still not definite, but Ray realized that if he were to do it, it had better be done quickly, at least while some boxing fans remembered who he was. That he didn't accept fight promoter Don King's contract offer is all the more amazing because it promised Ray about $200,000 up front and the opportunity to earn a good deal more. The contract, however, was typical of those offered by boxing's monopolistic promoters: Through a variety of option clauses it could have tied Ray's services to King for long into the forseeable future, and perhaps beyond.

In precisely this fashion has the flamboyant King controlled the careers—and the lives—of some excellent fighters. And ruined the careers of a great many others. A combination of financial need, a strong dose of greed, and the knowledge that King can offer national exposure through his television connections makes promising young fighters sign contracts chocked so full of option clauses favorable to King that the fighters are tied up for the best years of their boxing lives. That Ray Leonard, given the state of his life and bank account, didn't sign with King is testimony to his intelligence and strength of character. About the deal Ray has said he didn't like "the idea of someone owning a part of me." With that statement Ray avoided boxing's fatal pitfall.

It was clear now that Ray Leonard would become a professional boxer. Precisely how he would go about it was the main problem. And this is where, as had happened so many times before during his most difficult moments, that chance stepped in again and sent his career in a totally unique and fortuitous direction. By refusing to sign with King, or with Teddy Brenner, matchmaker for Madison Square Garden, or any of the dozens of promoters who had been hitting him with offers since the Olympics, Ray, with the help of Janks Morton and Dave Jacobs, had been saying no to the business-as-usual approach that was standard in the fight game. Ray knew what he didn't want to do, but finding a better way to open the door and shape a unique career wasn't going to be so easy.

That's where coincidence stepped in, in the unlikely form of a slow-pitch softball team. Janks told Ray about a guy he played ball with, a lawyer who might have some ideas about how best to crack the boxing business in a new way. Mike Trainer practiced in Silver Spring, Maryland, an upper-middle-class community just outside Washington. Trainer had a busy but fairly predictable practice at the time. Looking back at the day Ray walked into his office and changed both their lives, Trainer says, "One day Ray just walked in. I didn't know what'd happen. I was doing too many speeding violations; my life was getting boring. It didn't stay that way for long."

Ray, with his head spinning from all the things that were— and *weren't*—happening in the weeks since he'd announced his retirement on TV, didn't know what could possibly come out of his meeting with Trainer. In fact, Ray didn't know if he could trust the white lawyer. It helped considerably when Janks told him, "I'd trust Mike with everything I own." Janks Morton wasn't a particularly trusting man.

Trainer, of course, knew Ray from the Olympics and at their first meeting stressed the advisability of a college education. After a few more meetings, though, Trainer became convinced that Ray really wanted to box as a professional, so Trainer, who knew nothing about the ins and outs of the boxing business but whose legal-financial mind is a steel trap, came up with the unique approach to a pro career Ray was looking for.

Trainer knew that like any proposed business venture, Ray Leonard, Professional Boxer, required seed money or start-up capital. He estimated that about $20,000 would take Ray to his first professional bouts and the point where some profits might come in. Trainer actually raised $21,000 from twenty-four friends and clients—many of them members of the softball team—who wanted to be part of launching the local boy's career. There really wasn't anything very original about this approach: Businessmen had been bankrolling athletes to their starts in professional careers for years. In golf it's standard procedure.

In boxing, Cassius Clay had signed after the 1960 Olympics with the Louisville Sponsoring Group, and Joe Frazier had been supported after the 1968 Games by a group called Cloverlay, a far more financially modest organization. Although their deals differed, the general approach was the same. Clay received a $10,000 bonus and a guaranteed minimum of $4,000 a year thereafter from the eleven Louisville millionaires who had invested. The Group was to receive 50 percent of Clay's earnings for the first four years and 60 percent thereafter. When the arrangement was terminated in 1966, Ali had gross earnings of $2.3 million. Breaking with white "benefactors" who owned more than half of him cost Ali a bundle in settlement fees; staying with them would have cost a good deal more.

Trainer's approach was not exploitive. He and the investors had no intention of trapping Ray, so Trainer added an important wrinkle. The money was to be repaid within four years at 8 percent interest, regardless of how much purse money Leonard had earned. It was goodwill that had motivated these investors, not greed. Even Trainer, normally the most pragmatic of men, was caught up in the infectious spirit the young fighter seemed to engender. He didn't charge Ray for his time and expertise. Furthermore, in order to avoid the taint of any external control, Ray was made the sole stockholder in Sugar Ray Leonard, Inc. It cost Ray $35 to become a corporation in Maryland. Ray Leonard owned himself.

Under Trainer's direction, Sugar Ray Leonard, Inc. had its accounting done by Arthur Young and its publicity (called "public relations," naturally) handled by Charles Brotman, an institution in Washington who knew and was known by everybody who mattered in that town. Brotman, in fact, is a litmus test of sorts in the nation's capital. "If you can't get Charlie on the phone, you must not be important," a D.C. sports columnist once told me.

There was Janks Morton as confidant and personal adviser and Dave Jacobs as trainer. The team had formed itself, primarily by chance, but there it was. It lacked only an experienced professional boxing tutor to direct the ring career, to supervise the preparations, to orchestrate the bouts.

I'm inclined to say that Ray Leonard would have become a superb professional fighter no matter who masterminded his career. The skills, after all, would have been pretty much the same had any number of top managers stepped in to guide him. But the more I think about the proposition, the more I doubt my own inclination. Boxing is too full of very talented fighters who never fulfilled their promise. Most often, failure is their own fault, the result of a character flaw—unwillingness to train properly, a fatal attraction to booze or drugs or broads; in general, an inability to focus resolutely on a single goal and make the required sacrifices to attain it. That had never been Ray's problem. Sometimes, however, a fighter fails because he is mishandled, even by those rare and knowledgeable souls who would have his best interests at heart.

Sugar Ray Leonard, Inc. didn't lack for applicants as professional manager, nor for people with great credentials. After all, the kid had a ton of talent, everybody could see that. Eddie Futch, who had handled Joe Frazier, among other notables, was interested. So was Gil Clancy, who managed Emile Griffith in and out of a host of championships. Angelo Dundee, however, seemed to want the position more than the others, and his credentials were extraordinary. At the time he applied, he'd trained or managed a dozen different world champions. Maybe there's been a guy around who's prepared more champs, but you'll have to dig way down in the archives to find him.

Many of the applicants wanted absolute control of the fighter and a cut somewhere near the manager's traditional 33 percent.

Dundee had a different proposition. Although he would prescribe the training procedures, he'd leave the day-to-day work to Leonard's local people, primarily to Dave Jacobs. Then, a few days before a fight, Angelo would take over and bring Ray to precisely the point he desired. He would also take responsibility for choosing Ray's opponents, and this function, perhaps more than anything else Dundee did for Leonard, was his greatest contribution. It is doubtful that any other man could have orchestrated a career as well. For his services Dundee would receive 15 percent of Ray's purse.

When Angelo said, "If I'd had that same kind of deal with Ali, I'd be a millionaire by now," the ironies went even deeper than he was willing to admit. Not only did he work on a straight fee basis with Ali most of the time, but much of what he contributed to Ali's success was diminished by the political decision to make Herbert Muhammad, son of the Black Muslim's founder, Ali's manager of record. With Leonard, Dundee was listed as manager, and he had exclusive responsibility for all boxing decisions.

The first thing he did immediately earned him his percentage. Dundee ordered Ray's hands wrapped in Kotex, a trick that old-timers had known for decades and which all at once eased four long years of continuous pain for his fighter.

One advantage in Dundee's being absent and free to handle his other fighters was that the conflict inherent in the situation between him and Dave Jacobs was at least minimized, if it could not be eliminated. Often when a hot amateur prospect turns pro, the old coach or trainer, bound to the fighter by nothing more than a handshake, is cut loose. The new, more efficient managerial team usually doesn't like to carry dead weight and prefers to cut a fighter off from his adolescent tutelage. In the fight game this cruelty is considered a natural rite of passage into professional manhood for the young fighter—it's a cruel world out there, kid; let's see how much you are willing to give up to succeed. For the trainer left out in the cold, it's nothing less than theft.

Although the scene of the old trainer being sloughed off is a staple of most Hollywood movies about the kid who sells his soul for a shot at the championship, it has a strong basis in reality, believe me. I've talked to a good many such men, who've put in all those hours in the local gym only to have to watch the championship match on television. Let Earnee Butler, who trained Larry Holmes from his teenaged amateur days in Easton, Pennsylvania, until he signed a professional contract with Don King, represent the archetype. No one is scripting Butler's lines when he says, "I picked the kid off the streets and taught him everything. Bringing him along slow, the right way. Then, just when he's ready to be something, this guy shows us and tells him Don King is interested in promoting his career. But he's got to sign with them. There's no way to keep the kid then. They tell me that I'll go along with them since I developed him. But when it came down to it, they didn't take me. Now he's making the big money, and I'm still here in Easton teaching kids to fight." Ray Leonard didn't want to go that route with Dave Jacobs.

It's no mystery now that the unique path Leonard cleared to enter professional boxing was a remarkable success financially as well as artistically. Only by hindsight could it have seemed a sure thing. The gulf between amateur and professional boxing is roughly that between preparing a TV dinner in a microwave and tackling Julia Child's *duck à l'orange* over gas. And of all the possible pitfalls for a new pro, none is more difficult to negotiate than choosing opponents during the transition.

Dundee's problem in making fights for Ray was the one that A. J. Liebling, that most intelligent and eloquent observer of fistiana, nailed perfectly in his *The Sweet Science*. "In any art the prodigy presents a problem. Given too easy a problem, he goes slack, but asked too hard a question early, he becomes discouraged. Finding a middle course is particularly difficult in the prize ring. . . . The fighter must be confirmed in the belief that he can lick anybody in the world and at the same time be restrained from testing this belief on a subject too advanced for his attainments. The trick lies in keeping the fellow entertained while enriching his curriculum."

Or, as Angelo Dundee put it, "We'll let Ray get his feet wet first. But you can't start off against stiffs. All of us have seen kids who look like world- beaters, but for some reason they don't make it when the money is on the line." For Sugar Ray Leonard the money was on the line for the first time at the Baltimore Civic Center on February 2, 1977.

*   *   *

Team Leonard did everything right. Janks Morton particularly favored the idea of the local boy launching his career before the local folks. It evoked the image of honor and loyalty, the Olympic "good kid" resurrected after the bad welfare-paternity publicity.

Trainer loved the terms the city fathers felt obliged to meet. The owner of a local lumberyard guaranteed Leonard $10,000, and CBS matched that for the television rights. Leonard would also get $5,000 after the live gate passed $30,000 and half of everything beyond that. The city of Baltimore, nominal promoter of Sugar Ray's first professional fight, would get the other half. They promoted the fighter vigorously; attendance was almost a civic duty.

Brotman had soaked the Baltimore–D.C. area with an unprecedented shower of publicity. There were afternoons during Ray's workouts at the Civic Center when the visiting crowds almost got out of control. On the afternoon of the fight, a crowd of 10,270—an honest count—shelled out $72,320, almost double the record for any previous indoor fight ever held in Baltimore. When the accounting was completed, Ray's share of the complex package was around $40,000, more than had ever been earned by a fighter for his first professional bout, and a six-rounder at that.

Lightweight Luis "the Bull" Vega, a transplanted Puerto Rican living in Reading, Pennsylvania, was Angie Dundee's choice as a first lesson. Not that Vega, with an unimpressive record of fourteen wins, eight losses, three draws (which included some fights in Puerto Rico that were almost impossible to verify), figured to have much of a chance against the local Golden Boy.

Simple logic dictated that Dundee would never have picked an opponent who could possibly derail a million-dollar prospect and his 15 percent piece. If "the Bull" had any chance at all, it was what fight people call a puncher's chance, the long-shot possibility of taking Ray out with a single, lucky punch. But Vega hadn't knocked out another fighter for almost three years. Ray's risk of losing was minimal, actually infinitesimal, in fact nonexistent.

Yet there was virtue in Vega as a first opponent. He was very strong and very tough, hence the nickname. Low-slung, stocky, and belligerent in the ring, Vega was no cream puff or cutie but a very hard guy to fight. Difficult to back up and move around, he was tougher than anyone Ray had ever fought as an amateur, a man where boys had always stood before. He was also almost impossible to knock out. From Dundee's point of view, if Ray got the lucky punch in, fine, but his chief object was to put his elegant student in with a real pug. It was, when you think about it, a rather brilliant choice: Welcome to Professional Boxing, Kid.

In the first round Ray circled out of range—sometimes clockwise, sometimes counter—and pecked away at the short-armed Vega with that wonderful jab of his. A matador provoking a Bull with insulting stings. Vega, much slower, could do little more than turn in the direction of his swirling tormentor and get hit. At this point Sugar was a continuation of the flashy amateur boxer everyone knew him to be but that many boxing people didn't figure as tough enough to be the compleat fighter.

Dundee had a plan. Toward the middle of the second round he had Ray slide inside and throw some classic combinations. In the fourth, Vega was bleeding from the nose and cut in the corner of his left eye. Leonard, who was wearing white trunks, as he usually does, was displaying more blood than Vega, appropriately wearing red. Before the sixth and final round, Dundee told Ray, "Let's see you back him up," which meant, let's see how strong you can be with a guy like this, maybe even put him down. Vega had never been knocked out before. Although the fight was already won, Dundee knew that somewhere along the line, Ray would be required to out-tough an opponent. Might as well get a taste for it now. Also, Dundee wanted to see what his fighter had in him.

The obliging pupil hit the bloodied Puerto Rican with his best shots and, to the roar of the hometowners, moved the hapless Bull all over the ring. The crowd had almost demanded a knockout from the start; now they sniffed one. But Vega finished on his feet, the only badge of honor left to him.

After the fight Ray said, "It was like a replay of *Rocky*. I hit him so many combinations and he still didn't go down. He was the courageous underdog and he was still in there at the end. Vega is a champion too." This was still another aspect of a polished professional emerging: Sugar Ray Leonard, Salesman. Most of the consumers knew that Vega was not Sylvester Stallone and that the fight was merely a simple first test for a talented fighter.

Ray had passed the test. And he had learned some important things while doing it. He found out that although he'd trained rigorously, he was still not as sharp as he could have been; the six-month layoff since the Olympics had been too long. He learned that it was a big step up from three- to six-round bouts and that a fifteen-rounder, the championship distance, was a goal to be arrived at very gradually. He learned that professional fighters were a different species from amateurs. But he also learned that he could be an excellent professional fighter.

Reporters, photographers, TV cameramen mobbed Sugar Ray's dressing room, and Ray the Salesman was charming and magnanimous in victory, as always. He thanked God. He thanked his parents. He thanked CBS-TV. He thanked the city of Baltimore. Yes, he had invited President Carter but wasn't too disappointed that more pressing world affairs kept him from attending. And there was Ray, Jr., cute as a button, chip off the old block. Boxing, Sugar Ray was trying to prove, could be marketed as a wholesome sport conducted by and for wholesome people.

Elsewhere in the bowels of the Baltimore Civic Center, the loser's dressing room was a less uplifting scene. There wasn't much talk; what there was, was mostly in Spanish. A few reporters stopped by later to ask Vega how hard Ray hit, and the Bull said not bad, that he wasn't a bad fighter. Naturally Vega also said he believed he'd won some of the middle rounds, the fight wasn't that one-sided.

The unwholesome, it's fair to say debased, side of the fight game was exposed when it was revealed that Luis Vega's purse for the fight was $650. Six hundred and fifty bucks. Less than the bill for the printing to advertise the fight!

The real Rocky story and perhaps the best thing that can be said about the dark side of boxing is that Luis Vega never really believed for a minute he could beat Ray Leonard. He knew, in fact, he'd probably have to take a beating. Yet he gave it his best shot. And when in the last round he knew the fight was absolutely unwinnable, he made it a point of honor to finish on his feet. Courage could take him that far, at least. All for $650. The heartbreaking and ennobling thing about the professional boxing business is that there are hundreds of fighters who would have fought that final round adhering to the same code. Most professional fighters are surprisingly pure men in a very impure business. Fish in a polluted lake.

There was a time when the size of the crowd and how much money they kicked in determined the financial success of a fight. For the second Dempsey–Tunney championship match at Soldier's Field, Chicago, in 1927 about 150,000 turned up and paid $2.8 million. But the big money since the Ali era has come primarily through television, even though Ali could put fannies in the seats when he wanted to. Because he was an international phenomenon, a crowd of 65,000 in Kinshasa, Zaire, saw him regain his heavyweight championship from George Foreman in 1974. As late as 1978 he pulled 70,000 into the Louisiana Superdome for his rematch with champion Leon Spinks.

In each instance, even though the crowds were huge by modern standards, the television guarantee and percentage, either from the networks or from closed-circuit, constituted the lion's share. Ali understood that fact almost from the beginning when the second Clay–Liston fight drew 2,500 paying customers to the St. Dom's Youth Center in Lewiston, Maine, and more than 1.2 million viewers in theaters in North America. Clay earned half a million dollars for two minutes work; Liston the same amount for falling over, but that's another story. The live gate income has not been the main source of income for star boxers and big-time promoters for years.

Just as in the old days, however, when a fighter built his record and made his reputation in small local clubs and then on the road in good fight towns and finally got "the title shot—outdoors in the ballpark," as Terry Malloy had dreamed—there are now television equivalents for all the steps in the process.

First of all, after making a reputation as a crowd-pleasing amateur and young pro, a promising TV fighter will eventually get a match on a Saturday afternoon network sports anthology show. His fight might be sandwiched between a slalom competition and women body builders flexing their glistening gluteuses, but that doesn't matter. If he wins and looks good doing it, that's all that really counts.

Then, if the young fighter keeps winning and looking impressive doing it, he'll eventually get his title shot, sooner rather than later if he's well-connected. If the ratings have been good whenever he's been on the tube, he might even get to defend his title during prime time, especially if he's the heavyweight champ—that's network television's pinnacle, the "ballpark" of years ago. Unfortunately, to get there it's not always sufficient just to be an excellent fighter. That ineffable "star" quality on camera is every bit as essential; the audience has to care about him, if not love him.

If the rising star does have that certain something, if he's the "It" boy and the ratings reflect that fact whenever he's fighting in prime time, the price the networks can charge for commercial minutes between rounds rises as well. One minute of commercial time for an Ali fight went, at its peak, for about a quarter of a million dollars. Sugar Ray Leonard, amazingly for a non-heavyweight, surpassed that figure. Finally, in this ultimate media-star scenario, a fighter outgrows even network prime time: Instead of fans going to the ballpark and buying a ticket for the championship match, the ballpark (usually a small arena in Las Vegas or an auditorium at an Atlantic City casino) comes to them—for a fee, or course, on cable TV.

Sugar Ray Leonard, Inc. had begun the story line, but with a difference. Because TV had already made him a star as an amateur, he was salable as a weekend TV fighter even while he was learning his trade as a professional. The familiar old movie montage—you might say cliché—always had a fighter hitting the professional road by showing train tracks and a whistling locomotive, city names melding, knockout punches brought up from the floor, screaming sports-page headlines pinwheeling on the screen. Fighter makes rep.

Sugar Ray was doing exactly the same thing on the networks on the weekends. The road had come to us. We saw him going to professional boxers school every fifth or sixth Saturday afternoon, and making more money doing it than any student in history. Fight fans quickly developed a rooting interest in the Leonard matriculation, almost as many against its success as favoring it. A substantial boxing following resented what they perceived to be a fighter being manufactured by television, a slick-talking, pretty boy who hadn't met anyone the least bit accomplished in the ring. This overrated Leonard kid was still another example of the media trying to manipulate our judgment. From the point of view of fan interest in Sugar Ray Leonard, Inc., things couldn't have been better.

Three months after the Vega fight Ray came back to the Baltimore Civic Center to do it all over again with another Pennsylvania junior welterweight, Willie Rodriguez, winner of ten of eleven fights up in Pennsylvania. Rodriguez had beaten Vega twice, so he figured to be a slight step up in class for Ray. Lesson Two.

In the fourth round Ray got hit with two left hooks that staggered him, the hardest punches he'd been hit in his career up to that point, he later claimed. But for one reason or another— afterward he said it was inexperience—Willie Rodriguez did not follow up his advantage aggressively, and Sugar Ray pulled himself together and took control of the fight again.

Ray Leonard won the decision unanimously, as he deserved to, but not overwhelmingly. He'd shown he was vulnerable, making the anti-Sugar rooters out in Television Land surer than ever he was an imposter. Once again Ray's bad luck was simply the flip side of even better fortune: Now that an element of genuine doubt about his ability was added to the scenario, with it came controversy, drama, piqued interest. Was the kid anywhere near as good as the buildup? Stay tuned, ladies and gentlemen.

Although Sugar Ray Leonard, the fighter, was still an unknown quantity, Sugar Ray Leonard, the corporation, was hot. Ray had paid back his $21,000 loan to the investors after the Vega fight. The corporation paid $40 interest on each $1,000, causing Trainer to confess to his softball teammates, "It was a terrible investment." No one seemed to mind particularly. The original capital had never even been touched.

Furthermore, Sugar Ray Leonard, Inc. dumped CBS for a multifight package deal with ABC-TV that guaranteed him more money and regular national exposure while continuing to learn his trade. A few crank journalists objected to the fact that television networks had no business acting as *de facto* promoters in the fight business since they weren't licensed as such. Their criticism didn't change a thing. Boxing simply continued to be what it had always been, the most unregulated major sport in America, so why should media giants be excluded?

Although attendance at the Civic Center for Leonard–Rodriguez was down 3,300 (32 percent)—it was tough for working people to come up with ticket money a second time, even to show support for a hometown kid—the national TV ratings were very good. Ray made $40,000 for the licks he took from Rodriguez in that fourth round.

On the undercard, not seen on TV, Luis "the Bull" Vega fought his heart out and won a decision from a fighter who had beaten him two years earlier. Vega got the fight as partial repayment for being stiffed in his fight with Leonard earlier. So he went away happily with a few hundred more bucks and a win on his record.

Willie Rodriguez drove back to Allentown with $1,500 and a nagging feeling, a lifelong legacy, really, of "what coulda been" had he followed up those punches. At least those two left hooks will get him a drink on the house as long as he lives.

CHAPTER 6

My Fighter

Just as my old man linked himself psychically to Benny Leonard, most male Americans of different eras select a major sports figure to identify with. Theirs vicariously are the powers and pleasures of athletic excellence, which, in the mind at least, remain eternally young. Heavyweight champions, especially, like Corbett and Dempsey, Louis, Marciano, and Ali, were not only of their times; they put their unique, mythic stamps on very different generations of American consciousness, world consciousness in the case of Ali.

Naturally, I got caught up in the aura and sweep of the great champions of my lifetime. But the fighter I identify with—*my* fighter, in other words—was not as great a fighter as Benny Leonard or Louis or Ali. A knowledgeable boxing critic might rank him maybe a cut above a Hell of a Fighter. However, if you judged the totality of the man, boxer *and* human being, there have been few to match Richard Ihetu, the African who fought under the *nom de guerre* Dick Tiger.

As with the vast majority of professional boxers—along with the rest of us, come to think of it—the last act of Dick Tiger's life was bitterly tragic. The difference in Tiger's case is that it wasn't boxing that took the heart out of him but the dream he tried to support with the purses he earned after he reclaimed the middleweight title and then won the light-heavyweight championship.

If you tend to assume that winning a world championship automatically makes a fighter great or even good, you've got to rid yourself of that notion quickly. Very ordinary fighters can be and have been manipulated into championships. That is yet another corruption in a corrupt business. Legitimate champs, though, have to be at least very good fighters, and a legitimate double champion like Tiger had to be first-rate. Greatness in fighters, as with Presidents and novels, has to stand the test of time.

One thing that differentiates boxing from most other sports is its remarkable continuity and conformity. It is virtually impossible, emotions aside, to compare Babe Ruth and Henry Aaron as home-run hitters—ballparks differed tremendously, pitching techniques were revolutionized, night games began to dominate longer travel schedules, even the baseballs the two men hit were significantly different. In tennis, the size and materials of the racquets have altered the game's essentials. And pole vaulters now use modern engineering techniques to bend and snap themselves yards above their predecessors. In most sports, modern advances make true comparisons impossibly unfair.

Boxing, however, remains basically unchanged. It is one of the few sports in which weight classification attempts to equalize athletes, except of course among heavyweights, who have gotten progressively larger over the years. Comparative judgments of any sort are always debatable, but it really is possible to compare Jack Dempsey and Rocky Marciano in precisely the same manner that Laurence Olivier's King Lear can be compared to John Gielgud's or Paul Scofield's. Similarly, people who have seen them are very capable of comparing Ali and Louis, Kid Chocolate and Willie Pep, Ray Robinson and Stanley Ketchel, Ray and Benny Leonard. Of course the bias is almost always for the fighters of your youth, those good ole days when you thought you'd live forever.

Years from now, when a bunch of guys in a bar are grumbling about a mismatch on the TV, and they start talking about good, maybe great, light-heavyweights, Dick Tiger will not be the name they settle on—it could be Archie Moore, Bob Foster, or Philadelphia Jack O'Brien—but if they know their boxing, Tiger's name at least will be mentioned. Such is the nature of immortality in boxing circles.

I recall with rare exactitude the day and hour I first met Dick Tiger. It's possible because I have the information scrawled on the top of a page in a middle-sized spiral notebook: "Noon— March 10." The year wasn't written. It was 1965. I was in my sportswriter–imposter phase, if you recall. My UPI friend called and told me Tiger was meeting the press in his dressing room at the Garden. It was two days before he was scheduled to fight Rocky Rivero, a tough middleweight from Argentina known for a dynamite knockout punch. It didn't figure to be an easy payday for Tiger, who was thirty-five and had lost his middleweight championship fifteen months earlier to Joey Giardello on what was conceded to be, by everyone but Giardello people, a warped, hometown decision.

I flashed my friend's press card at the employee's entrance of the Garden and immediately discovered that I need not have worried so much during my trip crosstown about getting inside. The old man guarding the door waved me past without looking up from his racing form. Inside, some of the guys from the Boxing Department nodded to me, as did a couple of boxing writers; I'd become a recognizable ringside face. Only four or five reporters had shown up, and they waited at the door to a Fiftieth Street dressing room while the tap and slide of a jump rope was heard from inside.

Chickie Ferrara, Tiger's able little trainer, opened the door, and we filed in. I'd seen Tiger a couple of times on TV; one appearance I remembered especially, a vicious fifteen-round draw with Gene Fullmer. I'd never have recognized him in the flesh. He was the darkest man I'd ever seen. No, that doesn't describe it: There was a dusky, deep plum color to his skin, but even where he glistened with perspiration there were gray patches that looked dry, very much like the skin of the fruit. Never having seen an African before, I stared at his tone, at the knotty, heavily muscled body, almost oblivious to the questions being asked and to his answers, but not quite. Momentarily our eyes met and self-consciously I scribbled some words in my notes that make only partial sense to me now: "Giardello ducking me. Jersey isn't quitting."

The intention of the intimate press conference became quickly apparent as Tiger gave only the briefest answers to questions about the upcoming match with Rivero. I wrote, " 'Rivero presents no particular problem for me.' *Really!*" His special quality of voice and intelligence hit me when in clipped colonial British braided with a tribal African lilt he said, "The present champion refuses to meet me again. He has defended just once in fifteen months, once again in his home city. I put it that this is not a courageous posture for a so-called champion." *Courageous posture?* My God, who was this man!

At bottom, Tiger was using the great store of goodwill he'd built over the years with these boxing writers to try to pressure Giardello in print to give him his rematch. For more than a year there had been pressure applied to Giardello's people; they hadn't budged. They liked their championship, and they wanted no part of Tiger again. Seven more months would pass before Giardello finally agreed to give Tiger a chance to regain his championship.

"Why," a reporter asked, "did you agree to fight him in Atlantic City in the first place, knowing it was his backyard? Especially since you were the champ?"

"To a certain extent it was because of his problem in New York." The euphemistic "problem" was well understood. Giardello hadn't had a license to box in New York since '56. Although he'd served time in prison for assault, Giardello had had his license revoked because of what the commission called his "undesirable connections." Word was out that Giardello's management was mob-controlled, if not actually mob-connected. "But that is not," Tiger explained patiently, "the entire story. They offered me the most money to fight him there. I do not wish to seem the mercenary, but this is my livelihood, gentlemen. I am not utterly disappointed—with my purse I bought a beauty shop for my sister and a bookstore in Lagos. Yes, these are tribal scars."

His last statement didn't make any sense. I didn't realize he was speaking directly to me. I had been staring at his chest. His thick finger moved over a band of thin, vertical scars, each about two inches long, which formed a horizontal stripe almost from arm pit to arm pit. "Tribal scars," he repeated for my benefit. "All Ibo boys receive them when they have proven their courage."

I was surprised by his easy assumption that we would know what an Ibo was. I guessed correctly that was the name of his tribe, his people. Much of the world would come to know that name soon enough—shamefully and tragically.

"A bookstore," I asked, amazed that a fighter would own a bookstore, "why in the world would you want to buy a bookstore?"

He flashed a smile that revealed a gold tooth. "Because I like to read books. Har, har. Why else?"

I wanted to know more about his tribe, about life in Nigeria for a former middleweight champion who likes to read books. Dick Tiger, though, had not called his press conference to discuss matters anthropological; he continued to impress upon the real reporters his arguments for a rematch with Giardello without delay. They were, to a man, sympathetic.

Tiger made his best, most practical case one final time: The only decent payday left for Giardello was to fight the true champion, Dick Tiger. If Giardello did not come forward and offer him a rematch after he disposed of Rivero on Thursday night, Tiger would step up to fight light-heavyweights—the winner of Willie Pastrano–Jose Torres, who would be fighting for that title in a few weeks, was a real possibility. Tiger vowed that once he stepped up in class, he'd never come back down, and Giardello could kiss a profitable return match good-bye. "They needed one another" was the Nigerian's bottom line.

"You own a fur coat?" a bald reporter asked in dead earnest. The sweating fighter's brow furrowed. "Because Giardello will give you another shot just about the day after hell freezes over." There was more shuffling of feet than laughter.

Then there were some perfunctory questions about Rivero. Had Tiger seen the Argentine's two fights against Giardello?

"The outcome was already known. They were not title fights. These days Giardello doesn't fight anyone who could possibly beat him." Rivero had gone the distance with Giardello twice, one of them a close, tough match. "Rivero won't go the distance with me. No, I am not being arrogant. I have strong motivation to fight my best. There is too much to lose."

Is there anything you'd like to say directly to Giardello?

"I respect any man who is a champion. Truly. I do not blame him as much as the people who are behind him. But now he must finally act like a champion and defend against the challenger who has the strongest claim."

"Like you?"

"Not *like* me, sir. Me." He tapped his scarred chest.

"Isn't he waiting until you're too old, until you lose your edge?"

"But he is as old as I." Tiger suddenly jumped into a ferocious boxing position; his face contorted into a sneer; a snarl rolled from a curled lip. Then, while holding this position, he said ominously, "A Tiger never loses his hunger." And as suddenly he transformed himself back into the affable, relaxed man who had charmed the pants off us.

Finally, there was nothing left to say. Yes, he'd beat Rivero, but he refused to predict the knockout round. Some of the reporters waited to ask a private question or two and get a slightly different quote. Reluctantly, I moved toward the door, falsely occupying myself with my notes. Tiger said to me as I passed, "Just one moment." I waited around then until he'd finished with the others.

He asked me who I worked for. I chose a path between half-lie and truth. "UPI." He looked pleased; it was a national organization and could be very helpful. "But I'm only a stringer. Actually, I'm an English teacher."

"Have you read *Animal Farm*?"

"Orwell?"

"Of course, Orwell."

We spent the entire afternoon together, talking a bit about Orwell but more about the implications of *Animal Farm*, the terrible pitfalls of revolutionary politics. He seemed to have a personal interest. After he showered and dressed—his brown suit, by the way, was on the shabby side, the jacket a shade lighter than the pants, his black shoes had gray scuffs—we walked briskly down Eighth Avenue. He had a heavily twined package he wanted to go out in the afternoon mail. I saw it was destined for Aba, Nigeria.

I couldn't believe that I was, less than an hour after I'd met him, walking in Manhattan with the former middleweight champion of the world. Mistakenly, I assumed passersby recognized the celebrity and, by strong association, me too. In truth, almost no one noticed us; those who did happen to glance our way might have seen a middle-aged black delivery boy and a winded white intellectual.

The Ibo tribal scars on his chest, he told me as we wove through the crowds, were made by a very sharp, very hot knife when he was ten, unusually young for the initiation. No, they didn't hurt particularly. Then he corrected himself: An Ibo boy could not allow them to hurt. When finally we were forced to stop for traffic, Tiger looked at me carefully and said, "The politics of my country are a cause of great concern to me. There could soon be civil insurrection. The situation is classically Orwellian."

All the way to the post office and then back uptown, he explained the volatile situation in his homeland. "Although we are not the majority, my people have held leadership in Nigeria since the British have left. In recent years, military elements have taken control. We Ibo are not basically a militaristic people, but we will not permit ourselves to be shunted aside. Without the Ibo, my country would be a disaster." Then he said something that even now I recall with clarity even though I hadn't written it down. Perhaps it was because events have conspired to underline their bitter irony. "Our opponents call the Ibo the Jews of Africa. It is meant as an insult. I interpret it as a high compliment." Tiger's dark pupils focused on my chest; the whites were ivory-colored and marbled with thin veins.

A few blocks farther north—we were now on Tenth Avenue —he stopped in front of a tailor's shop. A heavy, gray-haired woman worked away at a sewing machine in the window. The sun cut a swathe across her hands. Tiger went inside and I followed. He pulled off his suit jacket and showed the man behind the counter a long tear in the satin lining. The woman at the machine glowered at the black man.

The owner convinced Tiger he'd be better off selecting a secondhand jacket from the racks in the rear than having his own jacket repaired. Tiger disappeared. The woman, I noticed for the first time, was repairing a small American flag; I watched her stitch a red stripe to a white. Dick Tiger returned wearing another brown jacket, a shade darker than the pants this time and a tad snugger in the shoulders and chest. The man wanted five dollars; they settled on two-fifty, his old jacket, and a ticket to the Rivero fight. I left the shop with a fighter who was not only tough on opponents but who confirmed the sportswriters' word on him— he was even tougher with a buck.

*   *   *

Rocky Rivero, the hard fighter he once was, didn't show up at the Garden. The Rivero who did show was paunchy and moved as though fighting under water. Every punch he attempted was of the KO variety. In fact, Tiger was hit cleanly just twice in five and a half rounds. The referee stopped the fight in the sixth after Rivero had been knocked down for the first time in fifty-four professional fights. Tiger must have known that Rivero was just showing up for a payday.

The stories after the fight were all Tiger. What would he say to Giardello now that he'd knocked out a fighter no one had ever knocked out? Would he move up to light-heavy immediately or would he give Giardello's people a time limit? But as the winner, Tiger was my friend's province; I was off to the loser's dressing room. Which was locked.

I tapped lightly and then strongly on the door.

"Yeah?"

"Press," I lied.

The door didn't open for a couple of minutes. When it did the scene was standard Madison Square Garden-loser-dressing-room. Only this time the men against the wall were all wearing narrow-brimmed hats with dark bands. The fighter was on a rubbing table lying facedown. On the concrete floor on either side of the table lay cut-away casts of his fists in tape. The entire side of Rivero's face had swollen like rising bread. An Hispanic trainer ran a hand over the loose flesh of his fighter's upper back in a tender solace.

I had only one question that mattered, one in which I had developed too personal an interest. "Was he tougher than Giardello?"

Rivero looked over at the men in the hats. They shuffled their feet. One glared at me; in spite of myself, I swallowed.

"I prepare bad for this fight," Rivero said, and with painful effort because his face had been pummeled by a heavy puncher. He turned toward the wall. He wouldn't say anything else to me. Interview over. I couldn't really blame the guy.

Tiger stayed busy after Rivero with his big win against rugged "Hurricane" Carter. If Giardello's people were waiting for age to catch up with Tiger, it didn't seem to be happening. It was true, however, and all experienced fight people knew it, that a fighter usually became an old fighter overnight. One fight, he's got it all; next fight, nothing. Call it the Dorian Gray Syndrome: The cumulative erosion over a career remains well concealed until, *voilà*, suddenly there's nothing left. Sometimes the loss takes place during a fight; a fighter can even lose it in a single round. Maybe some sign of deterioration was what Giardello's people were looking for, and maybe Tiger was foolish for not showing it to them by fighting a little below his top level, but he was, after all, an Ibo, and proud. At any rate, it was in Giardello's interest to wait as long as possible before committing.

Giardello, meanwhile, won an easy ten-rounder from a journeyman in Cherry Hill, New Jersey, his new hometown. "Home cooking," fight people called it. One of the New York papers did a Sunday photo spread on how well boxing had treated him. Sprawling suburban New Jersey colonial. Pink wall-to-wall carpeting in almost every room. French Provincial furniture. White. Rosalie, the wife, appeared to move through life under a blond bouffant wig. I imagined Tiger, with his secondhand suit jacket, living in a seedy Manhattan hotel room reading Orwell. I seethed with indignation over life's injustice to *my* fighter.

On the boxing beat, word was that if it were only up to Joey, he'd have fought Tiger a year ago. That he wasn't really such a bad guy. The problem was his management. They sure as hell weren't going to risk this championship with a beast like Tiger. They knew Tiger was already having trouble making the weight: He'd come in five pounds over the limit for Rivero. The thing that must have really thrown them was that the Nigerian, for all his threats, still refused to take on legitimate light-heavyweights. I knew that it was a matter of pride with him. The scuttlebutt also had it that when they felt Giardello had one good fight in him, and if Tiger was still available, they'd shoot for that last nice payday and, who knows, maybe even go out a winner.

The few boxing writers whose opinions I respected concurred that Giardello was a much better fighter than most people realized, and since boxing was essentially a matter of styles, might have the technique to squeeze out a decision. Of course that was easier for him to accomplish when he had the judges leaning toward him for one reason or another. It would matter terribly where they fought.

Giardello was what they called a "cutie pie," an excellent defensive fighter who could avoid being hit, counterpunch, and minimize the damage to himself with a combination of leaning, holding, spinning, and leverage tricks he'd learned and mastered in almost 130 professional fights.

The consensus was that Giardello, although not a big hitter, could still do a good deal of cumulative damage to a fighter as stationary as Tiger. The fight, if it ever came off, wouldn't be a walkover, that was for sure. A Philadelphia boxing writer, who was up covering a Floyd Patterson fight at the Garden, volunteered that one of the things that bothered Giardello as a man was that he wanted to fight Tiger to see who the better fighter really was. He just wasn't yet in a position to buck his braintrust. Because I'd made such a strong emotional bond to Tiger, I refused to grant credibility to anything positive said of Giardello.

Less than two months after Giardello's manager died, he was given a license to box in New York. The title match was then made for Madison Square Garden in October. Tiger would be thirty-six. Giardello, as champion, dictated the terms. Tough ones: He commanded $50,000 or 40 percent of the gate (live and home TV); Tiger managed $15,000 or 20 percent. When I saw Tiger again and asked him about the split, he said, "He takes the lion's share, but I will take the Tiger's." His wit should have caused him to smile in self-appreciation. He didn't. There was trouble at home, he told me. He had been saving, sending every penny to Aba to help the Ibo cause, but he worried about his family, his property, and particularly about his ability to concentrate on a boxing match, no matter how important, 5,000 miles away from the place and people that mattered most in his life. "The world is never without its ironies, Orwell understood that," said the man with tribal scars.

During the week before the fight the odds swung interestingly, and there was a heavy volume of betting. The early money liked the champ at 6–to–5. Then Tiger support came in and it was "pick 'em." Then Tiger at 6–to–5. Two days before the fight it was 8–5 Tiger. By fight time the odds were down to 7–5 Tiger.

The flow of the betting action convinced me we'd see an honest fight; it seemed to reflect the fact that a reasonable case could be made for each fighter.

The best argument for Giardello ran about as follows: Sure, he's a very used fighter, but they both are. Hell, the other guy's a year older. But Joey ain't had any tough fights for over a year, and he already beat Tiger once for the big one. Controversial, yeah, but he won it. And they split a pair of ten-rounders years ago. Styles favor Joey. Damn hard to hit, and he can hit the other guy enough to win on points. Don't forget, he's the champ—if the fight's as close as everyone thinks it's going to be, he gets the judges' nod. Right?

For Tiger the best scenario was like this: He really won the last fight, hometown decision. That won't happen in New York. This time he won't leave no doubt. He's been busier lately, fighting tougher fighters, beating them big; he's actually a better fighter than ever before in his life. He's a stronger fighter than Giardello, a bigger hitter—the next middleweight champion of the world. The biggest thing is that he wants it more.

That last point, I felt, was crucial. Dick Tiger not only needed the glory and wanted the revenge, he required the championship as a political platform and a means to help finance a civil war. I didn't realize in those days how difficult it was for an athlete to put such immense pressure on himself and still perform at absolute capacity. They always did it in the movies.

It was something to see the Garden packed on a Thursday night. It must have been particularly satisfying for the TV cameramen to be able to swing anywhere and have an authentic crowd as background. Over 17,000 showed up and paid more than $160,000, so both fighters earned a lot more than their guarantees.

I worried all afternoon that I'd be bumped out of my ringside seat. I wasn't. I was squeezed into the steps of the champion's corner, but not displaced. I took that as a good omen for Tiger. At ringside hardly anyone paid much attention to the preliminary fighters; there was too much celebrity excitement. Sinatra was supposed to show up. Mantle and Berra had already been seen. I spotted Sugar Ray Robinson and Rocky Graziano. There were more men in evening jackets and classy women wearing furs than I'd ever seen at ringside before. And they were all somebody or acting like somebody, which created almost the same effect.

Africans paraded through the crowd, some of them in tribal robes whose colors I not only couldn't describe but had never even seen before. Reds and purples and greens and golds, all of which had a dark intensity about them, through them, that made the robes seem not only exotic but vaguely dangerous. Most of the men wore flat hats in the style of prisoners in cartoons, but colorful and with golden tassels.

Tiger came out first from the Fiftieth Street side, and with his appearance a large West African drum (later an expert identified it for me as *apesi*), began to thunder rhythmically from the darkness of the end arena. Its beat was compelling but alien to the huge crowd of New Yorkers, most of whom were there to root the Italian champ home one more time. They clapped and stamped out a march beat. The drum, though, dominated underneath, foreboding as the drums in *The Emperor Jones*.

Although they each weighed the precise limit of 160 pounds, Tiger was two inches shorter, yet physically it looked like a mismatch when they met in center ring. Above his white trunks, Tiger's body was massive; his back and shoulder muscles had the bulk and sinew of a grave digger. Giardello seemed pink and soft by comparison; his dark trunks made his body seem even paler.

At the bell, Tiger rushed across the ring and met the champ before he was two steps out of his corner. The African threw punches behind his surprising jab with abandon—uncharacteristic for him—that backed Giardello against the ropes. A surprise tactic. Tiger had always been, like Giardello, a very cautious starter, especially in a fifteen-round fight. But now he was trying to set the pace and tone for the match immediately, trying to make his determination manifest. He didn't appear to believe he could be hurt, even by the master counterpuncher. Giardello couldn't get off the ropes and was taking more than his share of solid body shots. Significantly, each time Giardello smothered Tiger's attack and appeared to hook the dark arms, referee LoBianco quickly stepped in and had them fighting again. That favored Tiger. Tiger had complained that in their first title fight Giardello was allowed to grab and hold. From the steps next to me Adolph

Ritacco, Giardello's trainer, shouted, "He's too strong. Move, Joey. Use style, use style."

Joey simply could not. Tiger's fists worked the softening body. The great tribal drum thundered. Before the round ended, Joey Giardello became an old fighter.

To his everlasting credit, Giardello didn't permit the fight to become a rout. Even though he was taking a beating, he had his moments, tying the African up, countering sharply when it seemed he had absolutely nothing left. In the fifth round he hit Tiger with three clean left hands, causing the challenger's eyes to float, and the Nigerian staggered backward. Maybe Tiger had miscalculated; perhaps he'd begun to punch himself out with his torrid start. No, the setback was only momentary. Tiger cleared his head with a shake; Giardello didn't, couldn't, press his advantage. Tiger came on again. It's a disheartening thing when a fighter's best punches can be shaken off.

In the seventh Giardello delivered some hooks to Tiger's kidney that would have taken the heart out of a less determined man. They won the round for the champion. There was still some genuine rage and the touch of the maestro in Giardello's failing body. He did everything a used-up fighter could possible do— and some things that were impossible. The combination of courage and cleverness he showed could not be dismissed; in spite of myself, I'd begun admiring him. In the end, Tiger won the fight because of his superior strength and his transcendent desire. Their fighters' hearts were equally large.

No, it wasn't a great fight, but it was very interesting and very good. The decision was unanimous. I had it scored nine rounds to six. Africans in green and purple robes carrying a banner that read "BIAFRA MUST LIVE" leapt into the ring. No one understood its meaning. I took off for the loser's dressing room.

Giardello, sitting on a table, mopped his face in a bloody towel; his back was rubbed raw from having been raked along the ropes. He waited for questions. The room was full; the reporters' reticence was a sign of their respect for his enormous effort.

Your evaluation, Joey.

"Disappointment. With myself. I was throwing my right hand like a girl. I couldn't get started."

What now, Joey?

"Retire. Maybe one more fight for charity. Retarded kids."
Carmine, Joey's six-year-old, had been brain-damaged from birth.
I hadn't known that.

I flipped a page of my notebook and said, "At the start of the
fifteenth, you said something to him. You remember what you said?"

"Yeah. I said, 'Nice fight.' "

The middleweight limit became increasingly difficult, almost
impossible, for Tiger to make. Less than eight months after losing
the crown to Emile Griffith in 1966, he won the light-heavyweight
title from José Torres. But the pain can be traced back to the
Giardello fight. Not intense, but present as a continual discomfort
in his lower back and right side. The blood in his urine became
more common and stayed longer than previously. He understood
it as a small price to pay for his people, for his homeland. Biafra.

By 1967 people throughout the world knew that name. The
Ibo of eastern Nigeria had seceded from the central government.
They called their new country Biafra. Almost from the outset the
civil war that followed quickly became a rout. The Biafrans ap-
pealed to all the world powers for help, for arms, for aid. None
was forthcoming. The Nigerian central government controlled
the army and the oil in black Africa's richest oil country. "The
Jews of Africa" were slaughtered.

Shortly before hostilities broke out Dick Tiger returned to his
country to fight another African in what amounted to an exhibition at Port Harcourt, a few miles from his home in Aba. A
glorious day for the Ibo in Port Harcourt. Tiger donated his purse
to the Biafran government.

Then he came back to New York and gave Torres his rematch
at the Garden. Like their first match, it was fought before a pretty
good crowd, and Tiger, giving away about ten pounds, again won
by decision. The second fight was much closer; one of the judges
gave the match to Torres, eight rounds to seven. My experience
had led me to safety beneath the runway before the bottles came
flying out of the balcony.

Along with Biafra, Dick Tiger saw all else lost. Members of his
family were imprisoned; he received no word of their fate. He
could not go home. Rumors of the deaths of relatives and friends

floated to him in New York. His properties in Lagos had been confiscated. His apartments gone, the service station in Aba taken shortly after, the beauty parlor and cosmetics shop, the bookstore, the Mercedes—all gone. The tens of thousands of dollars saved by the man who wore secondhand suits, gone. Biafra, the dream, gone.

Dick Tiger was knocked out in the fourth round of his next title defense by Bob Foster, a truly great light-heavyweight, in May of '68. It was the only time he'd ever been knocked out. Perhaps he should have quit then. He was almost forty, a very old fighter. Too many tough fights. The pain in his lower back came in more frequent spasms. But he couldn't quit. He was a political exile in New York with no other salable skill. Dick Tiger fought four more times, all in New York, one of them a victory over Nino Benvenuti, a former middleweight champion. The fights gave him just enough money to live on.

After he retired in 1971 he worked as a guard at the Metropolitan Museum of Art, commuting by train from a room in the Bedford-Stuyvesant section of Brooklyn. He was recognized once or twice on the subway.

In October 1971 he was stricken by a stabbing pain in his back, right side, and abdomen, an attack so severe this time that he limped to the employees' lounge and fell to his knees. But he got up. He was taken immediately to St. Vincent's Hospital in Greenwich Village for observation. The Madison Square Garden Boxing Department picked up the tab.

No treatment was possible. Dick Tiger had cancer of the liver, very acute, very advanced. He told a reporter, "The United States is a very good country, a very nice country, but Biafra is my home. I will die in Biafra." Technically speaking, in 1971, no such place existed on the face of the earth.

The Nigerian government permitted Tiger to be returned to Aba after the war, to his Ibo home in east Nigeria. His plane landed in Port Harcourt. For days thereafter thousands of visitors—mourners, really—from miles around walked the hot, dusty roads to Aba. When they found his house they saw a muscular but pain-withered man sitting in the shade of a solitary acacia tree, his best fights behind him.

My fighter died December 14, 1971.

CHAPTER 7

Graduate, *Cum Laude*

Sugar Ray Leonard fought what Paddy Flood and similar hard-boiled fight guys called "pussies"—a category of boxer not on Angelo Dundee's classification list—for more than two years. Oh, you could make a case for a couple of his handpicked opponents, but the truth is there weren't many with a real chance to beat him. He didn't get around to fighting a world-ranked welterweight, Floyd Mayweather, until late in '78, Ray's fourteenth professional match, and even then Mayweather was ranked only seventeenth. So there was ample reason for tough-minded boxing folk to be critical of Leonard while at the same time admiring Dundee's ability to orchestrate a career for a pretty boy and TV bullshitter who still hadn't really fought anyone and was making a ton of money in the process.

Angelo Dundee can be a very patient man, especially when 15 percent of a multimillion-dollar payoff is on the line. If he was going to err with Ray Leonard's development, it would not be on the side of impatience. Not because Angelo is overly cautious by temperament. He's not. When it's time to shoot everything on a single roll of the dice, Dundee won't shy away. In the case of

Sugar Ray, however, Angelo realized that time was his greatest ally.

For openers, Ray was young and literally growing into manhood right before America's eyes. The change in his body on the TV screen from fight to fight might have been so gradual it could easily have been missed. But comparing a tape of Ray in his Olympic championship with him in, say, his fourth round knockout of Pete Ranzany three years later reveals a young man with markedly developed muscular definition in the upper torso and arms. And, happily for Team Leonard, without any loss in hand or foot speed.

Slowly, deliberately, Ray had been asked by Dundee to build his ring endurance. After three bouts scheduled for six rounds, he moved to eight-rounders. After eight such matches, he became a full-fledged ten-round, main-event fighter. The additional rounds required not only more stamina but a better-developed sense of pace, the ability to catch the judges' eyes with well-timed effort, learning how to rest and lean on an opponent without losing any points. The acknowledged master of pace and ring control among fight people was Willie Pep. Known as "Will-o'-the-Wisp," Pep held the feather-weight championship (126) throughout most of the 1940s. The legend that has grown about him is that Pep could win rounds without ever throwing a punch by making his opponent look so bad the judges would give the round to Pep's defense. Ah, there were little giants in those days.

In the years since his Olympic triumph Ray had grown naturally into a full-fledged welterweight (147), and occasionally he even went beyond that limit when Dundee wanted to see if he could handle slightly undersized middleweights. It was likely that toward the end of his career—if he stuck with it—Ray might become a true middleweight. Dundee wanted him to have a foretaste.

Partially because he was growing into his full size and strength, partially because Dundee was teaching him well, Ray began to score knockouts, eight of nine after the Rodriquez fight. Boxing skeptics, of course, attributed the run more to the "Tomato Cans" that were being flattened than to the fist flattening them. Dundee paid little attention, welcomed the criticism in fact. Someone would have to shell out megabucks eventually to see if the Corporate Kid could really fight.

Dundee knew that, other than in the heavyweight division, it was among the welterweights there was big money to be made. He watched and waited while his undefeated battler continued his profitable studies and settled in at his strongest natural weight. Angelo Dundee's imagination bubbled with possibilities. He dreamed of the money that would roll in from matches with the division's big names, Wilfredo Benitez, Pipino Cuevas, Thomas "Hit Man" Hearns, and, ultimately, professional boxing's Prince of Darkness, Roberto Duran, the man most admired by the boxing establishment. The key to all that green, however, was patience.

Dundee was waiting also for boxing's changing of the guard. He was waiting for the Ali era to pass. As Ali's trainer, he knew there wasn't much left, but Ali was still Ali and could be neither dismissed nor deserted. If Ali wished to diminish himself by continuing to fight with lesser skills, he'd earned that right, but Angelo clearly saw the end of the line for the remarkable champion.

The conventional wisdom was that "as the heavyweights go, so goes boxing." That meant the entire sport was expected to soften and sink back to what it had been when I was masquerading as a UPI boxing writer, back before Cassius Clay overwhelmed America's sensibilities. Angelo didn't accept conventional wisdom. Neither did Mike Trainer. They firmly believed it was possible to focus national attention on another personality, another fighter in another division. Their fighter.

Ray Leonard had already begun to fill the void in lots of small ways. By appearing on TV regularly in winning fights and by developing a special on-air relationship with Cosell, as Clay had. By cradling "Little Ray" in his arms after a victory and charming the camera with smile and style—we learned to care about the fighter and the man. He made a 7-Up commercial with his son that was so saccharine and so widely shown it should have carried a surgeon general's warning. His face and exploits found their way into not only sports pages but national news magazines as well.

This wasn't merely media hype. It was a first-rate buildup, a process to match Dundee's long, careful schooling of the fighter. An evolution in which we were asked to invest our emotions in that distant dramatic moment when we would watch the boy we had seen growing up on TV since Montreal in '76 try to win the professional championship of the world. Patience built suspense in the result. Suspense created anticipation. And anticipation paid off.

There were other good reasons for Sugar Ray Leonard, Inc. to bide its time. To start with, the Leonard team could afford to. These buildup fights, thanks to Trainer, were paying off nicely. Ray wasn't the only one learning to mix it with the big boys. Mike Trainer had learned quickly to play the networks against one another in order to produce the best deals for the young fighter.

Trainer realized that the networks, which had gotten used to what an Ali fight could do for them, now needed Ray and his consistently high ratings more than Ray needed them. So Trainer simply presented the fighter to whoever offered the best terms. The best deal, however, was not always for the most money. Selling the fights individually might have brought Ray more than the $350,000 he was guaranteed for his first six-fight package for ABC, but the assurance that his bouts would have regular national exposure was a greater consideration at the time. When the fighter finally scaled the heights, Ray Leonard could be sold in smaller, more expensive pieces.

Ray was twenty-three years old in May of 1979, and he had run his professional winning streak to twenty-two straight. If he had gone back to that intersection in Washington where he had suffered the indignity of anonymity, it would have been very difficult to find a pedestrian who *didn't* know who he was. And almost impossible to find one who knew that the World Boxing Council welterweight champion was Wilfredo Benitez.

Trainer had invested the fruits of Ray's labor so that the mutual funds and blue-chip stocks, the real estate, the tax-free bonds and treasury bills would go on producing important capital for Sugar Ray Leonard, Inc. if the president of that corporation never again laced a pair of Everlast gloves over a Kotex pad. And Trainer covered that capital with the protective tax sheltering that every American millionaire believes he not only requires but deserves. It was amazing. During his deliberate matriculation, without yet fighting a truly first-class opponent, Sugar Ray Leonard, Inc. had amassed a net worth of more than three million bucks. Naturally, Mike Trainer had long since stopped giving the kid his time and expertise; he had been working for Ray since the corporation's first profits rolled in on an hourly fee basis.

Until Ray finally got into a ring with a champion there would be no objective way to resolve the question of his true ability as a professional fighter. But even then there could be a situation—a lucky punch, an injury, a bad decision—that would still leave matters unresolved. Too often in boxing this is the case.

It wasn't only fight fans who wanted the matter resolved. Ray Leonard himself wanted to know how good he could be. He wasn't immune to what the skeptics were saying about poor quality of his opponents. He didn't believe them, and he was chafing for the chance to prove himself. Deeper, the artist in him wanted to know for himself just how good Ray Leonard really was. Somehow, even though he'd gained the financial security he'd sought, the artist was hungry for achievement and acclaim.

Ray had always been goal-oriented, and single-mindedly so. He sought the Olympic gold medal steadily for five years. Almost as hungrily, he desired security and came to accept professional boxing as a means to that end. He was now a rich young man.

During his three-year apprenticeship a number of important things had happened. In addition to becoming stronger and building his stamina, Ray's excellent training habits had been reinforced to the point of becoming second nature. He was always in peak condition for a fight; that readiness would make the difference in some of his most important matches. None of his opponents would ever outcondition him. Dundee matched him with middleweights who generally punched harder than welters so Ray would have a taste of the blows a true puncher could deliver. Probably Dundee was thinking ahead to welterweight KO artists like Tommy Hearns and Robert Duran, who hit like middleweights.

Dundee used all those fights to teach Ray every pugilistic trick he knew. There was so much to learn, it wasn't wise or fair to try to cram the course into half a dozen fights. Sugar Ray Leonard was as well prepared as a fighter could be in the TV era, schooled classically in spite of the enormous pressures to rush a "personality" fighter into bouts with contenders and titlists.

While the careful matriculation at Dundee U. continued, Trainer avoided the pitfall of network overexposure by taking the Leonard Show on the road without television coverage to towns like Hartford, Connecticut, Dayton, Ohio, and Utica, New York, where the live gates more than covered expenses and Ray wouldn't have to produce a blockbuster performance. A few other, more attractive matches were sold to Home Box Office and turned a tidy profit.

In the spring of '79, even while Ray was taking "Beating Middleweights 101," Trainer and Dundee were trying to make two fights that would come to fruition six and eight months later respectively. The first was not so much a fight as the centerpiece to a package of bouts that ABC was considering for prime time.

Muhammad Ali had slipped into one of his retirements and Larry Holmes had acceded to the World Boxing Council heavyweight championship. Although he would prove to be a good fighter and an enduring champion, Holmes lacked that special television magic to pull big prime-time numbers. ABC, realizing that a Holmes title defense by itself "wouldn't draw flies," as they say in the programming conference room, put together a three-fight card that also included Ray Leonard, who had become TV's biggest attraction, and Roberto Duran, the bellicose Panamanian generally conceded to be the best fighter in the world, pound-for-pound.

No, Leonard and Duran would not yet fight one another, and certainly not as a preliminary to a bout featuring Larry Holmes. Dundee, believing that older fighters—and Duran was almost twenty-nine—who have had lots of tough matches could lose it very quickly, realized once again that time was very much on his side. The ultimate showdown was inevitable; anticipation could only make the match an even greater financial success. ABC's scheduling was brilliant: Duran and Leonard would each be given journeymen to fight; the viewers could compare their skills and ring personalities, thereby developing a rooting interest in the showdown fight. It was as though fans were having their appetites whetted by delicious hors d'oeuvres. Naturally, ABC believed it had cornered the market for the entrée.

Things could not have turned out better in Caesar's Palace that September night in 1979. Duran looked sluggish against Zeferino "Speedy" Gonzales, an L.A. junior middleweight who had lost only once in nineteen professional tries. Duran won a unanimous ten-round decision in a lackluster performance. He looked slow and paunchy, causing widespread, but uninformed, speculation that he was ready to be taken by a strong, hungry, young fighter. Speak of the devil, here comes Sugar Ray in the very next bout. AND BLAM, he hits Andy Price a double left jab and a clean overhand right. Price backs against the ropes, where a dozen unanswered blows send him down and out for the count. First-round knockout for Sugar Ray, and how was that for a contrast? Dundee wasn't wild about the flash knockout; he'd scheduled the fight for twelve rounds precisely because he wanted to give Ray a feel for the championship distance.

But it was not Duran that Dundee intended next for Sugar Ray. Wilfredo Benitez was an extremely talented but erratic young boxer who in displays of brilliance had captured the junior welterweight title when he was seventeen and the welterweight title at twenty. Although at twenty-one he was two years younger than Leonard, Wilfredo had four more years of professional experience. He'd already faced some tougher fighters, much tougher. Dundee believed Benitez was beatable, however, and wanted Leonard to take the crown and wear it into the ring against Duran if at all possible. Making the fight with Benitez, Trainer's task, hadn't proven easy, he'd been working on it all spring.

The first sticking point, as it usually is, was money. As champion, Benitez, through his erudite manager, Jim Jacobs, felt he was entitled to the larger share of whatever package could be sold to the networks. Leonard, Trainer argued, was the draw, already pulling in far more money for a single fight than Benitez had ever earned as champion. A championship bout with Leonard meant prime-time scheduling, lots of media attention, and maybe ten times the size of any purse Benitez had ever seen. Trainer couldn't believe Jacobs wasn't buying.

Jacobs knew he had two things he didn't intend to bargain away: the championship and a very young fighter who lost nothing by playing a waiting game. So Jacobs continued to hold out for the principle that the champion must be given the bigger piece of pie. The package they finally agreed upon was $1.2 million for Benitez, $1 million for Sugar Ray. It appeared that Trainer had gotten outnegotiated. For the $200,000 disparity, however, Trainer received a very important, perhaps even crucial, consideration.

The fight would not be held in San Juan, Puerto Rico, where Benitez had won his championships and successfully defended each. The one thing the Leonard camp could not afford at any price was seeing all lost by a hometown decision.

Actually, accepting Las Vegas as the site meant that Benitez would be fighting in a town he'd never fought in before. Leonard, on the other hand, had become a Vegas regular, knocking out his last three opponents in that gaudy venue.

After some perfunctory bidding among the networks, ABC bought the TV package, and with Caesar's kicking in for the live promotion rights, the deal became by far the most lucrative ever for fighters in the 147-pound division. A division, by the way, that had produced some of the greatest fighters who ever laced up. "The Toy Bulldog," Mickey Walker; Tim-O's champion, Jimmy McLarnin, and his tormentor, Barney Ross; "Hammerin'" Henry Armstrong, Ray Robinson, Kid Gavilan—these were the ghosts of great welterweights who had preceded Benitez and Leonard. None of them ever saw that many zeros behind a whole number and a dollar sign on a contract in their lives.

Boxing's monetary rewards so favored the heavyweights that rarely did lighter boxers receive equal pay for equal, and sometimes far superior, work. So when old-timers talked about "the best fighter pound-for-pound," it usually meant the poor bastard was a lightweight or a welter somebody had to throw a benefit for when his career was over. Aesthetic approval, sure; money, not much. One of the things Ray Leonard will be most remembered for is how he changed the pay scale for fighters at the lighter weights.

Inherent in the disregard of the smaller fighters, especially during the television era, was an obvious ethnic-cultural bias. In much of the Third World, particularly in Latin America and Asia, people tend to be significantly smaller than North Americans. Diet and the genetic pool obviously have something to do with it. It's no surprise, then, that Hispanic and Oriental boxers are numerous and excell at the lighter weights. In recent years the names of the boxers who'll make most critics' "Hell of a Fighter" lists in classifications from middleweight on down would certainly include a disproportionate number of Hispanics. As long as Ali was holding sway, these fighters usually picked up compliments from knowledgeable boxing fans and crumbs from promoters.

Television required not only wonderful fighters but fellows who could charm viewers, or at least intrigue them. That meant interviews, and many of the best fighters of the era didn't speak English very well. It was a shame that some remarkable boxers—Antonio Cervantes and Carlos Monzon, to name just two of the best—worked in relative anonymity. And it was no accident that most of the fighters who figured to test Sugar Ray most severely were Latinos.

So important, in fact, had South American fighters and managers become in the structure of the sport that not one but two headquarters for organizations claiming to oversee its international activities were established in Spanish-speaking countries—the World Boxing Association (WBA) in Panama City and the World Boxing Council (WBC) in Mexico City. If these august bodies actually governed the sport fairly and with authority, they might have some justification for existence. They don't. They are, in essence, the "banana republics" of the fight game, corrupt governments that give the trappings of legitimacy to boxing's deplorable business practices. If baseball or football were supervised by agencies such as these, no self-respecting bookie would cover their action.

One such corrupt legislative body would seem to be quite sufficient to allow boxing to carry on as usual. Having competing groups is a brilliant con, particularly when it comes to sanctioning title bouts. Since the WBA and WBC rarely recognize the same fighter as champion in a division, there are usually twice as many fighters claiming titles than is credible. When you add the fact that a variety of "junior" and "super" weight classes have been added over the years, almost any decent fighter with good managerial connections can become a champ of something. It's a confusing state of affairs that makes it almost impossible for any but the most avid fans to develop a rooting interest in the sport.

The confused state of affairs, believe it or not, is welcomed by promoters and managers. If they can't do business profitably with one group, they just turn to the other. Some arrangement always seems possible given the degree of corruption that permeates these ruling bodies. Television sports executives don't seem to mind the chaos either: The abundance of sanctioned title bouts assures them fights they can billboard on their networks as "world championships" almost every weekend.

If and when someone tries to clean up the fight game, trashing these two organizations simply must be a priority.

Wilfredo Benitez was the logical choice as Ray's next opponent, not only because he held the WBC championship but because his style did not present any insurmontable problems for Leonard if he fought in the manner Dundee prescribed and up to the level of his ability. These are things, however, no one can take for granted. "That's why," as bookies like to say, "they have the guys lace up the gloves."

Benitez's credentials were legit. Since bursting on the scene he had beaten some of the best men around, taking the welterweight crown from Carlos Palomino, a very respectable champion. But although Benitez had a string of early KOs in fights around the Caribbean while he was making his reputation, in his more recent bouts with quality opponents he had won by decision. He was primarily a boxer type, with all the skills that come with great natural speed, a good young body, success, and acclaim. Wilfredo Benitez was in many respects a prodigy cut from the same cloth as Ray Leonard.

But he had been brought along in a very different manner. During his brief apprenticeship he rarely fought anyone difficult; nor did his father, who managed and trained him then, have the breadth of experience to teach his son much beyond the basics. It didn't seem as though he had to: Wilfredo was, like Ray in the amateurs, a natural, a genius, a wunderkind. Incomplete as he was as a boxer, there was enough pure talent in him to beat an aging Cervantes before a San Juan crowd in 1976.

No fighter, however, is without weaknesses, and Benitez's seemed to be related directly to his strengths. Things had come so easy for him, he put his complete trust in his remarkable talent. Call it arrogance, call it the ignorance of youth; however it was, Wilfredo Benitez was like the school kid who got "A's" without really trying.

Ray, of course, could easily have become that kind of student.

He didn't because Angelo Dundee wouldn't let him. The world was full of bright kids, Dundee understood, but a bright kid with a work ethic—that was something special, that was something that could get you through when, in those rare but inevitable struggles, simple talent can't get the job done. Dundee's curriculum recognized Leonard's genius and attempted to tame it without humbling it.

Benitez had no such structure imposed on him. As a result, Benitez was permitted too free a rein, so he lacked the control even over his temperament. He tended toward sullenness and great mood swings; he trusted his young body so completely that he did not like to push it in workouts—hadn't he gone the fifteen-round limit successfully twice before his eighteenth birthday? And, yes, he liked the girls enormously and was a familiar face at San Juan night spots.

The reasoning in the Leonard camp was that Ray would be meeting a slightly less dedicated and motivated version of himself. One, they believed, that did not have the punching power that the true Ray Leonard had developed without the boxing establishment paying heed or giving credence. If things went according to plan, the true should beat the slightly less true.

One thing that made Benitez tougher for this bout and was cause for a bit of concern was something the fighter had lost since his last fight. His father, Gregorio. No, he hadn't died.

During Wilfredo's first fight with Harold Weston, he returned to his stool to receive a slap from Gregorio harder than anything Weston had thrown during the round. In the second fight, father slapped son twice. And during the Palomino fight, Gregorio and Emile Griffith, then Wilfredo's trainer, almost came to blows over differences in strategy. Papa Benitez was so divisive an influence generally, it was deemed best for all concerned if he step out of the picture. That's when he agreed to sell Wilfredo's contract for $150,000 and 10 percent of the boy's future earnings. Jim Jacobs bought it and put some stability back in Wilfredo's career. Although Gregorio didn't step completely out of his son's life, at least he stepped out of his corner.

If Paddy Flood were still alive and cooking, I'm sure he'd put fathers right behind dames as the ruination of promising fighters. The father-as-manager is the real killer. It's tough enough for a kid to keep his concentration on the specific instructions from his corner without worrying about what Pop's expectations are. The dispassionate distance just isn't there, can't be; on the professional level a fight can rarely be won by making the old man proud of you. It doesn't much work in life either. Without getting too deeply into Freudian stuff, you discover by seeing the repeated failure of father-son combos in the ring that there are unconscious, unhealthy crosscurrents that interfere with boxing success. Pleasing Mom, possibly; but trying to win one to get the old man's everlasting approval is always a losing deal. Oedipus learned that the hard way.

Many of the fighters I've known have been indelibly marked by the "love-hate" thing with their fathers in childhood and beyond, even when it was not carried over into their boxing lives. And a surprising number tell of being knocked around, if not actually beaten systematically, by the old man when they were kids. Those who were actually abused as children carry terrible confusion with them, very often believing they deserved to be so punished. For these fighters the ring can become a scene of a muddled, guilt-ridden and brutal drama in which punishment plays too much of a part.

I recall spending a weekend with Gerry Cooney in his snowbound training camp as he was preparing for the biggest fight of his life, his match with Larry Holmes for the heavyweight championship of the world. I was certain Cooney would win the fight, giving the nod to youth and strength. Because all the roads were closed, we had lots of time to talk about all sorts of things. We talked with surprising frankness about our fathers. Cooney's had died of cancer in his fifties. Mine had died in the emergency room of a Queens hospital at fifty-five.

In most of the stuff I'd read about Gerry, he always mentioned how much his dad, a tough, hard-drinking iron worker, had meant to him. It was Tony Cooney who built the ring in the yard and pressured the Cooney boys to fight their way into manhood. Standard father-son stuff. I asked Gerry his most vivid memory of his father.

He said something almost frightening in its truthfulness. "He was a very hard man to live with. So hard on me, finally, that I had to move out of the house. One night I was driving him to the hospital for radiation treatments and he asked me to please come home. He was almost crying, and he never got that way. I said I couldn't. And I didn't. He died. I'll always feel guilty about that."

I can't honestly say I knew at that point Cooney couldn't beat Larry Holmes, but what I'd heard made me reconsider. That love-hate thing with a dead father, the complication of rejection, death, and guilt, that was a hell of a lot of excess baggage to have to carry into a ring against an excellent fighter at the top of his game like Larry Holmes. Maybe those guys who come from broken homes and who've never known their fathers have a leg up in the fight game.

From the point of view of family influences, Ray Charles Leonard, in this as in most things, was blessed. He had the best of both worlds: a father who was a quiet, stable supporting influence and a doting mother who had always known her "Little Ray" was touched with star quality. If fight judges were Freudians, Wilfredo Benitez stood no chance.

Papa Benitez could be kept out of his son's corner, but he couldn't be kept out of his hair. Just before the fight *The Ring* magazine, boxing's self-proclaimed bible, carried an article documenting all the reasons Wilfredo Benitez would lose his championship. The author was Gregorio Benitez. In his schematic of defeat the author cited the fighter's mental state as his greatest vulnerability. In interviews Papa B. claimed he was simply trying to psych his wayward son. Mind games on the eve of a big match, who needs them?

Also before the fight Ray and Juanita announced their plans to wed the following June. "Win or lose?" a reporter asked. Win or lose, Ray confirmed. The date was Juanita's choice, the June Bride thing. But there was more: Like Dundee, Juanita Wilkins had come to understand the virtues of patience in so unstable a profession. Marriage would come in time, like a championship.

Why, the same reporter wondered, had they waited so long to set the date, indirectly alluding to the fact that Ray, Jr. was almost six and they hadn't rushed to legitimize him. "I wasn't settled-minded," Ray explained. As long as there had been a core of unrest within him, he could not commit to marriage. With financial security came a very clear focus as a boxer—"I want to be something great," he said, "something special."

*   *   *

Ray knocked the defending champion, Wilfredo Benitez, out in the fifteenth round to take the WBC title. No one seemed to consider his performance either great or special. *The New York Times*'s evaluation was, like most of them, inconclusive: "The real judgment on Leonard must be suspended." The reasons the writer, Michael Katz, offered were that Benitez didn't mount enough of an offensive to test the challenger. At the same time, he frustrated most of Ray's attack with superb defense.

Harry Gibbs, an Englishman who was one of the judges, had Leonard ahead only 136–134 going into the last round. Afterward he said, "Boxing is the art of self-defense and Benitez made Leonard miss." (With a guy like that scoring, Willie Pep would never have lost; neither would Richard Nixon.) *Sports Illustrated*, too, came away with heaps of praise for Benitez, calling him "perhaps the best defensive fighter in boxing."

It was indeed true that Benitez made Ray miss more punches and miss them badly than any fighter he'd ever fought. But surely it was a punch from Leonard that knocked Wilfredo off his feet in the third round. A strong left jab it was that caught Benitez so cleanly it put him on his blue trunks for a fast two-count. In the fifteenth Ray found Benitez's chin with a clean overhand right that set up a barrage of left hooks and spun him to the canvas. Benitez was up and hanging on the ropes when Leonard charged in and measured the defenseless champ for the kill. After the third blow Carlos Padilla, the referee, stepped in and stopped the fight.

Ray Leonard knew he had become the welterweight champion of the world—or one of them at least—and ran across the ring, leapt onto the second strand of ring rope, and announced his triumph, his joy, by throwing his head back and thrusting his gloved fists into the air.

Padilla had stopped the fight with just six seconds left, and many observers believed Benitez should have been allowed to finish. The fact that Willie Classen, a middleweight who had been knocked out in New York one week earlier, died two days before this ABC extravangaza for a national audience surely was prominent in Padilla's mind. He was going to stop this one sooner rather than later if the need arose. And that's precisely what he did. But in this, too, Leonard's victory was tainted.

The fight was, for Leonard, a financial success, with even greater rewards now possible. For ABC Sports, the evening was a clean sweep: Their 40 percent share of the audience watching television whipped even *Dallas* and firmly established Sugar Ray as an Ali-sized attraction on the tube. But the evening hadn't been a complete artistic success; it did not wholly satisfy the critics who still believed that Sugar Ray Leonard was a flashy, overrated, manufactured media creation.

What in the world would it take to convince them he had become a Fighter? Perhaps an epic display of ring courage? More likely, nothing could do it.

CHAPTER 8

Boxing Theology

I'd never called anyone for a blind date before in my life. But her name fascinated me, probably because I was teaching the Puritans in my American literature class at the time. Faith Potter. Can you believe it? Right there on the East Side of Manhattan.

Faith Potter. The name conjured up an image of a stern-faced but irresistible beauty, a total change from your run-of-the-mill bimbos who populated the singles bars. In my imagination I created a clean, purifying face before I actually called Mistress Potter's number. It was a Thursday late in 1966.

For a number of months there had been a great void in my life. Mostly because my ersatz career as a boxing writer had ended abruptly when UPI suddenly transferred my friend from nights to days, from boxing to horse racing. Without a legitimate hook, it was good-bye ringside, good-bye losers' dressing rooms. Oh, I still picked my spots and went to the Garden on nights when there were fighters I particularly admired—Dick Tiger, Emile Griffith, Carlos Ortiz—or bouts I thought would be instructional in some way. However, with that core of fantasy missing from my persona, a certain savor had gone out of my sporting life. Perhaps that was why I sought romance in a blind date.

In appearance as well as name, Faith Potter didn't disappoint: She turned out to have the fresh, strong look I'd projected in my imagination. She taught English at a boy's vocational high school in Brooklyn, and did it with rare dedication, so this was clearly not just another pretty face. Faith Potter was someone to admire. But admiration wasn't love. Yet.

Love, it had always seemed to me, lived in deeper recesses, in the paradoxical, the shadowy undersides of human nature. For me, love for Faith Potter flickered first when she read the sensuous poetry of Wallace Stevens or recited a Shakespeare sonnet, all its levels of meaning suddenly becoming clear through her inflections and pauses. Here was much more than a New England name and the missionary zeal of a ghetto schoolmarm. Much more.

She told me that her mother ran a bar in a small town in New Jersey near Atlantic City, but off the beaten path. Her father was dead; he'd been a motorcycle cop in Philadelphia when she was a kid. That appeared to have been a sideline. His main activity was as bagman for numbers operations in South Philly. Love bloomed like a full night flower the evening this prim, lovely creature sat alongside me on the couch of her rent-controlled, East Side apartment and said, "One night we had to leave town fast. My father put us in the car and we drove to Florida. We stayed there a few years. That's where he managed fighters."

Fighters? Her father managed fighters?

"I spent my adolescence with boxers around. We lived in Miami. A lot of the fighters were Cubans. My father was one of Hector Gonzales's managers. I even remember 'Kid' Chocolate."

Eligio Sardinias, who fought under the name "Kid" Chocolate, had been one of the greatest featherweights and lightweights who ever boxed. "You knew 'Kid' Chocolate?" It was not a true question. I was actually saying, *I will never meet anyone quite like you as long as I live.*

" 'Kid' Chocolate was always around. He was retired by then, but he always gave my father advice. I used to play with him sometimes. Actually boxing is the only sport I really like. The boxers are usually wonderful guys."

"You like boxing?" This should translate into *I love you very much, Faith Potter, and want to marry you. Now. Tonight.*

We had met on a Thursday. We eloped the following Thursday. One week exactly, on our third date. To Elkton, Maryland, where everyone seemed to go to get married in the movies, not far from where ten-year-old Ray Charles Leonard was snuggling in his bed, now that I think about it.

In the cold, clear light of early morning, however, in a Baltimore motel room while we were still two hours from a justice of the peace, I got cold feet. The idea of marrying a total stranger, even one who loved boxing, suddenly came to me without the covering robes of romance and became very frightening. I said to this comely person on the bed, "I'm sure we'll get married, eventually, but we ought to know each other a little better. Let's just drive back to New York and date each other for a while." I picked up my shaving things and turned toward the bathroom.

From behind me Faith Potter said, "You're a gambler, aren't you? So, take a chance."

I froze. Who, I thought, would I ever meet in my life who actually said lines like these? Who, in fact, could even make up this kind of dialogue?

It hadn't been precisely the sort of engagement Angelo Dundee would have orchestrated. Or my old man, for that matter. Not the patient examination of matching styles and interests, not the careful analysis of aspirations and potential conflicts. Not at all the sort of match an experienced manager or matchmaker would have made. It could have been an absolute disaster. It wasn't. We got lucky—we were a match made in heaven.

We moved into my apartment. Tim-O was surprised, having me figured as a constitutional bachelor, but when he heard about my wife's pedigree, he fell for her too. Nevertheless, sharing the intimacies of life with a total stranger, however beautiful and qualified, took some getting used to. I'm talking about dinner by candlelight with classical music. Suddenly not just frozen chicken pot pies or fish sticks but something French and with wine. The week before I met Faith Potter, I'd tapped out at Aqueduct and supped on saltines and club soda. The contrast was a bit much. There were compensations, however—she could also read a racing form, a feat none of my friends' wives would ever master.

Because we were each very committed teachers in spite of our other eccentricities, and because our single lives had allowed us to be indulgent, we had neither the time nor the money for a major honeymoon. We set our sights on Europe for the following summer and began to plan and economize for that goal. I eschewed my twice-weekly visits to the track and felt pure and righteous by so doing. Married life was thrilling.

Still, we needed something celebrational, something appropriate to mark our nuptials and as a foretaste of the delayed honeymoon. It came as a wedding gift from my friend at UPI. Two fifteenth-row tickets to the World Middleweight Championship, a rematch between Emile Griffith, the champ, and Joey Archer. At Madison Square Garden. The old edifice was to see only a few more championship evenings before being flattened by the wrecker's ball.

The fourth Madison Square Garden, that commuters' special they were already building atop Pennsylvania Station, would present its first professional fight card the following year, on March 4, 1968. That night Emile Griffith would lose his title to the flashy Italian Nino Benvenuti before 18,000. I'd never seen the first Garden or the more famous second, which had been over on Twenty-seventh Street and Madison Avenue. It was in the roof garden of that old building where Stanford White, its architect and renowned New York womanizer, was murdered by Harry K. Thaw, creating the scandal of the century in 1906. The building was razed in 1925. And who claimed to have seen the last bout ever held there, a twelve-rounder in which Sid Terris decisioned Johnny Dundee? Right. My old man.

A sentimental journey uptown, he told me. The place held too many fond memories. He'd seen his fighter, Benny Leonard, battle there numerous times. Since Leonard was already in retirement by 1925, my old man rooted for Dundee, a remarkable fighter who had fought Leonard eight times to "No Decision" finishes. In those days "No Decision" bouts were too common: Matches didn't have judges, and unless there was a knockout or a clear beating, an inconclusive ND was awarded. My old man claimed to have seen all eight fights and told me he had Benny well ahead in each. Since one of those fights took place in Philadelphia and my old man had never been to Philadelphia . . . well, no matter.

Dundee, I might add, was no relation to Angelo. There had been a number of good Italian fighters who had simply taken names that didn't sound so *paisano*. Angelo and his brothers just did the same. Johnny Dundee's strategy was a bit unusual because he was also known as "The Scotch Wop."

Like Stillman's Gym before it, the second Madison Square Garden was destined to become a Midtown parking lot. To mark our marriage then with a visit to the building that had been synonymous with boxing, an arena in which every great champion and worthy challenger of the modern era had slipped between ring ropes in gleaming robes and danced and waved to the crowd— this should have been a bittersweet experience for us. Especially when I realized that an Oldsmobile would soon be parked on the very spot where Flash Elorde had knelt, where Dick Tiger had shown me his tribal scars. But it was no such thing. The crowd, which was divided in its allegiance pretty much along racial lines, was highly charged but also remarkably festive. So were the newlyweds.

The unusual crowd chemistry was the result to a great extent of Griffith's presence on the card. The champ, a Virgin Islander, was colorful, outspoken, and very much a crowd-pleaser in the ring. Not quite a great fighter, but an honest, hardworking one, winning most often by wearing opponents down, out-roughing and out-conditioning them. On his best nights, as when he beat Dick Tiger and Benny Paret, he could be formidable. Paret had died in this very ring.

Joey Archer was the latest in the tradition of clever Irish boxers. His older brother and manager, Jimmy, had been a boaster and a brawler—a slightly different Irish fighting tradition—who was memorable for the blood he left on canvases around New York clubs. Most of it was his. Jimmy Archer owned a bar not far from our apartment, and daily during the week before the fight Tim-O came back from his lunch hour at Archer's Sports Corner to report the Victory Gospel According to James Archer.

It really did figure to be a good fight. It had everything. Black vs. White. Puncher vs. Boxer. Out-of-Towner vs. Local Boy. And a very strong element of revenge. Their first match, Griffith's first defense of his crown, had left a bad taste. Griffith's people knew that Archer was the sort of fighter it was impossible to look good against, a cutie counterpuncher who slipped and slid and spun until frustration built and left just the opening he needed to score with that stinging left jab and hurtful hook. When he did get hit cleanly, rare though it was, Joey could take the punch well. As a result he'd been passed over by middleweight champs for a couple of years. When Griffith agreed to fight Archer for the first time the odds fell immediately to even money—speed, finesse, and even size were on the challenger's side. Griffith came into the fight ten pounds lighter than Archer.

One way to fight a boxer type is to swarm and smother him. That's what Griffith did in his first title defense. He rushed and drove in on the taller challenger incessantly, giving Archer no rest or time to think, pressing forward and leaning him against the ropes. Often Griffith's head came up into Archer's face; often he punched to the flanks and the kidneys and even hit while referee LoBianco broke a clinch. But the referee had allowed Griffith's roughhouse and Archer had no countermeasures for it much of the time. A lesser defensive boxer would have been eaten up alive.

Archer didn't succumb. When Griffith finally tired Archer came alive and took command with an exquisite jab and marvelous movement over the entire ring. It wasn't Astaire or even Gene Kelly, but it was Dan Dailey at least. The New York crowd, partial to the Bronx Irishman from the outset, booed the decision for Griffith, which was not unanimous for the champion. LoBianco had scored it a draw.

It was a dirty fight, therefore hard to score. Archer said afterward, "The guy led with his head all night." Brother Jimmy vowed the Brothers Archer would not allow the same thing to happen when Joey stepped into a ring with Emile Griffith a second time. That was why the anticipation was so great among almost 15,000 fans, which included at least one pair of newlyweds, as we sought our seats on a frigid January evening in the brave old building that was soon to be kicked over.

As on most big fight nights in the wonderful place, the crowd could not really focus on the preliminaries. Rather, like a junior high school class on a cultural field trip, it babbled and preened and wandered. The noise level was so high we couldn't hear the bell much of the time, and we were only fifteen rows back, farther away then I'd been used to, but fortuitously placed.

In front of us, dark blond hair slicked and parted near the center like a turn-of-the-century pugilist, Chuck Wepner, the "Bayonne Bleeder" himself. Back then he was still little more than a club fighter, although he had fought Buster Mathis, a heavyweight contender, and been kayoed in three. But after only three years in the pros Wepner already wore the nose and the scar tissue of a horror-movie monster. It wasn't until Ali picked him as "Bum of the Month" for March 1975 that the world would see the size of his heart as well as the color of his blood. It was supposed to be a workout for the flabby Ali, a TV date and an easy payday. Wepner took a hell of a beating for fourteen rounds; in the fifteenth he was knocked off his feet for the first time in his career but managed to stagger up. The referee stopped the fight with nineteen seconds left. By hanging tough for as long as he did, Chuck Wepner became the real-life model for Sylvester Stallone's celluloid exaggeration, Rocky Balboa.

Although the world did not yet know him, Chuck was big stuff in rows ten through fifteen. Just in case his leather coat, scarred face, and flashy pinky ring didn't draw enough attention, his broad could hardly fail. She was silvery, curved, and pointed, all at once, like a speared tuna fish. Repeatedly she left her seat for sojourns beyond the refreshment stand but never returned carrying anything but herself. All eyes followed her firm, jellied form. Chuck threw an arm around her possessively upon her returns. Spoils of war.

In the row directly behind us Dick Barnett and Emmett Bryant, a pair of guards for the Knicks, their ladies, and some friends were in remarkably high spirits. They bubbled in anticipation of the main event, evaluating their fighter's chances most favorably and vocally. It was the sort of talk that could elicit a bet from someone nearby. "Their" fighter in this case, however, was Joey Archer, whose name was always preceded by or substituted with "my man." As in "My man Joey was robbed last time. My man'll get himself straight tonight."

Something in the tone, though, a sarcastic stress, a mocking squeal and the slapping of palms afterward, revealed a complete reversal of their intention. They sure were having a good time making believe race didn't matter in the fight game. At one point Chuck Wepner's battered face turned back toward us; his eyes focused on the row behind. His basso said, "Yeah, and *my* man's Griffith." His wink wasn't as pronounced as he'd have wished because his eye, squeezed by a lumpy brow, was half closed to begin with. There was a peel of laughter and stamping of feet from the row behind.

Quite a few minutes before the main event was scheduled, the ring announcer tried to quiet the crowd. "Ladies and gentlemen," he kept saying and pointing to the timekeeper for short bursts on the ring bell. Very slowly and in diminishing stages the noise level in the old building subsided. Still, you could not hear every word: ". . . the passing of . . . champions the world has ever . . . Barney Ross . . . stand, please."

I hadn't known Ross died. How could I have missed it? We stood. Faith whispered, "My father knew him." Throughout the Garden people stood and after a few moments a deeper silence prevailed. The bell began to toll cleanly, counting Barney Ross out, a fighter who hadn't been knocked out in a career of eighty-two fights. One . . . two . . . three . . . If my old man had come along a few years later, it would undoubtedly have been Ross, born Barnet Rosofsky on the Lower East Side, who would have become his idol. Four . . . five . . . six . . . I recalled the elements of his tragedy: Marine, wounded at Guadalcanal in 1942, morphine treatments for pain, drug addiction, a life of torment, humiliation, despair. Seven . . . eight . . . nine . . . Death, finally, as a relapse for the former lightweight and welterweight champion who could spell "stethoscope." Ten.

When the fighters—first the challenger in a green robe with shamrocks, then the champ in white—finally came into the ring to cheers from their partisans, it was as though thoughts of Ross had been utterly forgotten. But they'd only been pushed under the canvas of consciousness. Life vibrated.

In the first row a fat lady in a bright yellow dress and hat with pom-poms rang a cowbell over her head with one hand and threw horns, the ancient finger sign of malediction, at Archer's corner with the other. Emile Griffith's mother. Flanking her, brothers and sisters, nephews and nieces, uncles and aunts—a row full of

Griffith blood and thunder that, around ringside at least, made the crowd noise, which favored Archer over all, seem more evenly divided.

Size and conditioning again promised to be the chief factors in this second match-up. A bad sign for the Archer camp was that Joey showed up for the weigh-in at 161¼, one and a quarter pounds over the limit. He took steam baths and had his hair cut to make the weight. He could have been weakened by the effort. Griffith, on the other hand, who is light for a middleweight, came in two pounds heavier than for their first match.

As they disrobed it was difficult to imagine two more different body types. Griffith, glistening dark, squat, terrifically muscular above the waist, pencil-thin legs. Archer, extremely pale, elongated, softly muscled, perfectly proportioned. I wished I'd known them as men, as I did Tiger and had come to appreciate Giardello.

When Archer was cut above the left eye in the fourth round, he began to box as though to protect himself from further damage. In so doing he started to show how well the classical techniques of the boxer could serve. For openers he was up on the balls of his toes and circling, circling, so even when Griffith decided to charge, Archer, like McCavity the Mystery Cat, wasn't there. Then, using his height and reach advantages, he popped the quick jab in Griffith's face; if there was an opening, he could follow with a hook and straight right, the classic combination, if not, pop the jab again and glide away. Joey Archer at his best had the ability to frustrate his opponent and score points. That could win this fight for him.

At the end of the sixth round I had him ahead four rounds to two. Faith had him up, 3–2–1 even. Both judges and the referee, when the scoring appeared in the next day's papers, had Archer winning the fight after six. Surest proof of Archer's superiority, though, was coming from the row behind us, where all pretense of objectivity had fallen away when the fight began to turn, decisively it seemed, toward Archer. The urging on of Griffith had taken on a plaintive quality. Even Emile's relatives in the first row, especially Ma Griffith, were throwing frenzied hexes and casting voodoo spells at Archer's corner. They weren't working. Perhaps they were being repulsed by a Hibernian band of invisible Wee People.

Movement had made Archer successful. And he would remain successful only as long as he stayed mobile and on his toes. Two things above all can take a fighter off the balls of his feet: fatigue and an opponent's body blows. Trying to determine which comes first is not generally easy. In the seventh round Joey tried to gain a few moments of rest and rehabilitation by tying up the arms of the enraged Griffith and dancing him along the ropes. A painful mistake.

First Griffith tore his left arm free and hooked twice to the body, so sharply you could hear Archer expel air and see his torso constrict afterward. Archer weakened then, and Griffith, with both arms free to work to the stomach, bent Joey over with body blows. The Griffith brood was stamping in unison and shaking bells. After a few moments Archer came forward and managed to tie up the shorter, lighter, but stronger man to lean on him long enough to steal precious seconds free of punishment.

Because the aggressive Griffith was, paradoxically, also often a cautious fighter when he had an opponent in trouble, or perhaps because he needed a respite from his own efforts—for whatever reason, he didn't press his advantage, seeming content just to win the round. Probably he knew something. The fight had turned.

It became evident in the next round. Although he again came out of his corner on his toes, Joey Archer was flat-footed and remained that way after thirty seconds had elapsed. His range and speed of foot had diminished, so Griffith was able to close and nail him with even more body blows, and, as a result, movement became even more difficult. Quite literally a vicious circle. To his credit, Joey Archer did everything that Griffith's tactics didn't take away. He counterpunched very well, finding the openings that were fleetingly there. And whenever he could summon up the strength, he did indeed stick and move. But essentially he was fighting his opponent's fight, and only remarkably complete fighters can do that and win. Joey Archer was not such a one.

From the row behind us, during the late rounds, there came more confident rooting. It was back to an occasional "Go get him, Joey" and "Stick 'n' move, my man," but the sarcasm carried far less mockery. At the final bell it seemed pretty clear that Griffith had won the fight. That, of course, didn't necessarily mean he'd get the judges' nod. Stranger things—much stranger—had happened in this old building. The Griffith clan in row one had no doubts: They were already celebrating the victory.

The decision, when it finally came, seemed fair—unanimously for Griffith, reasonably close on all the cards but not as close as for their first fight. In the crowded ring, immediately after the announcement, a scuffle broke out but was quickly controlled. Next day's newspapers said something about Archer refusing to shake hands, causing some shoving among some of the handlers, general bad feeling prevailing.

As the crowd slowly filed out into the frigid streets toward subways and buses, Faith and I remained seated, our fingers clasped. By having shared this evening, our first championship match together, it was as though our marriage had been formalized in some way by the official decision—"winner and still middleweight champion of the world. . . ." As though Wepner, Barnett, Bryant, and the rest of the crowd were witnesses to our marriage, the Griffith bell ringers our choir. As though Madison Square Garden had provided the church wedding we'd never had.

All that seemed to be missing was the clergyman to sanctify our marital-boxing union. As we finally rose and followed the few stragglers down the aisle past the ring, even our symbolic minister suddenly materialized. Love of boxing and of each other had such magical power. There, standing in the first row of the box seats, his tie loosened, collar open, suit and hair disheveled, as though he had rooted very hard and unsuccessfully, was Bill Buckley. No, he did not make the sign of the cross over us. In fact, he didn't even notice us passing below him; he was busy signaling to someone on the other side of the arena. We stopped and observed. When finally he got his respondent's attention he conveyed his evaluation of the fight with a hand gesture. It seems our priest was also Roman Emperor, and his judgment was *pollice verso*. Thumbs down.

It took a few years for the theoretical pull of suburbia to become real. Then, even though the Long Island Railroad deposited us right at the new Madison Square Garden, we, like Tim-O and thousands of fight fans, found our way to ringside far less often. At first, maybe half a dozen times each year; then, just a couple of times; finally, not at all. Nor did the TV fights pick up much of the slack. Oh, we did cook up some goodies and invite friends over when Ali was in a network fight, but he didn't usually peddle his best efforts to the networks, and normal weekend boxing fare on the small screen left a great deal to be desired in both the quality and the atmosphere we expected.

Occasionally, if Faith was dusting the books or I was vacuuming the rug, and one of us happened to turn on the set to a fight that displayed a boxer with demonstrable talent and tutelage, one would call the other and we'd postpone housecleaning until the decision. Those times were rare indeed. Television fighting didn't really suit our tastes. Too often kids were being rushed along; to build their records, they were given Tomato Cans to pound. When you put it all together, most TV boxing was not even old wine in new bottles; it was unready wine in cans. We considered ourselves connoisseurs.

So, as the years passed, boxing went from being a central part of our marriage to a tender memory of our "good old days." The fighters of *our* youth were, of course, the best, and we rated Emile Griffith, and even Joey Archer, higher in our romantically tinged estimates than boxing historians ever would. Only Ali, who bridged the first decade of our union, was exempt from our bias for the fighters of the late sixties. Twice—a one-sided decision against a blubbery Buster Mathis in '71 and a seventh-round TKO of White Hope Gerry Quarry the following year—we went to movie houses nearby and shelled out more than we could reasonably afford to see fuzzy Alis go through the motions. Naturally we absolved Ali of any responsibility; it was "closed circuit" that had disappointed.

Ali's name happened to be mentioned by a friend one morning in 1976 as we rocked into the city on the commuter special. This friend, an actor, was hustling between roles as a construction worker on a crew that was building a huge kitchen and storage area behind Joe Allen's, a playgoers' and actors' restaurant in the theater district. "There's this guy I'm working with," my friend said, "was one of Ali's sparring partners. Fought on the undercard of the Ali–Mack Foster card in Tokyo."

As much to pass as an expert as to pass the time, I said, with the hateful tone of someone sniffing cheap perfume, "Yeah. What's his name?"

"Willie Culpepper."

Good fighter's name, not the sort you're likely to forget. "Never heard of him."

"I checked him out," my friend said. "It was true. He knocked the guy out in Tokyo."

"How old is this Culpepper?"

"That's the point. He's young. Twenty-six, twenty-seven. He's got some fights in him. I've been talking to him about a comeback." My friend, a freckled Irishman, made his eyes twinkle. He said, with too much charm, I thought, "You wouldn't be interested."

Compressed into a fraction of a second, I saw these fantastic images: Me and Willie in identical sweat suits doing roadwork along the shore road near my house. Me, putting a robe over his shoulders and chugging down the aisle behind him, the leading edge of a phalanx, moving toward a boxing ring that lay in blinding light. Me, holding Willie, the heavyweight champion of the world, aloft by the waist. Hell, we had an extra room upstairs. Willie Culpepper could work off his expenses doing odd jobs while he trained. I said, "Let me check the guy out."

According to *The Ring Record Book*, Culpepper really had won that fight in Tokyo and a few others in California with quick knockouts before he dropped out of the picture in 1974. I asked a sportswriter I knew from the old ringside days for a scouting report. I got a call back the same day. Willie Culpepper, he discovered, was from Pasadena, so he'd put a call in to Don Fraser, a promoter who had booked just about every fighter who'd ever fought in California. "Sure, he knew your man, Culpepper. Remembered him fondly. Here's the bottom line—Culpepper hits anyone right, they go. Anyone. Doesn't like to train. If his head gets straightened out, he could still make some good money."

Interesting information, but since I didn't plan to act on it, purely hypothetical. It became a little less so when my actor friend called a week or so later and said he'd like to bring Willie by the house. That Saturday a very tangible Willie Culpepper, in plaid shirt, dungarees, and work boots filled the maroon wing-back chair in our living room. I drew up selective fragments of Fraser's scouting report: "Culpepper hits anyone right, they go . . . could still make some good money." Images of myself as manager of a heavyweight contender, hell, the champion, rolled again over the screen of my imagination.

Willie wasn't a big heavyweight, maybe six feet, 210 pounds. The construction work and biking on weekends had kept him only in reasonable condition, nowhere near fighting shape though. We all talked politely, avoiding the direct question we were there to address: Willie, do you want to try a comeback or not? We got close to it, finally, when Faith said, "How did you come to quit fighting in the first place, Willie?"

Culpepper smiled and said, "That takes some telling." And it did. Willie C. was a marvelous talker, knowing instinctively the value of both detail and digression. To make his long story bite-sized, here's what finally happened: In Newport News, Virginia, Willie Culpepper made the acquaintance of a group of evangelical Christians who convinced him it was not his destiny to wallop behemoths in short pants but to carry the word of Jesus to everyone he encountered. Make words not war, in other words. "*He* did not want me to be a prizefighter" was the conclusion to Willie's redemptive tale.

"And has He changed His mind? Do you think He wants you to be a fighter now?" Faith was using her no-nonsense tone, not her doubting-Thomas.

"That's the problem," Willie sighed. "I'm still looking for a sign from Him."

For the next few hours the discussion turned purely theological. We charged full speed into the thorny religious enigma of Fate vs. Free Will. Not Faith, though; she excused herself immediately after Willie said he was looking for a sign. She had student essays to grade. I recall waxing eloquent over the fact that human creation was most wonderful precisely because we were free agents: Choice was the greatest of virtues as well as of burdens. I think I recreated Milton's *Paradise Lost* right there in my living room. Faith's periodic groaning from the bedroom was almost as disconcerting as Willie's response, spewing New Testament chapter and verse in a literal manner I could neither understand nor refute.

When he left after midnight Willie Culpepper said he really enjoyed himself. Probably the only one of us. He enjoyed sparring with theology more than a gym partner. Naturally. No idea ever could lay a glove on his gray matter. As they left my friend said he'd stay in touch. I said sure. And after I pawed my way through the darkness and into bed, Faith's voice, not the least bit sleepy, said two things: "That's a head case" and "Do you have any idea how much a heavyweight eats?"

Later that summer my friend reported that Willie Culpepper had a change of heart.

"Has God sent him a sign to fight?"

"I don't know about that, but he's been running and he's been going down to Gleason's Gym to work out."

I remembered, *Culpepper hits anyone right, they go.* I said, "If he gets serious, we'd be interested."

A meeting was arranged, an audition, I guess you'd call it, at Gleason's, the storefront gym near the new Garden that has been as close to what Stillman's used to be to fight people in New York as we've had since parking places became more important than punchers. Willie, in tight sweat pants and basketball sneakers, was swatting the heavy bag when Faith and I arrived. All around him fighters in top-notch shape shadowboxed, jumped rope, worked the speed bags, sparred. Culpepper looked pathetic by comparison, sluggish and slow with his hands; perspiration ran in rivers down the brown flab of stomach and flanks. His body was a bit of a shock, but that should have been expected; He hadn't been in fighting shape for almost three years.

Willie was not only auditioning for us, he had a trainer interested in him as well, a man who looked distantly familiar. When the three-minute bell that ruled all activity in Gleason's clanged, a wheezing Willie Culpepper introduced us. The prospective trainer was Harold Richardson, a recently retired middleweight of fond memory. Although he had never won a championship, Richardson fought bravely but unsuccessfully against the great Carlos Monzon on the champion's turf in Buenos Aires, and in a widely traveled career Richardson had fought all the best men in the division. In fact, he'd been in one of the preliminaries on the Griffith–Archer card, so in a sense he had been a member of the wedding. When the bell rang again and Willie went back to work, I asked Richardson, "Well, what do you think?"

Richardson's toothpick slid along his lip warily and he leaned back against the paint-flecked wall. "Too early."

I told Richardson what I'd heard through the grapevine from Don Fraser in L.A.

"Sure. Willie could hit. And he could still make some money in this game. But it all depends."

"On what?"

"On how bad he wants it."

Faith continued to chat with Richardson while I went to the locker room with Willie. "Man, it's gonna be tough tryin' to make it back," he said while toweling off.

"Then you're going to give it a shot?"

"Sure, why not? You never know until you try. But I'm gonna need some stuff." He listed boxing equipment slowly. Shoes. Trunks. Mouthpiece. Gloves for the light and heavy bag. For sparring. Money for a license. Socks. Cup. Head gear.

"What's all of that going to cost?"

"Figure three, three-fifty."

"How much are you willing to put up, Willie?"

"Those are management expenses." Willie Culpepper smiled beatifically.

I went back out to the gym and saw my wife and Richardson in deep conversation. It looked important, so I stayed away. Faith came to me finally with an I've-got-the-scoop expression. "Harold's really a superb guy," she said. "He told me there's a sure tip-off to whether or not Willie's really serious."

"A lie-detector test?"

"Better. If he buys his own equipment, he's serious. If he wants us to buy it, he isn't."

"Oh. Isn't that interesting?" It was indeed. I did some incredibly fast thinking. I said, "You know, sweetheart, I'm not sure I want to go ahead with this thing anyway."

"How come?"

"I'm not sure *He*"—I looked up to a rust spot on Gleason's ceiling—"wants me to own a fighter."

CHAPTER 9

Getting It Wrong/
Getting It Right

Jazz players love to sit around and tell Thelonius Monk stories because the great piano stylist actually said and did the sorts of things that characterize the spacey yet unquestionable brilliance of his music. Comedians like to remember the things attributed to Lenny Bruce, or, in a less self-destructive mode, recount the off-screen madness of Mel Brooks. Through such insider yarns the subject becomes a "jazzman's jazzman" or a "comedian's comedian." Boxing people like to tell tales about Roberto Duran, the fighter's fighter.

Many of the Roberto Duran stories around the fight game hearken back to his life as an impoverished street urchin in Panama City, where it is said Roberto beat grown men to the cobblestones with his bony fists. They say he was ten. They say he swam two miles across the Canal with stolen mangoes from the other side to keep his family alive. They say he killed sharks en route with the knife he held between his teeth. They say he knocked down a horse with a single blow to prove he was a heavier puncher than Antonio Cervantes. They say he has a pet lion on his estate in Panama. There are a great many such Roberto Duran stories.

Who knows the reality. We are speaking here of legend. Undeniably, though, the street kid was very tough and more than slightly manic; even after he began to confine his rage to the more acceptable venue of a boxing ring, his hunger for violent action and the power of his punches remained. They called him the kid with hands of stone on the streets of Panama City; as a gloved professional he remained "Manos de Piedra."

A punishing hitter, to be sure, Roberto Duran was much more, more even than his remarkable ring record of seventy-one victories in seventy-two bouts coming up to his challenge for Sugar Ray Leonard's WBC welterweight title. Duran had lost just once in thirteen years, a close decision in 1972 to Esteban DeJesus, an opponent he knocked out twice in subsequent fights. Legend says that after that loss to DeJesus, Duran pummeled the locker-room walls until his stone hands were blood-raw. Admirers sometimes persisted in calling Roberto "El Animal," but for some reason he didn't welcome the nickname.

Ring records can deceive gaudily; they can be pumped up as easily as silicon breasts. Not the case with Duran—he'd fought everyone willing to step in with him on his way to the lightweight championship he held for almost ten years, through twelve title defenses. But Duran was considered a phenomenon not merely on the basis of KO statistics. Duran was Duran because of how he fought.

Always pressing forward, willing to mix and take an opponent's best shots in order to deliver his own. There was never in him even the faintest suggestion of "quit." Ever. And when he sensed he'd hurt an opponent, some deep, bestial instinct, a scent for blood, a possible kill, was aroused, and Roberto Duran moved thirstily forward for the finish. "It's a great fighter's sixth sense," Paddy Flood, whose admiration of the Panamanian was boundless, told me. "The man is one of the greatest finishers ever been around."

Roberto Duran in his prime was the kind of fighter other professionals, especially lightweights, did not really want to fight, not only because it was unlikely they could win, but because they would have to pay so dearly. Duran was not a one-punch knockout artist; rather, he beat on and came forward incessantly, finally putting the other fighter away after some invisible tolerance and survival threshold had been crossed. A typical Duran victory usu-ally evoked the same key words from the boxing writers, words like "savage," "disdainful," "brutal," "relentless," "pitiless." There were no other fighters around quite like him in the 1970s. He was a throwback in more ways than one, a mysterious, dark figure from some tropical and mythic past. Roberto Duran also looked the part.

His hair was long and blue-black; it fell behind him like a horse's mane. His mustache, goatee, and scruffy sideburns were villainous touches he cultivated and relished. The dark eyes glowed, perhaps with the same fire of the Mexican father he never re-membered, enigmatically, with a vestige of the Indian blood he also surely possessed. In victory Roberto Duran was never gra-cious. A sneer was his typical reaction to success in the ring. He had little inclination or the time to develop an honest respect for an opponent.

As champion of the world, Duran had come a long way from the untutored street fighter, even though the apparent style of a brawler led many fans to assume that he prevailed in the ring exclusively by force of muscle and will. But this was no Rocky Graziano, say, whose crude courage and lucky punch could win him a championship for a short while. At the highest levels of professional boxing, brute force, even when linked to physical courage, is not enough to win a fighter lasting respect among his peers. Skill matters considerably. Carlos Eleta, a Panamanian mil-lionaire and Duran's manager, understood this fact and went about hiring the best American trainers money could buy, Freddie Brown and Ray Arcel.

On the subway you'd give either one of these guys your seat. Brown, with a face like a battered ear, was seventy-three, Arcel, a pugilistic professor emeritus, was eighty-two when Duran and Sugar Ray Leonard fought for Leonard's welterweight title in Montreal in June 1980.

As unlikely a pair as you'd ever meet in boxing, they were the best in the game. Brown was assuredly one of the finest cut men in the sport, an excellent tactician and motivator; Arcel, the master strategist. In the nine years they'd been working with Duran, he had become a very good defensive fighter, learning to pick off punches as he came in and to minimize the effect of solid blows by bobbing his head and twisting his torso while fighting inside; he also developed his left hand as a significant weapon and to set up his devastating right. They'd helped make Roberto Duran a Hell of a Fighter, one boxing historians would probably be forced to consider Great.

Angelo Dundee knew that, strategically speaking, he was up against the best there was in the odd couple of Arcel and Brown. Even though he could more than hold his own against them in front of the press with classic lines like "Those guys, they're older than water," Angelo was going up against his own teachers. He'd carried water buckets for them decades earlier. He'd seen them work corners for fighters who constituted one wall of Boxing's Hall of Fame.

From Arcel and Brown, Angelo learned tricks of the ancient trade that had all but passed from the scene. Like the gambit he'd seen Arcel pull off over thirty years before when one of Arcel's fighters had knocked down but not out a tough opponent. Just as the referee picked up the count, Arcel leapt into the ring and jubilantly threw the robe over his fighter. The referee, momentarily confused by the end-of-fight celebration, concurred and hurried knockdown into knockout. Dundee admitted to using the old "victory robe" trick with success on occasion. But no matter how sharp Angie had become over the years, compared to Brown and Arcel he'd always remain the sorcerers' apprentice. Still, he genuinely liked Sugar Ray's chances against Duran and for a variety of reasons, some of them owing to Ray's now highly developed skills as a boxer, some of them the result of vulnerabilities he saw in the Panamanian that tended to get overlooked when the Duran legends are trotted out.

There is an old truism about knockout punchers that Dundee believed would be applicable here, namely that when a KO specialist moves into a heavier weight class, his big punch becomes less effective. It's not so much a matter of the power being diminished as of the larger opponent being able to absorb the hard shots better. For whatever reason, it is the case often enough so that smart boxing people pay close attention to hitters moving up in class. Dundee felt that although Duran was a punishing lightweight, those "Manos de Piedra" might not bowl over the muscular welterweight boxer Ray Charles Leonard had become.

Furthermore, the Leonard camp knew something that was not very widely perceived and would, in fact, take a good deal of proving even after it became known: Sugar Ray Leonard could take a hell of a punch. Because Ray never had to absorb the punishment that was Duran's modus operandi, it was widely assumed that a couple of blows from the stone hands would finally expose Leonard as the made-for-TV creation he was.

However, it was not in Dundee's fight plan to have Ray prove to the world how tough he was. You go fifteen with Roberto Duran, you take some wicked shots. Sure. But you certainly don't want to get in a mugging contest with a street fighter. Duran was not Andres Aldama, the Cuban slugger whose attack Ray smothered in this very same ring for his '76 Olympic championship. This was the legendary Roberto Duran.

Dundee wanted Ray to move and slide, but not to hide. Conventional wisdom. He wanted more; he hoped to use the fact that Duran was a stalking fighter against him. As Duran came forward to close with Ray or to punch inside, Ray was not to be in front of him but to step quickly left or right, set, and throw punches from eleven or one o'clock, never, never, from high noon. Ray's vastly superior foot and hand speed, his defensive skills and adaptability would all have to come into play for the strategy to work. Ray's stinging offensive jab that momentarily froze most of his opponents and set up the sparkling combinations was expected to be his most important offensive weapon. It's not accurate to say that Dundee was confident going in; he did believe, though, that if Ray carried out the plan, he had precisely the style and the tools to get the job done.

Usually comparing styles, records, and ages is sufficient to enable an experienced observer to project a winner in a big fight. Occasionally, though, things unseen and unknowable hold the key; shadowy matters buried in a fighter's past or in his psyche can tip the fight one way or the other. Rarely are fights won or lost primarily because of a fighter's psychological state, as they like to show in fight movies. But this was to be the case in each of the two remarkable Leonard–Duran matches.

*   *   *

Psychologically speaking, Duran was worth at least a chapter in a textbook on neuroses caused by deprivation. The abject poverty that pervaded his youth had scarred the adult profoundly. He compensated by becoming the "hungriest" fighter of his era, but his hunger was for food as well as recognition and respect, and it became insatiable as his boxing triumphs mounted. Roberto Duran literally ate himself out of the lightweight division. Between bouts the 135-pound fighter would balloon up to 165, 170. Tales of his enormous appetite became part of the Duran legend, as did tales of the deprivation and self-punishment required to get back down to fighting weight. The debilitating effects on a fighter of such extreme weight and mood swings would surely begin to take their tolls on the twenty-nine-year-old, who had been abusing his body for years.

Because he only had to make 147, the welterweight limit, for the fight with Leonard, Duran's prefight bloat didn't seem to be very serious; nevertheless, Freddie Brown had one hell of a job controlling Roberto's intake. With four weeks left to the opening bell, however, Duran was only six pounds over the limit; he would undoubtedly make the weight. Still, this could be the fight when the years of self-abuse conspired to transform Roberto Duran into an old fighter.

Not many students of the game were looking for chinks in Ray's psychological armor. Because he seemed incredibly well-adjusted or possibly because he'd succeeded in actually becoming the image he'd worked at projecting, most people didn't think there was a vulnerable human psyche in there. There was, and it turned out to be crucial in the outcome of the fight. One thing boxing teaches a serious student is never to assume the obvious —that's why referees wisely caution, "Protect yourself at all times."

There had been a slight intimation of something cooking in Ray's head at the Waldorf-Astoria's grand ballroom, where the fight was formally announced to the media and the fighters were introduced. It was at such splendiferous get-togethers that Ali first began to make his matches symphonies of hype and pizzazz. But when Sugar Ray leaned over the microphone, cast a sidewise glance at the Panamanian, and said deliberately, "When I fight Roberto Duran, I don't just want to beat him, I want to kill him," a breathy gasp filled the silence. The messenger and his message were totally out of character. Later, Ray tried to cover himself by saying it was just hype for the fight, something to catch the eye and ear on the six o'clock news. But the fight was a natural; it didn't require that kind of hype. Leonard's little slip was dismissed as misfired puffery. But, in fact, Ray had a bee in his bonnet, one that had a fatal sting.

Viewed purely as a financial venture, the match couldn't miss. So potentially profitable it was that Mike Trainer did the impossible—he put together a deal that attracted the antagonistic and mutually exclusive talents of boxing's heftiest promoters, Don King and Bob Arum.

Rivals in almost every respect, King and Arum grudgingly agreed to try to work together in promoting the fight because it had a chance to be the richest match in boxing history. Money is balm for deep wounds, at least temporarily. Of course you could never be certain how big a big fight will actually sell, but when all the closed-circuit and residual moneys came in, Duran was expected to earn $1.5 million, far more than he'd ever dreamed of when he was merely considered the best fighter in the world by the experts. Simply stepping into the ring with a "star" fighter brought greater rewards than simple artistic excellence ever could. As the "star," Leonard's lion's share guaranteed him $7.5 million. Trainer had played his cards perfectly. If the world was not a fair place, the boxing world was less so.

Some promotions run smoothly from the start, some don't. This one didn't. The Quebec Olympic Installation Board bought the fight for $3.5 million U.S. In order to cover that nut, they scaled the arena from $500 at ringside to twenty bucks for seats in the far-distant balcony. At both extremes, sales were brisk. But tickets going for $75 to $300 didn't move well at all. A few days before the fight less than 30,000 tickets had been sold. Montreal's Olympic Stadium held 78,000.

The selection of the site had been a sentimental one, not a hardheaded commercial choice. This was where Sugar Ray had won the hearts and minds of fans as a sweet kid who could fight like a whirlwind. Here he announced he'd reached his goal and would retire to a less violent life. But, as Sugar Ray should have known from harsh experience at that Washington D.C. intersection, memory is short, allegiance even shorter. He was not the same kid, not the aspiring innocent he was made out to be in '76. He was a hard defending champion in a hard business. Nor was there a widespread interest in the challenger, Montreal not being particularly well-known for its vast Latino population. In New York or Texas or in Southern California, the fight would have played very well. Fortunately, closed-circuit would blanket those places and most other major boxing markets in the States.

The most frightening moment for the investors and the principals came at what should have been the *pro forma* prefight physical about a week before the fight. Duran's electrocardiogram recorded a strange and troubling arrhythmia sometimes associated with hardening of the arteries. Four hours of tests at Montreal's Institute of Cardiology finally cleared Duran to fight. It had been touch and go for a while. This incident, too, would eventually become part of the Duran legend. Said Ray Arcel to reporters, "They took him to the hospital to check out his heart. But everyone knows that Roberto Duran hasn't got a heart."

Although the matter finally played no part in the fight itself, it is entirely likely that Duran had been taking pills to help him lose weight—as we discovered Ali had for his fight with Larry Holmes. Weight-loss medication could have accounted for the irregularity in Duran's cardiac exam.

When at last all the obstacles that intruded themselves with this promotion had been overcome, all the sparring and training completed, all the interviews and hype finished, all the aimless, empty hours of waiting killed off, it was time to see who could beat whom. That is, after all, the elemental purpose and attraction of the blood sport. Within such a simple objective, however, are stirred, like swirls in a marble cake, the complex variables of boxing. Courage and speed, reflex and will, strength and imagination, and unknowable, incommunicable variables as well. Between well-matched fighters such as these, you can never be certain until they punch and are punched what will unfold.

A strange thing occurred even before the bell rang. When Sugar Ray was introduced the overwhelming support he expected from the crowd was not there. Boos, in fact, could be discerned peppered in the din. Boos. Had he been perceived as too smart-alecky now that he had become TV's darling?

When Carlos Padilla, the referee, called them to the center of the ring, gave them instructions, and told them to touch gloves, Ray automatically reached out. Nothing. Duran had turned away, leaving the champ alone in the center of the ring with his arms extended. That single small gesture of disdain by Duran, Leonard's confused and momentary humiliation, may have tipped the outcome of the fight.

Ray Leonard did not fight the fight Angelo Dundee had planned. Ray Leonard did not fight a smart fight at all that Friday night in late June. He fought according to his own lights and made an elemental mistake. Rather than taking advantage of his superior skills as a master boxer, Ray opted to brawl and maul, slug and mug with the man who had written the book on such tactics. To the consternation of his brain trust and over their urgings and objections, Ray Leonard fought Roberto Duran's fight.

Ray's irrational and uncharacteristic behavior did have a certain logic, at least in retrospect. Unfortunately, it was the logic of losers. Ray suddenly saw very clearly his chance to bury all his critics along with their criticism. Not merely a championship to be defended and a fighter of great reputation to be defeated, the fight became for Ray Leonard a chance to prove to everyone, once and for all, that he had lots of heart. To out-tough Roberto Duran, he reasoned, would do just that. A twenty-four-year-old believes in once-and-for-all.

Perhaps Ray had been baited into the trap by Duran's constant needling, maybe that final insult in the center of the ring had caused Ray to dismiss Dundee's best-laid plans. Depending on your point of view, it was either arrogance or ignorance that caused Leonard to spring for the obvious bait. However it was, Sugar Ray fought the wrong fight against the wrong fighter as a result.

From the opening bell, Duran bulled forward. Ray did not circle. He did not move to eleven or one o'clock; he took Duran's direct charge, an admirable tactic in college basketball but dumb as dirt when you're in with Roberto Duran. A stiff jab was Ray's strongest statement of the opening round. Just one. Duran worked inside beautifully, raking the champ along the ropes roughly, and

Padilla let them fight out whenever they were momentarily entwined, a judgment that favored Duran, the infighter supreme.

Ray was pinned in the corners for most of the second round. A left hook caught him early and put him in trouble that Duran maintained the entire round. Later Ray would say, "I can't remember taking quite so long to recover from a punch." For his wife, Juanita—yes, wife finally; they'd married six months earlier—watching Ray take more punishment than in any round of his career was sheer agony. She began to weep and would do so on and off until the eighth round, when she fainted dead away in the arms of Ray's sister, Sharon.

Through the middle rounds Ray seemed to get progressively stronger and, still fighting Duran's fight, began to hold his own as a roughhouser. All three judges scored the seventh and ninth rounds even. There was still time to turn the fight around if Ray Charles Leonard could reach down and find the grit and guts and staying power to quell the fury of the most furious fighter of recent decades. The thirteenth was Ray's proudest moment. It also happens to be one of the best rounds in modern boxing. Bob Waters, the late boxing writer, realized the fact as it unfolded and filed the following in his *Newsday* story: "If great moments were really *golden moments* then some method would be found to immortalize the 13th round of the contest—one of the greatest rounds of boxing, if intensity and savagery are the things by which we judge boxing then the round deserves to be etched blow by blow and saved for whatever posterity remains. . . ."Fortunately, such a method does exist: On video tape the thirteenth remains as brilliant a round as it did the night it was fought.

Two of the three judges gave the round to Leonard. Of course it had been tactically wrong for Ray to try to bull a bull, but once he adjusted to Duran's *in extremis* approach to the sport, Ray sure as hell wasn't being blown away, not by a long shot. As the fight wore on the rounds were becoming increasingly difficult to score.

As he had throughout the fight, over the last two rounds Duran kept boring in; Ray managed to maintain enough room to counterpunch very well. Although they could not match thirteen for intensity, they were very up-tempo for the final rounds of an extremely rugged fight. He'd been taunting Ray in little ways throughout the early rounds. Now toward the end of the fight a confident Roberto Duran mocked his opponent brazenly by blowing kisses at him and clutching his throat disdainfully. Roberto Duran was playing Roberto Duran. This was, he said afterward, merely his way of expressing his exuberance at having the fight won. When the bell rang at fight's end Duran thrust his fists in the air and shouted insults at Ray in Spanish. He refused to shake hands when Ray offered his. Some exuberance.

The judges gave the unanimous decision to Duran, but their scoring indicated their uncertainty. A total of nineteen rounds were scored "even" on the three judges' cards. French judge Baldeyou scored it 6–4–5 even; Englishman Harry Gibbs had it 6–5–4; Angelo Poletti, a son of Italy, believed he had witnessed *ten* even rounds and gave Duran three of the remaining five. More than the closeness of the fight, the scoring revealed the judges' collective incompetence. The decision belonged to Duran, I believed at the time, because he had fought a typical Roberto Duran fight and because Sugar Ray Leonard had fought a typical Roberto Duran fight too.

There was no doubt that Duran had been the busier and more aggressive fighter for most of the match, far more effective with head and elbows, shoulders and knees. But there were some writers present who believed Ray had landed the cleaner, harder punches. Bob Waters gave Ray the nod by the slightest of margins, as did Pete Bonventre, the good boxing writer for *Newsweek* and *Inside Sports*. To this day he contends, "If you look at the replay carefully, you'll see that while Duran was mugging, Ray was doing some very effective punching. I don't believe Ray fought a smart fight, but I think he did do enough to win."

I've looked at the fight repeatedly on a video cassette and agree, but only sort of. However, because Duran dictated the way the fight was fought—and because Ray acquiesced—it always *feels* like Duran's fight every time I watch it. A matter of the whole seeming greater than the sum of its parts.

Ray Leonard took a pretty good beating that night. His face was badly swollen, his body ached, his back had been rubbed raw along the ropes. The closed-circuit millions that were being counted even as Ray and Juanita, limp from emotional exhaustion, made their way through the darkened tunnel of Olympic Stadium were not at that moment a reasonable consolation. Slightly more satisfying, but not at all sufficient, was Ray's knowing that the courage he had shown that night would surely undercut the rap against him that he lacked "heart." Nothing, however, could divert him from the hard realization that he had not only lost his championship but lost it because he fought so stupidly. Here he was, finally a doctoral candidate, given a major problem to solve, and he'd gotten it wrong. The truly galling thing, though, was that he'd known the right answer all along.

A fighter with a different temperament would have kicked his own ass for a week or so and then told his manager, "Get me Duran again." Financially speaking, nothing would have been easier for Mike Trainer. Ray Charles Leonard, however, when confronted with a setback or an overwhelming success, seems to yield to paralysis and malaise. Immediately after the fight Ray once again said, "This is it. I gave it all I had, but this is it." With Juanita supporting his inclination to retire, the next weeks had Ray bending precipitously toward quit. It was as though Ray had a deep psychological need, win or lose, to be able to say at any moment, "Boxing is not my master," the way a gambler or a drinker needs to be able to pass up a martini or a tip on the double.

This injury to Ray's pride hurt particularly because it was to a great extent self-inflicted. Maybe, if he had been cleanly whipped by a better fighter, he really could have walked away and stayed away. Ray didn't believe that.

The rematch was made for the Superdome in New Orleans five months later, in November.

The simplest task was Mike Trainer's. Duran–Leonard II was as easy to sell as a Japanese car. Certainly Duran, the new champ, had a right to claim the larger cut, but it would be a bigger pie than had ever been baked in boxing—a guaranteed $15 million, $8 million to Duran, seven to Ray.

Dave Jacobs, the man who had been in Ray's corner since the kid first walked into the Palmer Park Recreation Center in 1970, took the opportunity after the loss to Duran to drop off the team. Ever since Dundee had come aboard when Ray turned pro in '76, Jacobs' position had become increasingly untenable. On the one hand, Janks Morton had become the fighter's ring confidant; on the other, Dundee called the shots professionally, at least until

Ray decided to follow his own foolish counsel with Duran. That left Jacobs a supernumerary wrapped in a proud man's character. He'd flirted with quitting repeatedly and actually had quit once before, but he came back when Sugar Ray Leonard, Inc. sweetened his paycheck.

The reason Jacobs offered for his resignation now was a difference of opinion with the brain trust. He didn't think Ray should step over the ropes and into a ring with Roberto Duran again without a couple of tune-ups under his waistband. A legitimate position. Let your fighter sharpen up and regain a little confidence; at the same time, let the champ get a year older, forty pounds overweight—maybe then Duran's will, if not his hands, would erode as he passed thirty. Jacobs knew how fast a fighter can become an old man.

Jacobs was overruled by economics and emotion—an overwhelming combination. Too much could happen if they waited. The interest and therefore the money were there right now. Additionally, Ray wanted to undo what he perceived as a humiliation as soon as he could. To his normal desire to prove himself as a great fighter in the ring, a thirst for personal revenge had been added. Patience might have been the wiser course; it wasn't going to be.

Normally, no one could out-patient Angelo Dundee, especially when he had the younger fighter. In this instance, though, there was a mitigating factor in addition to the lure of windfall profits. Angie was more convinced than ever that Ray could beat Duran cleanly *if he fought the proper fight*. Furthermore, word had gotten out weeks after the first fight that Roberto had already started eating.

Many experienced observers of the Battle of Montreal believed it was Duran's dominating style that had forced Ray into his atypical, counterpunching posture. No one had ever controlled or eluded Roberto Duran, his backers contended, and it was foolish even to try. Freddie Brown asked rhetorically in his postfight analysis, "Why did Leonard fight Duran's fight? It's hard to think when you're getting your brains knocked out . . . this ain't football, you know. And Duran, like Marciano, never gives you the ball." Angelo demurred silently; he believed, as he always had, that Ray could take the ball away with lateral movement.

Since so much that had done in Ray Leonard was psychological, clearing the air, psychologically speaking, was a necessary pre-condition to any tactical preparations for the rematch. Ray had fought extremely well in that first fight, maybe he even deserved to win it. He'd proven to most doubters that he had gobs of heart. But that wasn't the point. He had lost. Dundee hammered away at that.

Like a sinner, Ray had first to admit and then to confess he'd fought stupidly. Rid himself of any lingering illusions and non-essentials before he was truly ready to get right what he had gotten wrong.

Fortunately, Angelo had learned from that first fiasco that the "right" fight for Ray against Duran was not the artistic *tour de force* of the dancing master. It was not going to be an easy thing trying to take away a championship with footwork and a jab. But Dundee now knew that Ray could take the best Duran could give and still have something of his own to give back. "You play checkers with a guy like this," Dundee was fond of saying, by which he meant something quite different from a coy and clever tit-for-tat.

It's no accident that most boxing gyms of my acquaintance have a corner in which a checkers game is a constant diversion. Checkers, in Dundee's sense, is a game of angles and traps, the traps sprung successfully because the angles are so well-hidden and -conceived. "You play checkers" meant that Ray would have to be able to change his position quickly and constantly and be able to strike from positions the lunging Duran did not expect. "Everything has got to be short and timed perfectly," Ray said; he ought to have added, "And coming from a different place each time." Very few fighters could carry out so new and complex a strategy.

Dundee also had Ray trying to develop quickly a very difficult maneuver: throwing a right-handed uppercut while pivoting on the right foot, then switching over and doing the same thing from the left side. The pivot would angle Ray automatically to one side or the other as Duran came forward; the uppercut was to be the punch the crouching Duran would not be able to avoid.

There are very few boxers a trainer would dare mess around with before an important fight, since for most boxers a style of fighting is as personal and well-defined as a thumb print. But the artist in Ray rebelled against repetition and loved the challenge of breaking new ground—perhaps that partially explained his foolhardy and impetuous decision to become a pure slugger with Duran in the first fight. Putting in the new moves also gave the training camp a sense of intellectual challenge and immediacy that kept the idea of "getting even" from becoming too obsessive. Revenge can easily feed on itself if you aren't careful.

Ray tried not to think too much about the first match, tried hard in interviews not to let too much of the bitterness come through. The grudge-match quality of the fight was simply there; it certainly didn't have to be hyped. As fight night approached, impatience became a problem for Ray. Certain he now owned the key to dispossessing Duran of the title and could atone for, if not erase, his only loss as a professional, Leonard became edgy waiting for the opening bell. A good sign, Dundee, Morton, and Trainer believed.

Ray dared not think about the possibility of losing again. Such an outcome, he knew, would pretty well finish any dream about becoming a boxer highly regarded by posterity, a dream that had taken center stage in his mind. Sugar Ray Leonard would become, by losing, merely a name that enhanced the legend of Roberto Duran.

Some things about the rematch were the same as for the original fight. The seats at the Superdome were also scaled way too high—$1,000 for a prominent perch at ringside—and the live crowd would fill less than half the 80,000 seats. Nationally, however, the closed-circuit sales were excellent.

Other things were very different. Ray wore black—black trunks, shoes, and socks—for the first time in his professional career. The choice subtly announced his darker purpose—"No more Mr. Nice Guy." It was as though Luke Skywalker had become Darth Vader.

In a masterly psychological touch, the national anthem was sung as a soulful blues by Sugar's namesake, Ray Charles. A hand-held TV camera caught Ray the Singer in the foreground, his head bobbing unself-consciously to the afterbeat; Ray the Fighter took the background, glowing with sweat from prefight exercise, his intense eyes smiling with joy. He seemed to understand the song as a personal encouragement and inspiration. ". . . and the ho-ome of the brave," seemed nothing so much as a reminder from Ray to Ray of what he needed to win.

There had been salsa rhythms rolling out of Duran's supporters before and after the anthem, but from the opening bell, Leonard, the jazz fighter, dictated the tempo. He was the virtuoso, the innovator. Flicking the jab to the head, to the body, and then spinning suddenly away—these were things he hadn't done in Montreal. Halfway through the first round, Duran rushed at Leonard, who was caught off balance and standing directly in front of him. He quickly muscled Ray into the ropes—that familiar and effective Duran tactic—but Ray pivoted away and landed a nice right hand while bidding adieu. Dundee beamed. Brown and Arcel winced.

The rounds that followed, except for a lapse in the fifth, when Ray allowed himself to get caught for too long on the ropes, proved that Ray had learned his lessons very well. Almost everything he tried worked. Rarely had any boxing strategy and execution been more successful in a rematch.

In the eighth, a round that has already become an indelible part of boxing history, one that will forever tarnish the Duran legend, Ray Leonard sensed the level of Roberto Duran's frustration at not being able to have his way. Now it was Sugar's turn to taunt and mock the man with hands of stone. A payback for all the insults and humiliations in Montreal. Ray dropped his hands in mid-ring and exposed his chin, a look of teasing stupidity playing on his face. By merely twisting this way and that, he made Duran miss the too-tempting target. Frustration mounted. A few seconds later, again in the center of the ring, Ray wound his right arm like a pantomiming softball pitcher. The so-called bolo motion is not one of boxing's classic punches, but as Duran watched the right hand winding up, Ray popped him with a quick left jab right on the schnoz. It was the sort of move my old man would have pulled on me during our first few weeks of sparring. Duran heard the crowd's derisive laughter.

With only sixteen seconds left in the round and with Ray working *him* along the ropes, Roberto Duran turned away and said to Octavio Meyran, the referee, *"No más, no más."*

Meyran said, *"¿Por qué?"*

Duran's nonanswer: *"No más."*

Roberto Duran's quitting, unhurt in mid-fight, was so big a story that Ray Leonard's strategic and technical brilliance was overlooked. His problem, Duran explained insufficiently afterward, was stomach cramps, not Ray Leonard. Something he had drunk, something he had eaten before the fight. Other, more plausible theories emerged. He had lost too much weight too often; this time it took its toll in a sudden wave of weakness his rage could not help him overcome. There were strong rumors of mysterious drugs that had sapped his will. More logical was the theory that the macho man could handle anything except being made a fool of in public—it had never happened during his life on the planet; now it was happening for the world to see. So he chose dishonor over humiliation.

For Sugar Ray revenge was sweet enough. He said, "I proved to him what I could do. I *made* him quit. To make a man quit, to make a Roberto Duran quit, was better than knocking him out."

Before the fight Duran was the hero of the boxing fraternity. They held him up as the shining example of what a professional fighter should be. After *no más, no más*, he became an instant pariah.

Still the *¿Por que?* remains. For a while I subscribed to the macho-humiliation theory. And I still do to a certain extent. But there was more.

I recalled reading a remarkable profile Gay Talese wrote on Floyd Patterson for *Esquire* in 1964. When I dug it out of the attic it fell open to a dog-eared page. Patterson had been trying to explain why he brought false whiskers and a mustache to wear as a disguise after fights he feared he might lose. Admittedly, not your conventional manner for preparing to cope with defeat. After his first fight with Sonny Liston, in which he was KO'd in 2:06 of the first round, Patterson put on his disguise and drove from Chicago to New York. In New York he continued directly to the airport, still incognito.

Patterson confessed, "I had on this beard, mustache, glasses, and hat—and I also limped to make myself look older. I was alone. I didn't care what plane I boarded, I just looked up and saw this sign at the terminal reading, 'Madrid,' and so I got on that flight after buying a ticket. When I got to Madrid I registered at a hotel under the name Aaron Watson. I stayed in Madrid about four or five days."

Talese was a wise enough writer not to mention his own reaction to what the former heavyweight champion of the world was telling him. But when I first read those words, and as I read them again, my mouth fell open in disbelief.

Almost to fill the silence Talese had left, Patterson added, "You must wonder what makes a man do things like this. Well, I wonder too. And the answer is, I don't know . . . but I think that within me, within every human being, there is a certain weakness. It is a weakness that expresses itself more when you're alone. And I have figured out that part of the reason I do the things I do . . . is because . . . I am a coward. . . . My fighting has little to do with the fact, though. I mean you can be a fighter—and a *winning* fighter—and still be a coward. . . ."

After a while Talese asked, "How does one see this cowardice you speak of?"

"You see it when a fighter loses. . . ."

"Could Liston be a coward?"

"That remains to be seen," Floyd said. "We'll find out what he's like after somebody beats him, how he takes it. It's easy to do anything in victory. It's in defeat that a man reveals himself. . . ."

Patterson's remarkable insights are stunning in their implications. Of course it takes a certain kind of bravery for a man even to step into the ring, but Patterson believed that courage in the face of defeat was the acid test. Sugar Ray had his mettle tested in Montreal: Then, after struggling mightily within himself, he survived his dark night of the soul. When it was Duran's turn to lose, he simply could not cope. Roberto Duran was, that night in the Superdome, at least in Floyd Patterson's sense of the term, a coward.

Just in case anyone thinks that is a smug judgment of Roberto Duran, let me remind myself and whoever else is interested that in time we will all have to confront certain defeat—it comes automatically with our mortality. Only then can each of us know what we are in our deepest, most private selves.

Fighters simply get to explore these frightening places sooner than the rest of us. From them are kept few secrets of the human heart.

CHAPTER 10

Phonies, Fakirs, Frauds

Willie Culpepper fulfilled my deepest fantasy indirectly. No, not the one about managing the heavyweight champion of the world. The other, older and deeper one about becoming a big-time boxing writer and not having to fake credentials to get a seat in the press section.

Willie Culpepper, as Faith had predicted, never got in shape. He never fought again. The Lord probably just told him to move on along and spread the word, for after a few months he simply dropped out of sight.

Using a generous amount of a fiction writer's license, I wrote a story about him anyway as a former Ali sparring partner struggling to decide whether or not to lift his fists again in anger. It was a nice piece I thought, and another friendly sportswriter helped me sell it to *SPORT* magazine.

I rested comfortably on my laurels for a few months, wondering how next to let the boxing world know of the arrival of its new Liebling. But although I'd gotten paid for my Culpepper profile, it hadn't been published. And it still hasn't been. Why, I began to wonder, would a magazine buy an article and then not print it? It would take even a few months longer to find out.

In time I heard from Berry Stainback, the editor at *SPORT*. He didn't particularly want to talk about the Culpepper piece. Something better. He wanted to get together with me to discuss some other boxing stories. The Culpepper article, it appeared, was an audition, but one it seemed I'd passed pretty well. I was high on my prospects. It hadn't struck me that the time of our meeting—7 P.M.—was a bit unusual. Magazine people, I told myself and shrugged it off.

The lobby to the building on Lexington Avenue was formally closed. The security guard required a signature and some identification. A curious mood had been struck. No one toiled in the cubbyholes of the magazine offices, and Stainback, Ellie Kossack, the executive editor, and I withdrew to the conference room to talk about boxing in general. It seemed to me we were waiting for someone.

After a while Dave Wolf entered. He was a real boxing writer, the magazine's very best, and one of the best around. Wolf's a hard man to take seriously when you first meet him because he appears to take himself so seriously. And also because he wears a red hairpiece that undercuts his no-nonsense manner. Wolf was who we were all waiting for. He's often late.

He began asking me directly what I knew about boxing. There was the feel of being recruited by the CIA about the interrogation. I opted for honesty. Don't ask me why, sometimes I just do. Wolf quizzed me particularly on the televised boxing tournament that ABC and Don King Productions were calling the United States Boxing Championships. I knew just enough I guess because we all went off to a small restaurant on Second Avenue where the darkness and the first round of drinks began to loosen tongues. En route, some invisible border had been crossed.

It was hard trying to stay cool. Something thrilling was up and I knew it. I ordered gin straight up with a twist—it seemed right for the image, hard-boiled yet stylish. It didn't work. I had a coughing fit.

Wolf was explaining that he had a contact inside ABC who had proof that the tournament was rigged, if not actually fixed. This informant, he explained, must at all times be protected. Wolf himself was too well-known, he claimed, to get any information from the principals, but someone like me, a college professor and a boxing buff, might be just the type, nonthreatening and naive, they'd talk to, especially if I said I was doing a piece on, say, the resurgence of boxing under Don King, the man who was masterminding the renaissance. Wolf would feed me the inside stuff and I'd try to discover corroborating evidence. Well, what did I think?

"And by the way," added Stainback, "we might have to wire you so we can prove some of this stuff."

"It's up to you," Kossack said benevolently.

So what did I think? Fortunately, I was still coughing.

Wolf outlined the formal setup and the scam. It was a subtle piece of work. King had gone to ABC Sports in 1976 with an idea for an elimination boxing tournament to determine the best American fighters in the major weight classifications. A very attractive programming idea because it would fill the demand for competitive fights, create ongoing interest in individual fighters as they advanced in the tournament toward the finals, and highlight new boxing talent, maybe even discover future stars, the lifeblood of TV boxing. ABC Sports went for it; all it required from King were assurances that Don King, as their contract stipulated, ". . . agree to use your best efforts to establish the tournament as one of creditability, merit, and equality."

In order to assure that those conditions would in fact be met, Don King Productions vouched that ". . . the quality of the fighters participating in each weight category be the best possible, determined by rankings established by *Ring* magazine at the time the tournament starts." Not content merely with meeting the letter of the law, King went even further. He established an oversight committee consisting of James A. Farley, Jr., chairman of the New York State Athletic Commission, *Ring's* publisher-editor Nat Loubet, associate editor John Ort, and two former members of the New York Athletic Commission.

The viewers, it appeared, had legal assurances, theological assurances (since *Ring* was known as boxing's bible), and the personal assurances of important people in high places—from Farley, son of a former national chairman of the Democratic Party and postmaster general, to Howard Cosell, who was a lawyer and by his own modest admission the finest judge of boxing acumen extant, to Roone Arledge, resident genius and president of ABC Sports, who was assumed to be by definition beyond reproach. So much for assurances from on high.

In reality, not most, or even very many, of the worthy fighters eligible for the tournament were approached. In fact, fighters who had been inactive for a year or more could find themselves suddenly ranked in the top ten by *Ring* and tapped for national exposure in the tourney. Investigation proved them to be fighters whose managers had agreed to kick over to some of King's associates and employees a few thousand bucks. Once they had "earned" their ranking in *Ring*, they were chosen to participate in the tournament. To the exclusion, I might add, of some very good fighters who were not even approached or who would refuse to do business.

When I finally hit the road and began interviewing some of the chosen ones, I found, thanks to Wolf's info, more than one case like a junior middleweight from Texas named Ike Fluellen. Without having fought in a year, Fluellen was invited to participate in the tournament after he agreed to accept Washington, D.C., fight promoter Chris Cline as his new manager. Cline, by the way, had three other fighters in the tournament, including his own son, all with falsified records in the annual *Ring Record Book*. Immediately after accepting Cline and still without having had a fight, Fluellen found himself mysteriously ranked tenth in his division. One month later he was miraculously elevated to third. Two fights that never took place were listed as victories in the 1977 edition of the *Ring Record Book*, and the redoubtable Mr. Ort, who was in charge of the rankings for *Ring*, granted this very same Ike Fluellen honorable mention for the magazine's prestigious "Progress Award of the Year." And they say boxing's such a rough business.

I was finally able to document half a dozen such "inaccuracies" in the records of tournament fighters. There were undoubtedly many more. My particular favorite was a draw listed on the records of two fighters who had qualified for this tournament of "creditability, merit, and equality." The match, on one fighter's record, occurred in Wilkes-Barre, Pennsylvania; on the other fighter's record it was Winston-Salem, North Carolina. Hell of a stretch for a draw. Even more so when you realize that one boxer was a welterweight (147 pounds) and the other a lightweight (135). Obviously the match was a figment of someone's imagination. "Clerical errors" would be the pathetic defense when the story broke and ABC was forced to pull the tournament off the air.

Just about half the fighters in this tournament of "creditability" were represented by managers who had close ties to King, in some instances by blood. King's two sons were listed as manager of record for a number of fighters; so was Don King Productions' production manager Rich Giachetti, a King associate from the Cleveland days. Paddy Flood and Al Braverman, two hard-boiled old-timers who had trod just about every runway in every boxing arena on the continent, had offices in the basement of King's Manhattan town house. They had a "Boxing Department" sign slapped on their door. Even Connie Harper, King's secretary, had been assigned fighters' contracts from time to time. Further down the line were promoters and booking agents and managers who'd done business with King for years. It didn't take long even for an investigative imposter like me to corroborate most of Wolf's suspicions.

I recall sitting late one night at the kitchen table. I'd made out three-by-five cards of every fighter, his manager of record, and all the tourney officials. It was not difficult to see that the U.S. Boxing Championships formed a perfectly closed system. King chose the fighters; *Ring* supplied credentials wherever necessary; King's *ad hoc* commission played arbiter; ABC Sports, having covered itself contractually, gave it all its tacit stamp of approval.

Still, the very nature of the setup, the questionable associations among the individuals involved, ought to have made executives at ABC Sports much more vigilant, especially if they truly had the mass of their viewers—who knew nothing of the selection process—in mind. Since they were so concerned at the outset that the tournament be above suspicion, why hadn't they investigated at least to the point of note cards on a kitchen table? And why in the world would Don King jeopardize such a great idea with what was essentially nickel and dime stuff?

No way to know, really, but it was just possible that the unregenerate con man in King couldn't help itself. Perhaps the years of being Cleveland's numbers baron had left a legacy of reflex habit; he and his cronies simply could not overlook the loose change that was right there for the plucking. I discovered a far more practical reason for the hanky-panky when I finally got my hands on a fighter's contract with Don King Productions. A clause in each contract gave King promotional control over tournament champions for two years, and with his penchant for tying fighters up with options on options, Don King could tie up a promising fighter for years. So by controlling the tournaments entries, King could, to a great extent, select the talented fighters whose careers he could ride profitably as far as they'd go. Since ABC Sports executives had copies of the King contracts with the fighters, there was no legitimate reason for their hanging back and letting matters run their course, especially if they wished the tournament to be truly open and fair.

When the story finally broke and ABC was forced to pull the show off the air, everyone accused everyone else of betraying a sacred trust. Mostly they did it in that special tone of indignant sorrow used by convicted politicians on the courthouse steps, a victimized expression that says at once, "Where has loyalty gone? What's happened to good old-fashioned trust? I've done nothing wrong, as the world will discover when the new evidence is introduced. All I'm really guilty of is putting too much faith in the word of others." That's pretty much what ABC Sports said of Don King, what King said of his commission, what the commissioners said of *Ring*, and *Ring* of the fighters' managers, who it claims fed it inaccuracies.

Because a magazine's lead time is weeks, my article came out after the story broke in the dailies and on TV. I didn't have the scoop I dreamed of. I did have, I think, the best, most complete, and well-documented rundown of how the scam worked and who was responsible for how much. The piece was reprinted in *Best Sports Stories of 1977*. I couldn't have been more pleased with myself as a crusading journalist who had begun to clean up the sport I loved. I was certain at the time that one or all of the investigations—the FBI, the IRS, the U.S. Justice Department, a Baltimore grand jury—examining evidence of malfeasance, conspiracy, fraud, tax evasion, perjury, or extortion would be able to nail at least some of the spoilers.

ABC, far more adept than most governments in dealing with a messy situation, set up its own inquiry under Michael Armstrong, who had been the tough chief counsel of New York's commission to investigate allegations of police corruption. As such he'd grabbed headlines as a crusader for months. I believed his investigation of the U.S. Boxing Championships would unearth some hard evidence. I smile bitterly even now at my naiveté.

No one served a day. Nothing even mildly felonious could be proven. *Ring* magazine was taken over by cleaner hands. Farley was forced to resign as chairman of the New York Athletic Commission. ABC lost a hot property. The episode got a lot of play for a little while. Cosell, who had been the tourney's on-screen voice, became grandiloquent in calling for the establishment of a federal boxing commission that would "once and for all clean up this cesspool that calls itself a sport." King continued promoting championship fights at roughly the same championship pace. All too quickly what had become an obsession for me skipped out of the public consciousness like an opening-night bomb on Broadway.

What I'm left with years later, much to my confusion and consternation, is the enduring fondness that boxing's charlatans held for me. In spite of the fact that I repeatedly reminded myself it was always the fighters who paid in the end, every time I was in the presence of Flood or Braverman and, to a lesser extent, King, I was attracted by the force of their personalities. A hilarious Irishman, a raffish Jew, a jive and shucking black man—among them, they had the classic ethnic American styles covered.

I was hooked wihin moments of walking through the "Boxing Department" door. Braverman was older and much more bloated than Flood. His maroon leisure suit, however, was overmatched by Paddy's flowered sport shirt and checkered slacks, but the laying on of gloved hands in their youths had given Braverman's face the clear decision. Both of them had been willing but mediocre fighters. They handled me from the outset like a college professor—with gentle derision. They particularly made a point of calling me "Sammy" when they answered my questions. Terrific.

When I asked something semitough—such as how did they happen to have so many fighters in the tournament (between them they had eleven)—a low-boil hostility flashed and faded across their faces. At such moments I was very glad not to be wired for sound. Braverman made it perfectly clear he perceived no conflict of interest: "Now let's get this straight, Sammy. King ain't our boss. I don't want none of that shit. We're consultants, not employees. There's a big difference. He pays for our boxing advice, that's all. Truth is, he don't know shit about boxing!"

The "consultant" schtick turned out to be enough of a moot legal point to cover their asses when the crunch came. Braverman and Flood could dissemble so entertainingly that their vigorous justifications and denunciations were much more alluring than an honest man's simple truths. Of course, come to think about it, I really didn't get to interview any honest men.

If I had to choose between these greedy consultants and any of the ABC Sports executives I interviewed, it would have been no contest. Like their suits and their haircuts, the ABC guys had their morality cut to order too. Unlike Flood and Braverman, who were sweating bullets while hustling up their bucks, the corporate gents were wired into the ratings.

Seemed to me, finally, that ABC Sports had known something was rotten in their tournament but had opted to see if they could ride out the rough spots, at least for that year. Although they hadn't actually rigged anything themselves, theirs were the cynical sins of omission. No accident then that they were more polished, better groomed and educated than the street hustlers. I hated their umbrella ethics and their attempts always to take the moral high ground.

Consider as an alternative style Paddy Flood's response to this simple question—"How did you first come to meet Don King?" He gurgled laughter at the memory. "We ran into him about five years ago in Cleveland. We put together a show for him there. He was just over his prison trouble and he tells us that he can produce Ali for an exhibition. And you know something? *He does.* So we say to ourselves—*that's some nigger!*"

Why in the world have dinner with Roone Arledge (who as president of ABC Sports okayed the U.S. Boxing Championships and who during the fuss was promoted to president of ABC News as well) when you could have it with Paddy. Or could have until 1983, when Flood died.

Don King was not so easy to love from up close, or for very long doses. When he wanted to dazzle an interviewer in the flesh or on TV, he couldn't be topped, and my first session with him in his office was an absolute Don King blitz. Once he learned I was a college prof, he threw a stream of intellectual one-liners at me, the best *bon mots* of Nietzsche, Thoreau, Shakespeare, Voltaire, Freud, *et al.* I had a sense the quotes didn't mean anything to him: He simply pushed buttons in his head and up popped an appropriate tag line. No matter, the lines were all correct enough.

More impressive was the fact that when he'd become a reader in prison during his four-and-one-half-year manslaughter term, he knew that those words had the power to serve him well someday. He memorized long passages accurately. Now he just called up a representative line or two he believed served him. What I didn't want to admit to myself was that this huge, self-educated black man with electric hair pleased me just by indicating he knew who Freud and Nietzsche were. It gave each of us a smug satisfaction that he approached me on my terms.

When I finally asked him what would happen if it were discovered that something illegal had been going on in the tournament, his already large body appeared to expand. He laughed bitterly and said, "Man, I've been to jail. It was hell in there. But I survived. If they put me back, I'll come out again. I'm one of the world's great survivors." He flashed his huge diamond and a smile as big as the Ritz. "You see, Sam, I'll always survive because I got just the right combination of wit, grit, and bullshit."

Nearby was a photograph of King shaking hands with Jimmy Carter that corroborated his survival assertion. It was incredibly easy to forget in his presence that here was someone who had killed another man with his bare hands.

Each time we met thereafter I became aware of a gaping hollowness in Don King that he seemed bent on trying to fill with gab and frantic activity. As an individual human being, he was simply unfathomable. I sensed this quality most deeply when I accompanied him and his wife in his platinum limo from a hotel in San Antonio to nearby Randolf Air Force Base, site of some of the tournament matches. (Don King Productions was of course staging the tourney at various service bases. King always crowed about how proud he was to be giving our boys and girls in uniform some high-quality entertainment. Most Americans still hadn't heard Samuel Johnson's one-liner: "Patriotism is the last refuge of a scoundrel.")

Sitting in the rear of the limousine, I discovered that for the moment I had no more questions. I demanded nothing. It should have been a quiet time. King couldn't abide that. He virtually interviewed himself. The only memorable thing he said was, "I never get tired because it ain't *my* energy that's being dispensed. It is *God* speaking through me."

When I looked into his face I was sure that he'd absolutely convinced himself of that. It gave all his words and actions total self-justification. Like Willie Culpepper, he believed he was a mere vehicle for some great superplanetary force that had singled him out to do its will. So it was not venal self-interest, after all, that had King write those option clauses into all the fighters' contracts. God had directed him. Immediately such righteous hypocrisy put him far lower in my estimation than Braverman and Flood, who had chosen their unsavory professions, made them their calling, and flaunted them in the best Damon Runyon tradition.

Two things about King that I didn't write about at the time strike me now as the most revealing of his essential character. His wife and his eyes. Mrs. King appeared in public very rarely, preferring the isolated, bucolic life on their Ohio farm. She was along on that trip, I realized, to reinforce the image of Don King, husband and family man. She said nothing and gazed out the window sadly. She didn't listen to a word her husband said. She bore the mark of a shy woman who had seen and heard too much that was sordid in her life and seemed barely able to carry the weight of that legacy. Life with this man had marked her severely.

King's eyes are absolutely dead. Watch him closely when he's on TV. Even in the midst of his most animated story, with his hands cutting the air, his huge teeth glittering, Don King's eyes never come alive. They reveal no human feeling. It's particularly frightening because their emptiness suggests there are no boundaries, no empathy, nothing.

So dominant was Don King's position as a middleman between the networks' insatiable appetite for good fighters in good fights and the fighters' need to be served to America as the networks' blue-plate special that his leverage worked mightily in both directions. The networks usually met his terms because he could produce fighters like Ali, Larry Holmes, and Roberto Duran. Young fighters usually accepted his terms of glamorous servitude because he could guarantee national exposure. Because boxing is the least regulated of major American sports businesses, King's position was invulnerable, unless of course his greed caused him to break the bounds of civil law, which I believed he'd already done with the tournament fiasco.

During the brief period when it appeared that an indictment might be coming down, King pulled the brothers together for a very vocal and very predictable defense. On Don's behalf, Ali announced, "They're out to get the coon, and I ain't gonna let it happen." The Reverend Jesse Jackson issued a statement condemning, ". . . the endless vitriolic attacks . . . on brother King." A group of respected black publishers stated that ". . . the white press [was] conspiring to discredit Don King in the boxing world, and therefore restore white promoters to the control of boxing." The very last line of defense, then, wasn't patriotism at all—it was racial solidarity. The indictment never came.

It's amazing, when you think back to Ray Leonard's confused days after the '76 Olympics, that the kid didn't yield to King's enticements, especially when that welfare scandal broke in the papers. That Ray intuitively knew enough to say "No thanks" to Don King and to keep on saying "No thanks" boggles the mind. That he ran into Trainer, who developed the "Inc." gambit, was sheer good fortune. Most young fighters, however, have neither a salable reputation nor a salable TV personality coming out of the amateurs. Or the good sense and good luck of Sugar Ray.

No one, King has argued, forces any fighter to sign with him. Maybe that's why he stuck that two-year agreement into the U.S. Boxing Championships contracts. Some lucky fighters would have "won" Don King along with their titles. Sometimes, losing is a hidden blessing.

If you don't want to sign with King and you're not really equipped to go it alone, the other well-connected promoter is King's anti-self, Bob Arum. King's antithesis in every important respect—short, white, Jewish, Harvard Law, the Justice Department—Bob Arum is a boxing promoter who pulls off just about every promotional coup that King doesn't. Together—even though they despise one another personally—they are boxing's all-powerful Yin and Yang, a two-headed, schizophrenic Octopus, Inc.

Arum's special sideline, you might say speciality, in professional boxing has been promoting South African fighters in the U.S. and exporting American fighters there. It's not the benevolent peoples-to-peoples program he'd like it to seem. In 1979 he promoted a match in Miami between Kallie Knoetze, a South African ex-cop who'd shot a black youth in both legs during a racial disturbance, and Bill Sharkey, a mediocre American black heavyweight who'd served thirty-one months for manslaughter. Jesse Jackson, trying to call attention to South African racial policies, picketed the CBS match with a group of his supporters.

Arum also promoted the Gerrie Coetzee–John Tate WBA heavyweight championship bout in Johannesburg. South African Coetzee lost the unanimous decision; Arum pocketed over a million and a half bucks up front for delivering the black American contender. In addition, Arum had the Ali–Leon Spinks rematch scheduled for the Sun City resort in Bophuthatswana, a spurious South African "tribal homeland," before the fighters were forcefully reminded of the political implications of such a show and backed out.

I thought at first that like any purely venal fight promoter, Arum was simply going where the gate and residual money would fill his coffers to the fullest. Then by chance I saw a story in *The New York Times* that gave me other, darker thoughts. A scoundrel named Eschel M. Rhoodie, information secretary of the South African government and a strong apartheid propagandist, had absconded with millions of dollars in secret government funds; he'd just been apprehended by police on the French Riviera. Rhoodie was fighting extradition by threatening to go public with details about a secret project funded to break the boycott and isolation South Africa had been subject to because of its racial policies.

One element of the project he revealed was the use of monies, diverted from other sources, to break the athletic boycott that most civilized nations either practiced or honored. The fund to break the sports boycott, according to Rhoodie, amounted to around $60 million. Rhoodie managed to stir up enough trouble in South

Africa that various ministers and other appointed officials were forced to resign.

Rhoodie's allegations made perfect sense and seemed to explain Arum's single-minded commitment to promoting South African fights and fighters. I finally got to ask the promoter how he justified his doing business with people who had a racial mentality roughly equivalent to the Nazis' for Jews. Arum maintained that he was doing more to improve the system by bringing fighters over than boycotting would. Stadiums, he argued, were integrated for the racially mixed matches he promoted. Sometimes they were, sometimes they weren't. None of them ever remained integrated permanently.

Although I was never able to go to South Africa to investigate the facts fully and could not produce Rhoodie's smoking gun, the Arum–South Africa connection, for whatever reason Arum had maintained it throughout the years, has been ethically despicable. In fact, my worst experience at any fight—worse by far than the riots in the old Garden—was at an Arum promotion in Monte Carlo. The feature was an important heavyweight elimination between Leon Spinks and Gerrie Coetzee, the winner to fight John Tate for the WBA title, in South Africa as it turned out.

When Spinks was introduced only his family at ringside rose to cheer. The crowd was the whitest fight crowd I'd ever seen. And it was, except for Prince Rainier, the press, some French movie stars and international socialites, almost exclusively South African. Coetzee knocked the toothless Leon senseless in the first round and the partisan crowd carried their champion off to his dressing room in glory. All well and good and as it should be.

However, in the starlit darkness by the dressing-room door, three burly Afrikaners began pummeling a solitary black man to the ground. He was wearing press credentials. I couldn't get to him, held away by a wall of beefy men. I heard the word *kaffir* (nigger) amid the laughter and mocking comments. Then, ever so slightly, the milling crowd began to still itself. Male voices were singing. Louder, more deeply, and with fervent feeling. The language, Afrikaans. All the thick-bodied men around me stopped motion and stood proudly erect.

The solemn singing rose to the heavens filled with stars. Beneath short blond hair, all the pale eyes filled with emotion. The words of their anthem must never have held so much meaning for them. The love of nation and the pride of white men for it and themselves existed so palpably at that moment that I could almost pull it out of the air and pocket it. But at that moment I could do nothing but realize that this place, this time, could as easily have been Munich in 1938 with me the *kaffir* lying on the ground.

I got my ass out of there.

With time so many things I didn't fully understand about why people did what they did began to fall into place. Dave Wolf's man inside ABC Sports, who it turned out had tried to warn his superiors that the tournament was rotten, eventually had to use whatever means he could to save his network even worse embarrassment. When the smoke cleared and Armstrong's investigation found the men at ABC Sports to be nothing worse than careless and gullible in dealing with King, Wolf's "mole" was glorified and promoted up the corporation.

Wolf's own motives in exposing King's operations took a while to emerge from the haze. He had been making the very unusual transition from boxing writer to boxing manager—in other words, to putting his money and his time where his mouth was. Trying to resurrect the career of once-promising heavyweight Duane Bobick had become his full-time job. It didn't hurt Wolf's—or any other independent manager's—interests a bit if he could weaken Don King's omnipotent position in the boxing business. Not exactly the purest of journalistic motives, but what the hell.

When I noticed about a year later that Bobick was fighting in South Africa, my eyebrows arched. Wolf's next fighter, Ray "Boom Boom" Mancini, began to have Bob Arum promote a great many of his major bouts; in fact, he was even scheduled to defend his WBA lightweight championship against Kenny "Bang Bang" Bogner in South Africa before a prefight injury caused Mancini to withdraw. It was an Arum promotion.

A very plausible, but very cynical, thought came to me in time. Even though everything he'd tipped me about King's operation was perfectly true, Dave Wolf may have used *SPORT*—and me —to further not only his own interests in boxing but those of King's chief rival, Bob Arum. The realization had two effects: It made me smile for days and also made me realize how absolutely overmatched I was in the boxing business.

Oh, yes, there was another remarkable piece of fallout from my role as an investigative journalist. About six months later I was sitting in the university cafeteria munching on a cheeseburger and leafing through Camus (who had been, by the way, a very impressive young boxer in Algeria, the only activity in which he was a lightweight). A senior stepped up, introduced himself, and inquired if I were the same Sam Toperoff who'd written that story on the Don King tournament. I overcame my false modesty with false struggle.

He, it turned out, was not only an aficionado but also published a monthly boxing newsletter. Quite friendly, he told me, with good old Paddy and Al. After the publication of my piece I somehow neglected to stay in touch. I said, "How are the boys?"

His face clouded. Considering carefully his response, he said, "They're not exactly wild about you. But I think you'll be okay."

"Be okay?"

"For a while they were thinking a little about some kind of retaliation. Busting your kneecaps, torching your house."

I examined his face, and it seemed to me that he wasn't trying to scare me but merely to report accurately what he'd heard from the consultants in the Boxing Department. I laughed unconvincingly.

He remained perfectly serious. "Finally, they didn't do anything because of your wife."

Chivalry, I thought. "My wife?" I said.

"She being a cop and all. They didn't want to mess with any of that."

"A cop!"

I walked away from the cafeteria on wobbly legs. Faith was not a cop. But she was teaching college English courses to New York City policemen in their precinct houses. The boys had made a mistake. But they had actually *checked things out*. And if they'd gone that far . . . Torching. Kneecaps.

CHAPTER 11

Jewish–Goyish
Showdown

Thomas Hearns, the undefeated WBA welterweight titleholder, claims never to have liked his *nom de guerre*, "The Hit Man." It smacked, he said, too much of the wrong kind of violence, as though he were the faceless, efficient out-of-town assassin who got the unpleasant job done with the help of a .350 Magnum and a silencer. Sure, he could hit, but not the way a hireling did it. Hearns much preferred to be called "The Motor City Cobra." Deadly, yes; efficient, certainly; but the force was his own, not someone packing a gun.

Nicknames in boxing, like early reputations, don't get corrected very easily, and "The Motor City Cobra" never really stuck. Hearns didn't force the issue. He was a timid kid outside the ring who was made even more shy by a self-conscious awareness of his minimal education and his personal lack of confidence in public. Remarkably and untypically successful as a boxer, Thomas Hearns could stand as the archetype for the sort of black ghetto kid who seeks in the ring what he cannot otherwise win outside it—respect and wealth. Perhaps when the more intellectual forms of personal expression that are the result of education are cut off, the frustration that fills the void seeks a more physical and sometimes violent outlet. Perhaps. If such was the case in a brutal fighter like Thomas Hearns, some other theory will have to be developed to explain the attraction to violence for Ray Charles Leonard, Jr., who seemed to be in no way deprived as a kid.

There are other ways in which the Hearns story is archetypal—and very different from Leonard's. As a child Thomas never really knew his father, a void he began to fill when at four- teen he walked into Detroit's John F. Kronk Recreation Center and caught the eye of boxing coach Emanuel Steward. It's a story that's been played out thousands of times in inner-city gyms across America. When Thomas Hearns got Emanuel Steward as a trainer and manager, he was getting a surrogate father as well. (That put him one up on former light-heavyweight champion Matthew Franklin, who was abandoned and named after Philadelphia's Franklin Bridge on which he had been found. And Hearns was certainly better off professionally than Wilfredo Benitez, who had too much father.) After directing Hearns brilliantly as an amateur and then to a professional title in less than two and a half years, Emanuel Steward's results turned criticism into quibble.

Emanuel Steward was a little man (a former national Golden Gloves bantamweight champion) with an immense dream. He had quit a successful and secure job as a master electrician and projects manager with Detroit Edison to run the boxing program at the Kronk Gym full time. Steward's dream was to transform the gym's boxing team into the finest amateur group in the country. By the late 1970s there was proof and a consensus among boxing people that Steward had done precisely that. Kronk fighters, led by Hearns, Hilmer Kenty, Milt McCrory, and Mickey Goodwin, had won a host of national and international titles.

What the amateur boxing world came to know respectfully as "a Kronk fighter" was really a very carefully programmed Eman- uel Steward fighter. There was, in fact, a sense in which Steward the master electrician and Steward the boxing coach were one and the same—it was all presumably a matter of correct wiring.

A Kronk fighter was typically very lean (almost emaciated) and very mean. Steward kept the heat in the gym close to 90 degrees. Training in a sweat box, he believed, was a test of a fighter's character as well as his stamina. It was the "if you can't stand the heat in the kitchen . . ." attitude transposed to the gym. "There's not as much oxygen in that hot gym and I think it's great for conditioning," was the little trainer's simple explanation.

Stylistically, a Steward fighter kept his legs fairly wide apart: Balance at all times is Steward dogma. Kronk fighters are body punchers; they tend to carry the left hand low—a little too low for some purists. Steward is also a master needler who likes to stick the pins in deeply enough to get his fighters riled up while they're sparring with one another. Kronk has more than its share of training wars. Working in the Kronk Gym is synonymous much of the time with the "survival of the fittest" school of sparring.

You could disagree with Steward's approach—and lots of professional trainers did—but you certainly couldn't argue with his results, unless you were sucking sour grapes. Kenty and Hearns won championships quickly after turning pro. Many other Kronk fighters embarked on promising careers. Nevertheless, in spite of the rousing success of so many Kronk fighters, Steward was not my kind of trainer, Hearns not at all my kind of fighter.

The difference in philosophy between Steward and Angelo Dundee was the essential difference that Lenny Bruce, the hip comedian, worked into his famous "Goyish–Jewish" routine. The world, according to Bruce, was divided culturally along "Goyish–Jewish" lines. Dallas, he contended, was essentially "Goyish," but New Orleans was very "Jewish." Barbershop quartets "Goyish," rock 'n' roll "Jewish." Football "Goyish," basketball "Jewish." Richard Nixon "Goyish," Lee Iacocca "Jewish." Bruce, of course, didn't mean literally; he was talking about an essential difference in style that has historically been understood as the Classic vs. the Romantic. Put still another way, it is the difference between the externally ordered and the internally inspired. Structure vs. Feeling. All subject to personal perception, naturally.

In the profession of teaching, the distinction between the externally structured (what we usually mean by discipline) and the internally developed (intuition) is absolutely crucial. The classicist imposes. He imposes a structure, usually in the form of hard and fast rules. Precisely such a task master was Emanuel Steward. At the Kronk things were simple: It was his way or the highway. Steward's way, when it worked, was remarkable; when it didn't, no one really heard about it because the student didn't hang around long enough to demonstrate what he was unable to learn.

Angelo Dundee, although perfectly versed in every formal technique, taught his fighters in a far more flexible way, trying to shape and extend the talents that were already present rather than rigidly imposing a set of rules. Working from the inside outward rather than the other way around was his method, especially with fighters who had an abundance of natural skills. Of course he could be tough as hell, but only when something inherent in the situation called for it; that's why he was more psychologist than drill sergeant with most of his fighters.

Steward's "survival of the fittest" approach worked beautifully as long as you were dealing with very willing young fighters in sufficient numbers. It was perfect on the amateur level for turning the Kronk into a powerhouse team of very tough kids in a hurry. Another important difference in these coaching approaches is that when the disciplinarian is successful, much if not most of the credit goes to him. When the nurturer succeeds it is the athlete on whom the plaudits fall. And that's as it should be, it seems to me. At the heart of the matter, finally, is the size of the teacher's or trainer's or coach's or parent's ego. Angelo Dundee had grown wise enough to understand that, as with Ali, the more room he gave Ray, who was growing intellectually as well as physically, the better he'd develop as a fighter also. Dundee did not have to put his stamp on the kid for the world finally to come to know how fine a trainer he really was. Ego was the enemy.

Although it is almost impossible to minimize Dundee's influence on Leonard in the early years, Sugar Ray had become the controlling agent in his ascent to the championship. Angelo's role had become what it should have been under these new circumstances—a master teacher who encouraged his student's independence and experimentation, all the while reminding him of the importance of the classic fundamentals. It is a rare teacher indeed who encourages his student to need him less and less.

If young Ray Leonard, reluctant as he was about committing himself to boxing as a kid, had walked into the Kronk, chances are he'd not have lasted out the first week of Steward's drill-sergeanting. Hearns not only lasted, he thrived. He was, in fact, so much an extension of Emanuel Steward, it was virtually impossible to tell where the master left off and the disciple began. It bothered me that Steward had achieved such dominance and even more that Hearns had permitted it. Although Ray's intuition and impetuosity had cost him the first Duran fight, it was a characteristic excess of genius, the flip side of his extraordinary ability to improvise and anticipate, that did him in. Hearns was too much a manufactured fighter and bore too much the Steward stamp to be extraordinary. So it was on purely philosophic and stylistic grounds that I liked Ray's chances when the match was made for Las Vegas in September 1981.

The most intriguing thing about the Hearns–Steward union for me was precisely how they'd managed to become so potent a knockout combination in the pros. After thirty-two professional fights, Hearns had recorded thirty KOs, by far the best knockout percentage of any active fighter with as many bouts. As an amateur, however, he had 163 fights, 155 victories, but *only eight knockouts*.

Steward naturally took most of the credit for the incredible transformation, saying that Hearns had finally solved the mystery of punching leverage that he'd been patiently trying to teach the fighter for years. Perhaps. Some of those knockouts, though, came against fighters frozen with fear because of the "Hit Man" image and the string of KOs Hearns had already begun to put together. A knockout reputation was a little like Roger Bannister's breaking the four-minute barrier for the mile: Once accomplished a few times, they seem to want it to happen some more. It's not quite accurate to say it was all done with mirrors, though: Hearns really had become a big puncher with the right hand. Half a dozen times on television I'd seen him punch straight across and slightly down with the bony right arm from his daunting height and shock an opponent into instant paralysis. Other times the victim toppled in sections; occasionally Hearns had to mug him to the canvas. The results left little doubt that Hearns was a dangerous one-punch artist.

As a fighter turns from boy to man it's natural for him to become bigger and stronger. Generally that strength shows itself in improved knockout ability, dramatically so with Hearns. But it had happened with Ray Leonard as well, even though very few of the experts were taking particular notice. He had knocked out twenty-one opponents in his thirty-one fights, but because he didn't do the job with Hearns' sudden devastation, he tended to be over-looked as knockout artist.

How legitimately powerful was that miracle Hearns's right seemed to be the central enigma of the fight. The gamblers thought they knew, and once again Sugar Ray, underappreciated still by much of the fight crowd, came into the fight the underdog at 7–to–5.

The most important thing in analyzing an upcoming fight—or anything else in life, for that matter—is first to ask the right questions. The right answers to the wrong questions can be very misleading—and costly. Asking the right questions, of course, is a lot easier said than done. It's a knack, however, that begins to come with time well spent, spent around gyms watching and lis-tening, time spent at ringside or in front of the television set when the fights are really competitive. And the knack begins to be there one day, like an invisible accumulation that feels a little like wisdom.

So while Hearns's knockout power had become the object of most attention, only the truly sagacious were posing other ques-tions. For example, what about Hearns's chin? Since he'd domi-nated all his professional fights, how would he respond if Ray hit him a good lick? And wasn't it possible that Ray could take the best Hearns had to offer and stay right in there? What would the "Hit Man" do then? And, most important, how would Ray, since he had developed such an impressive variety of ring skills, decide to fight Hearns?

For those who would like to smarten up quickly, that last ques-tion is the most important. What it tells us is that Ray Leonard had many more options than did Hearns, who was a known quantity—a stalker-puncher not likely (or able) to depart from what had been Steward's strategy. He never had to in the past, and he'd always been successful. If one thing about the fight was certain, it was that the neat mind of Emanuel Steward had not planned anything esoteric, exotic, or extreme.

Sugar Ray Leonard, with his range of possibilities, becomes the key fighter, the one to focus on for analytical purposes. If he indeed has the solution for the menace of Thomas Hearns's right hand somewhere in his repertoire, and if he selects the correct solution (as he did not in Duran I), Ray Leonard should control the fight. Furthermore, given Ray's abundant possibilities for attack, it became extremely unlikely that Hearns would be flexible enough to parry or avoid his offensive maneuvers. There was no reason to believe that either Ray, a seasoned professional who learned from his mistakes, or Angelo Dundee, a container ship of boxing wisdom, would make strategic or tactical errors this time around. Of course one clean right from the "Hit Man" could make all analysis academic. In a good fight, let X always equal the unknown.

As a rule of thumb, however, it is what I like to call "the control fighter"—the one with more ways of winning offensively and defensively—who's usually worth wagering a fiver on. I bet mine on Ray with our garage mechanic. All he saw in the papers was Hearns's thirty knockouts in thirty-two fights.

A. J. Liebling in *The Sweet Science* structures most of his essays in precisely the same way: The fight is made. Liebling visits the training camps. Liebling evaluates the fighters. Fight night comes (here there is usually a detailed description of the author's— always the gourmand—dinner and the ensuing trip over to the Garden, the Polo Grounds, or Yankee Stadium). Then the fight itself is followed by Liebling's understanding of the fight, which is more important. It was a very tidy and serviceable structure for a tidier and probably saner era.

There was a historical and financial inevitability to making the Leonard–Hearns match—the WBA and WBC welterweight champions had to meet eventually to see who the true champion was. Naturally the money maneuvering and hype in themselves became a story on the sports page weeks before the fight date, an irrelevancy Liebling never had to deal with. Ever since Ali, however, the making and building of a major fight had become a complicated piece of show business. For a headliner like Leonard, at the top of his form and earning power, each championship match took on a bloated financial importance, with dollar figures that could only make the great welterweights of Liebling's heyday—Mickey Walker, Jimmy McLarnin, Henry Armstrong, Ray Robinson, Kid Gavilan, Carmen Basilio—think the world had gone completely mad. It had.

Without minimizing Mike Trainer's efforts, I had come to lose interest in the enormity of Leonard's payoffs. Suffice it to say that once again Sugar Ray Leonard, Inc. figured to receive the grandest sum ever paid a pugilist, a tad more than $11 million. Hearns would get more than $5 million.

Nor was it usually feasible to visit training camps in the epoch of the Las Vegas venue. Leonard was training at Caesars Palace, where the fight would be staged—that's the right word these days. According to the papers, he was working against tall, rangy sparring partners, but it was impossible to determine from reports whether he was trying to smother their reach advantage or opting to move and stick. That was the crucial information.

Steward had virtually made Hearns incommunicado by setting up early camp on a secluded jut of land in northern Michigan more suitable as a hunting setting for a Hemingway short story. If Liebling had been alive, he'd not have bothered to make the trip. He'd have hung out at Stillman's (if it, too, were alive) and found out from Charley Goldman and Whitey Bimstein, the Marciano brain trust, exactly what Hearns was doing. The grapevine knew those things. Most likely Hearns would be sharpening the left jab, for that was the punch that Steward counted on to set up the dynamite right. That, and learning to gain some punching room in case Leonard chose smothering tactics.

The night of the big fight Faith and I opted for Chinese cuisine in a suburban temple that adjoined the movie theater where the fight would be shown. The epicure in Liebling would have been revolted by our choice, and I'll bet his spirit still is.

The egg drop soup was just a bit too heavy on the MSG (no, not Madison Square Garden), but all the more flavorful and dangerous for that. The spare ribs were singed just to my liking. The fried rice, when sprayed with sufficient soy sauce, met minimal standards. The dessert was resplendent under its gay umbrella—six chilled lychee nuts partially submerged in thick syrup. Alongside, a single fortune cookie. I have its message taped to my typewriter; it gives me a reason to persevere: SOMETHING WONDERFUL WILL HAPPEN VERY SOON.

The specific wonder predicted may have happened even while our bodies were processing our oriental repast. Hearns–Leonard was a remarkable fight. Even now, after five years of reflection,

I'm inclined to call it a great fight, especially as far as Sugar Ray was concerned.

We contributed $20 apiece to the ancillary rights pot. A little steep we thought going in. The crowd was probably very different in the other big-city outlets, but in our affluent North Shore Long Island salon, people filing in seemed remarkably subdued. Many more well-dressed loners and floaters than we ever saw at the old Garden and almost no women. "Doesn't seem like a real title fight," Faith observed. "Where's the bevy of bimbos? Where are the guys with pinky rings?"

It wasn't only the absence of bimbos and little guys with pinky rings that tainted the ambience, it was the movie theater itself. The mind simply could not bridge the psychic distance between the dark anonymity of a place where you've watched Hitchcock films for years and a hot arena full of bursting passions. One— not the most significant, but one—of the reasons fight movies always seems phony is that the movie theater itself removes us from credibility.

Perhaps it all just came down to the seats in this place. Sitting in cushioned splendor, against a backrest that slid into semireclining, was simply not the same as having to accommodate your buns to an unyielding piece of hardwood. Boxing was, after all, the most spartan of sports. And when the action gets fierce, a natural impulse makes you want to rise and move toward it. Not so easy when your seat slides and reclines at thirty degrees.

During the introductions of the fighters our crowd revealed itself politely but overwhelmingly in favor of the gamblers' and sportwriters' choice, Hearns. Faith and I smiled knowingly at one another. More troubling were the announcers, Don Dunphy and Ferdie Pacheco, whose partiality toward the "Motor City Cobra," as Hearns was introduced, was less easy to ignore. At home I could turn off the sound, and usually do. At a live fight, as Liebling so well appreciated, the events required no commentary, only some charged quibbling among partisan neighbors between rounds. Here, I was a damned captive.

There are many ways for a fight to be excellent. In general, though, if each fighter transcends himself in artistry and courage, and if each of their styles complements the other to produce a lot of attacks and counters, you've got a fine match. If, in addition, the progression of events as the rounds unfold provides unexpected reversals, then you've got a hell of a fight.

Hearns didn't come out storming, as had been his normal M.O. Rather, he boxed Leonard early, moving and sticking the left. He was not the masterful boxer, more the careful student at Emanuel Steward High, but he was a better pupil than I'd expected. Ray was content to explore with movement and feints. Hearns's long jab was effective, surprisingly so, probing for possibilities for that finishing right. Late in the second round it was there, the opening, the jab cleared the path for a clean right hand to the head. First big punch of the fight. A sound somewhere between a gasp and a squeal came from the darkness around us. But Ray, hit cleanly, didn't seem to be hurt. He moved out of further danger immediately. When a hitter connects and nothing happens, it is a worrisome early warning.

The critics' rap on Hearns was that he had no staying power. Of course he usually had no reason to hang around very long since he took care of business early most of the time. He'd never gone more than ten rounds, and was required to do that just twice. But his body type indicated a limited endurance. The ring was very warm under TV lights on a Nevada desert evening. Hearns had to dehydrate himself, or believed he did, to make the 147-pound limit, which he misjudged, coming in at 145. He could have used those extra pounds on this night. Time was Leonard's ally; his strategy seemed to be to make Hearns move and work, then come at him late and try to finish him. A risky business because Hearns was winning the early, light-hitting rounds on points.

Ray's patience wore thin in the fifth, probably because the Hearns' jab was getting to the left eye, swelling it and beginning to blur his vision. Leonard began exchanging heavy punches with the "Hit Man" in the center of the ring. A perfect left hook to Thomas's exposed flank with seconds left in the sixth set up a barrage of unanswered blows that almost put Hearns away. The Detroit fighter could not find a straight line back to his corner. It was perfectly reasonable to expect the next round to be his last.

It wasn't. Hearns took a terrible beating to the body and, when he covered up, to the head. He reeled around the ring, badly hurt for the first time in his career, but he fell into the ropes instead of to the canvas. During those interminable seconds Thomas Hearns did what at some point in life many of us are required to do—simply refuse to yield. Whether it is pride or shame or sheer perversity that keeps someone going when the only rational prospect is more punishment remains one of the great mysteries of the human heart. It's a shame that this special heroism is so often cheapened by a compromising reason on the one hand or by sentimentality (à la *Rocky*) on the other. Thomas Hearns survived.

Then an amazing thing happened. Hearns gathered strength. Not enough to hurt Ray. But enough to move away, stick that long jab in Ray's advancing face, and avoid being tagged while standing flat-footed. This was his dance of survival. Sugar Ray, normally the masterful boxer, now found himself in the unaccustomed role of the stalking destroyer. It didn't suit him at all, for although Leonard had become a knockout artist of sorts, his effectiveness generally came from blows thrown in series during the normal context of an exchange. As a stalker, he stunk.

The fight I've been describing was not the fight Dunphy and Pacheco were describing. Nor was it the one the judges were scoring. They all were giving a Hearns jab the equivalent value of a Leonard body shot, and since there had been more jabs, they all had Hearns ahead on points. In the thirteenth round a devastating series of unanswered blows put an exhausted Hearns through the ropes, but referee Davey Pearl ruled the last blow a push and discounted the knockdown. Later in the round two clean rights sent Hearns deeper through the ropes in the same spot, no push this time. The Hit Man found himself knocked down for the first time as a professional fighter. Our theater was silent except for Faith, who was whooping at the count. The bell rang at six. Since a fighter can be saved by the bell only in the last round, Pearl's count continued. He got to nine before the brave Thomas Hearns struggled up. (Even at this point in the fight the judges and the expert commentators had Hearns ahead.)

Sugar Ray ran out of his corner at the bell for the fourteenth. It was hard to tell if the hooks to the body or the rights to the head began the final, irreversible decline. Later, Emanuel Steward said the left to the ribs in the sixth round was the punch that did in his fighter. The sheer volume of unanswered blows caused Pearl to stop the fight at 1:45 of fourteen. A memorable title fight.

Sugar Ray Leonard, in essence, now held three championships—the WBC and WBA welterweight titles as well as the WBA junior middleweight crown. But he'd taken another pretty good beating in wresting Hearns's title. At twenty-five he'd made a ton of money, more than all other boxing champions put together, if you excluded Ali. And he'd made more than Ali. His son was beautiful. His marriage was solid. There was a time when the kid from Palmer Park would have said, "That's it. I've reached my dream. I quit."

Not now. Ray was now in a position to put himself and his accomplishments alongside all the great fighters of the past. The "other" Sugar, the "other" Leonard, Ali, Marciano, Henry Armstrong, Dempsey, Jack Johnson, Willie Pep, all of them. A fighter only had those few years to become immortal, and Ray Charles Leonard decided to put aside his ever-present reluctance and go for the once-in-a-lifetime chance.

The climax of his career seemed predictable—some tune-up fights and then the showdown with Marvelous Marvin Hagler, the very good WBC and WBA middleweight champion. Again, the money would set a new record. Again, time would be on Ray's side. He could take Hagler whenever he was ready, when he had grown strong enough to take on a particularly powerful 160-pounder. And when, of course, Hagler was perhaps just on the verge of losing it. What a great fight it would be.

There were some easier, bit-money fights in the offing about which Mike Trainer had his own little dreams. Trainer believed it was time to make Sugar Ray an international figure in the Ali mold. Usually the title "World's Champion" reflects only a level of attainment, not of true world recognition. Ali was the exception. In his day Ali was a world figure on the grass-roots level, a phenomenon unparalleled in sports, probably the best-known figure on earth. Could Ray attain the same stature? Trainer was sure he could.

Leonard detractors would have bet the ranch against such a likelihood. But they'd been dead wrong in every other evaluation, from the range of his talents to the depth of his courage to his incredible impact on the sport by filling the void left by Ali, and filling it to overflowing. Who was to say that Sugar Ray Leonard, Inc. could not sweep the international market.

The dream was never to be. Not Hagler. Not the world. Ray Leonard would not have the chance to show what he could do in Europe, Africa, or Asia. Other than his sortie across the border into Canada for Duran I, all of Ray's fights as a pro were destined to be in the U.S. of A.

In commenting on the judges' scoring after the Hearns fight, Ray said, "I don't know why I'm an exception to their rules." It sounded like pouting, but in fact if Hearns had managed to finish on his feet, he would probably have gotten the decision even though he was a soundly beaten fighter. In a number of Ray's fights the scoring had struck me as more biased than merely arbitrary. The boxing establishment, it seemed, was only reluctantly going to give its best fighter his due.

In time I began to understand that the reluctance, the resentment, was not really personal. It was profoundly philosophical. As a throwback to a darker age, boxing and the keepers of its flame assume the worst about human nature. Thomas Hobbes could have been describing a boxing career when he described the human condition as being "nasty, brutish, and short." In the professional boxing world there is always the presumption of personal worthlessness akin to original sin; that is precisely why an individual fighter's worth must be proven continually at such great personal risk and cost. A Golden Boy like Sugar Ray, then, is an insult to boxing's cynics because he refutes their basic premise about the dark underside where boxing's soul resides. As a result, nothing Ray could do to show his worth in the ring could change their basic antipathy. His due, if it came at all, among the fraternity, would come only with the passage of time, which sets fights and fighters more truly in history.

Sugar Ray Leonard was a fighter, like the young Ali, who seemed to be untouchable and above the rules under which everyone else was required to operate. Too pretty, too talky, too good, too rich. With Leonard there was the feeling that he was in the boxing world but definitely not of it. And unlike Ali, there was every indication that he was one of the rarest of fighters, someone who would be able to walk away from boxing finally without having paid enough of a price physically, someone who had beat the system.

Maybe that's why the fates that ruled the dark domain of boxing stepped in to do to Ray Charles Leonard what other men and the system could not.

CHAPTER 12

No More Sugar

In the spring of 1982, while training for a busy-work fight with welterweight Roger Stafford, Sugar Ray Leonard took a thumb in the left eye from a sparring partner. Commonly in boxing it's an errant—or intentional—thumb that does disproportionate damage. The action was stopped immediately. Ray's eye reddened and ran with tears. His vision was blurred for a short while; the spots stayed longer. It was unpleasant but precisely the sort of accident that happened to fighters all the time.

Occupational hazard in this instance became occupational disability because the spotty vision in Ray Leonard's left eye did not go away; it hung on like a scary dream. Ray Leonard's luck had run out. A detached retina was diagnosed and confirmed. Quickly and expertly a retina attachment operation was performed by Dr. Ronald G. Michels, the Sugar Ray Leonard of retinal surgery, at Johns Hopkins Hospital in Baltimore. Although the detachment was undoubtedly caused by a blow of some sort, according to the best medical knowledge available there was no way to be absolutely sure which punch or punches that Ray had received during his career might have caused the trauma. It could as easily have been the jab of Thomas Hearns as the careless thumb of a sparring mate.

If a detached retina were to occur in most of us, it would scare the hell out of us, even though the damage would be easy enough to repair surgically. For a fighter, it is a descent into hell itself. Even though some of the most prominent retinal specialists are absolutely convinced the repaired eye is actually stronger than the originally vulnerable one, a fighter who has lived through weeks or months with those shadow spots returns to the ring a chastened man, burdened by doubt, if not outright fear. And a doubtful fighter isn't really a fighter at all.

There wasn't a fighter around who didn't know the sad story of another Sugar Ray. The only standout on the 1972 Olympic Team, the one Ray Leonard didn't make because it wasn't his time, was Sugar Ray Seales, who won the only American gold that year in Munich. Immediately thereafter he launched himself on a professional career. Seales, although ranked consistently among top-ten middleweights, came up a little short in fights with future champions Alan Minter and Marvin Hagler. Much too good to be a mere club fighter but not quite good or lucky enough to scale the peak, Sugar Ray Seales found himself to be the excellent journeyman who fought the tough fights wherever the pay was decent—and sometimes when it wasn't. More often than not Seales won.

Nowhere Seales fought—and he boxed in most of the major arenas in this nation—did the cursory prefight eye exams reveal the fact that Seales was fighting with detached retinas. Done properly, they should have. Nor did Seales, who was learning to live with smoky and shadowed vision, tell the examining doctors about his symptoms, so badly did he need another payday. Sugar Ray Seales is now blind.

Retinal tears and detachments are not picked up by quickie eye exams or by any but qualified eye specialists. For this reason an exam by a retinal expert ought to be a mandatory procedure in all prefight examinations. It ought to be assumed, furthermore, that the fighter's judgment of his own vision is irrelevant. Such supervisory care would also save the deteriorating vision that occurs in some older fighters.

When fight people talked about eye injuries, it was the pathetic Ray Seales story that you heard most often. Few remembered that

Earnie Shavers's sight was saved by a retinal operation that repaired a massive tear in his retina—and he was able to fight again. So, medically speaking, the odds were good that after his retina healed, in about six months, Sugar Ray Leonard would be able to fight again without risking loss of vision. That was medically speaking. Favorable medical odds didn't mean much, though, compared to what Ray was feeling. The Sugar Ray Leonard Golden Boy scenario now had a catch; the vision problems were real, they also had a foreboding, symbolic quality.

Everything else in his life was so perfect. Juanita was a superb companion and anxious to enlarge the Leonard family. Ray, Jr. was a pure joy, a nice kid his father loved spending time with. There was the rambling new house in Potomac, Maryland, and all the money any of the Leonards would ever require. Things were so good, in fact, that Ray couldn't help perceiving his sight-threatening injury as an omen rather than merely a setback.

Here he was, a perfect physical specimen in the full power of his manhood and athletic excellence at twenty-six, intellectually alert, professionally and personally confident and secure: Suddenly all was jeopardized by these vague spots in his left eye. Ray Leonard began to understand in a real way for the very first time how incredibly delicate is the balance of our well-being. How illusionary and fleeting is our power, our independence. The shock to Ray's psyche was the true realization of his own mortality. It simply came a little earlier and with more subtle drama to him than to most of us. Ray Charles Leonard, already mature for his years, jumped into middle age as a fighter.

During his rehabilitation Ray had time to think, perhaps too much time to think. He knew he had a gut-wrenching decision to make. Did he retire one final time, prudently opting for home and family, for the ease and security of the essentially uneventful and vicarious life of the sportscaster? Or did he risk his vision again by seeking Marvelous Marvin Hagler's middleweight championship, thereby attempting to match a feat accomplished by only the greatest of welterweight champions? Sugar Ray Robinson had done it and become a boxing immortal in the process. The same level of recognition would be there for Leonard. There would be the added bonus of still another "biggest purse in boxing history." If Ray won, he'd have proved everything any reasonable boxing historian could have expected of a great fighter. He'd never have to fight again; he wouldn't have any serious reason to.

For months Ray grappled with his decision. Given his track history of quixotic retirements and equally quixotic changes of mind, there was no reason to take a retirement seriously. Even less so because of the manner in which Ray planned to announce his decision. Sugar Ray Leonard, Inc. orchestrated a glitzy media event.

On November 9, 1982, Ray Leonard rented himself a hall, the Baltimore Civic Center, scene of his first triumph as a professional fighter, to tell the world what he would do. In six short years since launching his career Ray Leonard had earned an unprecedented $37 million as a fighter—and he wasn't a heavyweight! With every tick of the clock the corporation's capital was earning even more money for itself. The Leonard family would never want.

Depending on your point of view, the style of Ray's melodramatic announcement could be seen as either classy or crass. On the one hand, it was a benefit rally for a summer jobs program for local youths, a black-tie affair for the capital area's elite. On the other, it was so blatantly a publicist's creation that it made Sugar Ray look grotesquely self-important. However you saw it, though, it was at least suspenseful: No one attending really knew whether they were there to hear Ray announce that his eye had healed perfectly so he would be going for Hagler's title after all . . . or that he'd be hanging 'em up once and for all.

I was certain it was all pre-Hagler hype because among the 10,000 present were the special invitees, most prominent of whom —after Ali, of course—was the Marvelous one himself. It was extremely unlikely he'd have come just to hear Ray tell him to kiss off the biggest payday any middleweight ever dreamed of.

A bell rang. The huge crowd quieted slowly. Wearing a spiffy tuxedo, standing in the familiar ring amid a glaring spotlight, Leonard, never one to leave a dramatic moment unwrung, cleared his throat and with heavy voice, while gazing directly at Marvelous Marvin, said, "A fight with this great man, with this great champion, would be one of the greatest fights in history. Unfortunately, it'll never happen." There was a gasp. The young man with this strange and irrepressible penchant for finality had done it again.

When Juanita ran to him in the ring, Ray began to sob. Marvin

Hagler didn't cry but surely had ample reason: A gate of at least $30 million had been a certainty.

For a while, even more than a while, the decision felt good to Ray. He was busy enough. He was a ringside analyst for CBS and Home Box Office; as a result, he worked a match virtually every week. It was pleasant work because he was being paid to talk about something he understood better than himself. The traveling wasn't so bad; he was usually only away from home two or three days each week. His ego—necessarily large for an athlete driven to accomplish great things—was soothed by the recognition and praise he received all over America in airports and hotel dining rooms. Like an ex-President, a former champion of Ray's stature never loses his title in public—he's "Champ" for as long as he breathes. A great many distant admirers felt close enough to call him "Sugar Ray" with an intimacy that surprised no one. People seemed to go out of their way to be pleasant to him; it was pretty well established that history would treat him well enough.

As keeper of his own flame, Ray Leonard made the rounds of TV and radio talk shows explaining his decision, talking up some of the fights he was working, and otherwise being what they call a personality. He stayed in good shape by taking tap-dance lessons and messing around with karate as well. He ran and exercised. For someone who had never known the lonely and surreal thrill of standing in a shower of blazing light in a boxing ring, the waves of human sound rolling out of the darkness, about to face a professional fighter with the outcome unknowable—the very different life Ray Charles Leonard lived since retiring would have been extremely satisfying. Pleasant work, time for himself, time for his family and friends, money for anything he or they wished. The fulfillment of the Dream.

Only by degrees did Sugar Ray come to realize that there was a detachment in his life greater than the one that had been corrected in his eye. The more he realized it, the bigger the hole got. When he quit he had known that boxing was the thing that defined him in the world, the thing that gave him wealth, prestige, respect. But Ray believed he'd accrued enough of that stuff to last him a lifetime, so he didn't think he'd have to go back to the old well to bucket up any more cash or esteem. In that respect he was close to correct.

What very few fighters who retire with some good fights still in them—and even those who haven't—realize too late is that they miss boxing mostly for its own sake. They miss the roadwork, the exercise and the jumping, the heavy and light bag, the sparring —the perverse agony of boxing; they miss the sounds and smells, the ambience of the gym, the close attention of other fight people. It is paradoxical as pleasant pain, but it is the way a fighter loves fighting. Ray loved his family. He was proud of this stature in the world. But those were qualitatively different feelings from what he felt as a fighter. They were external to him; fighting put him in touch with parts of himself that nothing else could. There would come a time in the not too distant future when his body would simply not be able to love him back in the manner to which he had become accustomed. That would be a sad time, the time to quit. Maybe he had been a little premature.

One evening in November '83, Ray was sitting ringside at Caesars Palace in Vegas to work the Hagler–Duran middleweight championship rumble for HBO. It looked like a mismatch going in, with Hagler figuring to be much too big and too strong for the overused Duran.

Duran, the 4–to–1 underdog, fought the fight of his life. In the sixth round Hagler hit Duran with everything but the dollar slots. Duran didn't fall. He was not only still around in the twelfth and thirteenth but won those rounds decisively. The fight came down to the final two rounds. Hagler won them and retained his title.

It was widely reported that when the fight was over Duran came over to Leonard and shouted, "You knock him out, Leonard. No problem." Even without such a strong first-person endorsement, Ray Leonard liked his chances against Hagler. Sugar Ray Leonard, Inc. announced it was back in the boxing business the following month. Ray said, "I'm coming back because fighting is what I do best. It's why I was born. It's as simple as that."

Marvin Hagler's credit rating leapt to Triple-A. You didn't have to be a cynic to suspect that the whole scenario had been dreamed up to stoke up even greater interest in the Leonard–Hagler climax after so ingenious an *interruptus*. I don't want to be placed in the unenviable position of arguing that Ray actually meant to stay retired this time, but that's what I believe, even though I can't prove a word of it. A substantial part of Ray Charles Leonard, who was in fact a man of complex and often unrelated parts, believed his retirement every time he announced it. He believed his comebacks too.

Selecting a comeback opponent after a very long layoff is not an easy matter. In this case it was particularly tricky because Ray would have to be in there with someone who was credible and tough enough to give the repaired eye a serious test. A fighter who shouldn't be able to beat Ray, even on an off night, but who would test Ray's skills and his desire. In addition, a fighter who could prepare Ray for Hagler in a single fight; therefore, he'd have to be something of a hitter so there would be present that unknown factor fight people called "a puncher's chance." For such a fighter, it was the chance of a lifetime.

Any opponent who couldn't hit would be suspect because there certainly was no one around who would be able to box with even a rusty Sugar Ray, not that Ray ever let himself get out of shape even during his rehabilitation. The brain trust settled on Kevin Howard, a durable welterweight who was not in the top ten but who had two things going for him: He was a big puncher and a Philadelphia fighter. For people familiar with boxing, that last thing meant that Kevin Howard was also tough and well-schooled.

One stipulation in the contract that Sugar Ray insisted upon was that the match be fought with thumbless gloves. The glove was an experimental innovation in which the thumb was attached to the fist to form a single piece. It prevented all thumbing, accidental as well as intentional, but it felt slightly awkward to fighters, so naturally the boxing establishment was reluctant to accept the change. Ray's insistence on thumbless gloves, self-protective as it was, also kept everyone's attention focused on the fight's main drama—Ray Leonard's eyes. The thumbless glove issue was Leonard, Inc. at its best: benevolent and brilliantly commercial at once. Kevin Howard didn't welcome the thumbless gloves; he did welcome the hundred grand he'd get for the match, so he bit his thumb, so to speak.

Ray's overprotective, possibly gun-shy posture was played for all it was worth to hype the fight. Forget the two-year layoff for

Sugar, the real question being presented in this one was, would he be diminished as a fighter by uncertainty and anxiety, would fear take away the small but razor-sharp edge that had left him totally free to do in a boxing ring whatever had to be done to defeat an opponent. Would he no longer be alone with his other self when a bell rang, or would there be another small voice counseling prudence? That would be the end of Sugar Ray as surely as if his great boxer's heart gave out.

For his part, Kevin Howard brought the garish art of boxing hype to a new low point. Naturally the media asked him about any reservations he might have in punching at Ray's eye. No reservations, none. In fact, Howard offered, he'd shoot for the eye to win the fight because that was where his opponent was most vulnerable. Ray Leonard wants to fight after retinal surgery, that's Ray Leonard's problem, not Kevin Howard's. Kevin Howard, he said, would do whatever was necessary to win. Whatever. If it means popping that eye, so be it. It was important for credibility to sell the idea that Leonard's opponent would not take it easy on the eye. Howard went beyond credibility to morbidity.

A few weeks before the fight an eye examination by a Massachusetts Boxing Commission ophthalmologist—yes, they were taking special precautions for the controversial match scheduled for Worcester, a venue off the beaten path on the boxing circuit—revealed a slight hole in the retina of Leonard's *right* eye.

The discovery prompted a small medical debate. Dr. Michels at Johns Hopkins didn't believe the hole was any more than an individual irregularity and not in the least sight-threatening. Dr. Edward Ryan, the Boston surgeon who finally operated on the eye, counseled preventive surgery. The medical point was moot because once the problem was made public, it became almost impossible for the Massachusetts Commission to sanction the match and too risky for any other state commission to put itself on the line by accepting it. The appearance of danger was every bit as discouraging to boxing officials as danger itself.

If he really was committed to a comeback in the ring, Ray Leonard would have to undergo a second operation, minor compared to the first, but surely a psychological setback of major proportions for a man who had been trying to subdue his fears for months. It also destroyed his concentration: Ray had been focusing only on a specific opponent at a specific time; now, with that time and that opponent at hand, it was blown. Marvin Hagler, watching all these bizarre turns of fortune, must have thought he was tuned in to *General Hospital*.

Because Ray was completely committed to the comeback, the sooner the operation the better. Dr. Ryan performed a five-minute repair job using a freezing technique that bonded the retina by forming scar tissue, and Ray was back in training ten days later. The fight was rescheduled for May '84; that meant a layoff of twenty-seven months since Ray's last fight.

Kevin Howard, who had been placed on hold for a few months, proved he could sink even lower than morbidity by telling the press his chances for winning had doubled, he now had two vulnerable targets to shoot for. Thank you, Kevin.

All comebacks, regardless of the sport, are extremely hard. You are dealing above all with uncertainty, not the conventional sorts about the situation or the opponent—those have always been part of the equation—but about yourself. And there is enormous self-consciousness. What the body, the instincts, the reflexes used to do automatically, cannot be counted on with any degree of certainty. So you try to recapture the moves, the patterns of moves, the attitudes of the successful days to take you to the point where the body and the blood remember and take over as they used to. But you can't be sure it *will* happen until it *does* happen and happen when it counts, not in training but when you're alone with an opponent in the spotlight.

They say, "Be nervous, of course be nervous, that's a good sign. Means you're ready. When you take that first hard punch or throw that first combination, it'll be there. It's like swimming or riding a bike, you never forget. It'll be there, don't worry." But you can't be absolutely sure it's there until you feel it there. What they don't tell you is that even if the old feeling comes back, it might not be all there. Maybe just enough of it to get by, or even to be good. If you've been great, however, good isn't good enough.

You could be kind and call such thoughts reasonable concerns, but in the privacy of a man's soul at odd moments of his day they distort into overwhelming fears it takes a great effort of will to subdue. The eyes, always the eyes, whenever the journalists discussed the risks of the fight. It got to him at last. There was something mysteriously sacred about the gift of sight; it was as though Sugar Ray Leonard was tempting retribution from the gods themselves.

The day of the fight was strange, and if you believed in omens, you'd have anticipated trouble. That morning Ray tipped in for the official weigh-in at 149. In the dressing room after dinner he weighed 156. Maybe the scale was wrong, but he felt logy. Nerves, he guessed.

Ray had used the early rounds of lots of fights to evaluate an opponent tactically. That's what he planned to do with Howard. Besides, he sorely needed the active time if he intended to scrape away some of the ring rust and was seriously preparing for a Hagler match in the not too distant future. Never, though, had he moved against an opponent in quite the manner he did against Howard. It was as though a puppeteer were working Ray's head with a broken finger. Whenever his body and arms tried to do something offensive, the head swiveled and tilted backward; it could as easily have been on someone else's shoulders. As a result, his punches either missed the target or landed without force. After the fight, Ray admitted, "I was apprehensive, afraid of being hit." You didn't have to be an expert to notice. There were boos in the crowd, a particularly unsentimental lot.

But it was early. Ray hadn't been hit a good shot yet, and I believed that if and when he was, the hidden power of the blood would assert itself and reclaim the true fighter. Ray moved better in the fourth; you could have sensed a fight plan developing. If you looked away just then, you'd have missed it. Ray hung out a jab and *bam*, Howard came over it with a right to the left side of Leonard's head, perilously close to the eye. Sugar Ray Leonard was on his ass in the middle of the ring, knocked down for the first time in his professional boxing career.

The punch caught him perfectly and, yes, he was slightly off balance, a rarity with the true Sugar Ray. But the likes of Benitez and Hearns and Duran hadn't even come close to a knockdown of the kid from Palmer Park. He was hurt, but he bounced up immediately. He was also very angry. The hell with the eyes now; he was a fighter.

He stood in his corner before the start of the fifth round,

waved and blew a kiss to Ray, Jr. and Juanita, who was eight months pregnant with their second child. Ray wanted them to know he was okay. The round was better for him, not vintage Sugar but a reasonable enough facsimile. Ray was up on his toes, moving in and out, beginning to go to the body when he was close enough. The fear was just subdued, not banished. The timing appeared to be slightly out of sync on the combinations, but some of his single punches were getting in.

Leonard's attack to the body began to wear Howard down, and his hand lowered with each passing round. Individual punches Ray threw did a cumulative damage; the combinations simply weren't there. In the ninth a clean left hook wobbled Howard, but he was able to clinch with Leonard, who couldn't manage to shake him off cleanly. When Ray got loose he went for the finish like a raw kid, flailing wildly—and missing for the most part—at the cowering Howard. The referee did everybody a favor and stopped the fight. TKO Sugar Ray.

Finally, it wasn't the eyes, no, not the eyes entirely, that had caused Ray to fight so poorly. He said it immediately after the fight: "I knew even before the knockdown it was over for me. In the first round I tried to establish a rhythm; I tried moving. But when it didn't come, I said, 'Damn, I'm in trouble.' I kept trying to get my hands to work, but they never did. He'd throw a jab, I'd see it coming—and it would hit me. And my right hand was stuttering. It wasn't *my* right hand."

His body wasn't *his* body anymore. The Sugar had gone out of it. Ray Leonard knew it was never coming back. As it had happened to so many great fighters before him, Ray Charles Leonard had lost the magic. He had had one tough fight too many. I wondered if Angelo Dundee had seen it leaving after the wars with Duran and Hearns.

The comeback fight hadn't been an artistic success and would probably be remembered more for the knockdown than anything else, but at least Ray had reached down and found the resources to win. In his dressing room, he told his wife and son, "Don't worry, that's it." His statement to the press was only slightly longer. There. Done. Not with a flashy bang this time, more like a whimper, but it was final. Ray Leonard was twenty-eight.

CHAPTER 13

The Blood Sport

Professional boxing is a throwback, a vestige of our dark, irrational past. That's one reason it is usually under sharp attack in a society that likes to believe it has evolved very different and superior values.

You surely cannot reason people into an appreciation of boxing. For many years I tried and I failed. Instinct will rise up at the sight of the first flurry of punches and make them either hate it or love it instantly, more likely hate it. Impartiality toward boxing is almost impossible to maintain, and those who hate it can mount the stronger logical arguments. Strong, even perfect arguments, however, do not lead inevitably to understanding, rarely to truth. Some things are comprehended less through language and logic than by the heart, the blood, or in the pit of the stomach.

I first discovered an irrational "understanding" in myself about the time my old man began teaching me to box—or rather to receive punches while trying to box him. I don't know how the tooth got loose; it might have been one of the stiff, double-clutch jabs I allowed to slip through my pillow-glove defense. In a week the tooth, a baby one, came close to falling out. He wanted to attach a string and yank it immediately. "A little pain and then it's over," he said. No, I said. "Be reasonable," he said. No, I said. It seemed to me even then supremely *un*reasonable to opt for pain whatever the promise of release. I was ten.

So why do I still remember sitting at my desk at school that week diddling at that dangling tooth with the tip of my tongue, bringing on excruciating pain and tears to my eyes? It hurt like hell yet I persisted. Why? Not, as I rationalized then, because I was trying to push the damn thing out, or not entirely so. Part of me actually enjoyed it. I was discovering the perverse pleasure that commingles with certain types of pain. More than that, I discovered human complexity of a sort I'd never known existed and that doesn't yield to simple reason. I discovered a deeper, nonrational self. And it was scary. Don't get me wrong, the discovery didn't loose all my demons; it just let me know that there were at least two of me in there, and one of us seemed to be a very mysterious customer. And that life was going to be a lot less rational and more complicated than I'd been led to believe.

Blood is the mystery element in the human equation. It is supposed to remain pulsing quietly beneath our skins, out of sight, carrying out its pure magic as though it didn't even exist, as though we were not extremely vulnerable biological creatures linked by this very same blood to other creatures on the planet with whom we share a dark history. Perhaps I am not alone in my double and very confused reaction to blood running freely: I am revolted and tremendously curious at the same time.

Professional boxing is a blood sport, though not to quite the same degree as *la corrida* or cockfighting because blood is neither essential nor inevitable in the boxing ring. But human blood is there often enough to be more than a mere side effect. It is close to being integral. So if your distaste for blood—or for the very tenuous animal nature it symbolizes—is strong, boxing will be repellent to you. But you knew that already.

In the ring blood has great theatrical significance. The raw and elemental drama hearkens back to primitive times when subduing natural and human rivals violently meant nothing less than survival. To the extent that technology has allowed us to forget that fundamental reality, it deludes us. And just as modern reason claims an exclusive superiority to passion, so does the brain automatically try to suppress what the blood understands. It does the intellect, smug as it tends to get these days, some good, I think, to have to confront the blood drama in the ring. Boxing's ultimate lesson, you see, is modesty. Never has "civilized" man needed it more.

But the fight game is corrupt. I knew that from all the movies I'd seen as a kid, and my old man confirmed the fact around the time he first took me to Stillman's Gym. It only really became necessary for a fan to justify its utter and profound corruption when a prominent boxer died in the ring or when a not-so-prominent boxer died in dramatic fashion. A ring death could always be counted on to bring out "abolish boxing" sentiment and evoke some of the most affecting writing you've seen on the sports pages since the last tragic death in the ring. A few state boxing commissions would then institute a reform or two—the standing-eight count, more discretionary power for the referee and the ring doctor—then, after the passage of a couple of weeks without another fatality, the old blood drama would be staged again with a few new regulations, but with its essence unchanged.

Not all ring deaths, however, create equal public outcries. When Duk-Koo Kim died on November 17, 1982, as the result of a fourteenth-round TKO by Ray Mancini in a WBA lightweight championship fight in Las Vegas, the soul-searching ran unusually deep. The shock waves reverberated a little more powerfully this time because only the night before, in a televised fight from Miami, Alexis Arguello, the excellent and widely admired multi-titleholder, was knocked senseless by the rugged Aaron Pryor. Arguello lay unconscious on the canvas four deathly minutes. He came around finally. Kim, however, lingered on life-support systems for days.

The Mancini fight, a surprisingly tough one given the fact that Kim was virtually unknown outside Korea, was televised nationally on CBS. Kim's credentials, his top-ten ranking, and resultant eligibility for the title match had been suspect from the beginning. Mancini, the champ, had become a small-screen attraction. Most observers believed he'd achieved his mini-stardom because he was a willing battler who exuded boyish charm in his interviews. He had another rare commodity among world-class fighters—he was white.

I believed Ray Mancini was something more. He was really, in spite of the Ohio twang and engaging gift of blue-collar gab, a 1940s Italo-American club fighter who'd battle his heart out whenever and wherever a bell sounded. Every time I saw him wonderful names floated back from my youth—Sammy Angott, Tony Janiro, Charley Fusari, Steve Belloise. With Mancini in the ring, suddenly it was the summer of '42. In an age of designer jeans and gold chains (both of which he wore, by the way), such a throwback as Mancini was more than refreshing in the fight game, he was downright necessary.

Ray "Boom Boom" Mancini was not an old-timer by accident; the original "Boom Boom," his father Lenny, had been just such a fighter. The son became the father's immigrant work ethic made manifest in the ring. I could never begrudge this Boom Boom a six-figure payday. With some very attractive and big-money fights just ahead, it didn't seem logical that Mancini's manager would jeopardize that future by agreeing to an opponent who might beat Boom Boom. The Korean lightweight filled the bill.

Inside boxing types could not help admiring the brilliant way Mancini, a fighter with the single virtue of heart, but a ton of that, had been handled, finessed, in fact, into the lightweight championship without having to face many dangerous opponents. The feat was accomplished by manager Dave Wolf. That's right, the same guy who had led me carefully and seductively through my investigation of boxing's corrupt byways for *Sport* magazine.

Like a lot of writers, novelists as well as guys on the boxing beat, Wolf found the lure of the blood game overwhelming. So Hemingway tries the gloves on with Dempsey and Tunney. George Plimpton has absolutely got to taste Ali's jab, or its nonlethal facsimile. And a huffing, puffing Norman Mailer tries to keep up with Ali during predawn roadwork before dropping behind and giving up. For Wolf, the challenges were, first, to discover a promising kid who'd been overlooked by sharp-eyed and sharp-talking managers and then moving such a cull toward a title. That, and the delectable pleasure of negotiating contracts with the game's sharks and still coming away with enough meat for himself and his fighter. The sweat and chatter and roughhouse of the gym, those were delicious bonuses.

It was Wolf who perpetrated the great "Too Tall" Jones swindle of 1979, thereby earning the eternal respect of every hustler in the fight game. Ed Jones, the huge, all-star defensive end for the Dallas Cowboys, believed—or was led to believe—there was more fame and a great deal more fortune to be gained as a heavyweight contender than an NFL defender. Boxing people knew of course that the transition would be impossible: Size and football toughness had absolutely nothing to do with taking a punch on the point of the jaw (no face masks allowed between the ropes, Ed) or learning to throw combinations and mastering foot and body movement. Ed Jones never learned any of it very well. Nevertheless, with Wolf's Barnum-styled media blitz behind them, the "Too Tall" circus wagon hit the road. Even after six wins, five of them KOs, it was painfully obvious, especially to Jones, that he really had been born to anchor that left side of the Cowboy's defense. The experiment more than earned its way as far as it went.

So when Dave Wolf came up with an amateur lightweight named "Boom Boom," whose old man had been a contender before he took some shrapnel in the Battle of the Bulge, there was absolutely no reason to believe that kid was anything but another Wolf media con. To the extent that it got people's attention it was precisely that, but Ray Mancini could fight. He couldn't box, but he could fight. Winning the lightweight championship, even though achieved against unusually weak opposition, proved that much at least. It also showed that Wolf could handle a legitimate fighter brilliantly.

Fighters, managers, trainers, and writers take delight in describing a particularly violent match in which each fighter takes the best shots of the other and keeps hanging tough as a "war." Too often mere skirmishes these days tend to get exaggerated into battles, and battles inflated into full-scale wars. But Mancini– Kim was the real thing. Not a match for purists, it was nevertheless a remarkable test of wills. Unfortunately, it was to a very great extent Kim's will to prevail that killed him. During a fifty-second period in the thirteenth round he took thirty-nine punches, most of them to the head, but he not only stayed right in front of Mancini, he ducked very low and came back with enough powerful punches of his own to make it impossible for referee Richard Green to stop the fight under the existing rules. When the bell rang for the fourteenth, Mancini drew on some unfathomable reserve of energy and ran out of his corner directly at the challenger. A strange tactic given the wearying slugging of the previous rounds. But Mancini didn't close with Kim; he sidestepped at the last moment and unleashed a withering barrage of punches, the last of which, a right cross, toppled Kim backward. Even though the Korean struggled to his feet in time to beat the count, referee Green finally had the situation he needed to stop the fight.

Duk-Koo Kim collapsed and left the ring on a stretcher. He was rushed to Desert Springs Hospital, where Dr. Lonnie Hammargren, a neurosurgeon, performed an emergency operation on the right side of Kim's brain and removed a 100-cc blood clot. The prognosis was familiarly depressing: Kim was critical; if he lived, Hammargren said, he would do so "with terminal brain damage." Hammargren also opined that Kim's "trauma was caused by one punch, since the hemorrhage was quite fresh." He also doubted if a fighter already hemorrhaging could have fought back as effectively as Kim had in the thirteenth.

Because the fight was part of CBS' *Sports Saturday* anthology, the audience included many more than hard-core boxing fans. Hundreds of thousands of channel switchers had stuck with what was obviously a hell of a fight. Millions of Americans had developed an emotional bond with the valiant Korean underdog. It was probably the most widely witnessed ring death in history.

Most boxing fatalities come by degrees. Knockout or TKO, collapse and coma, days or weeks of vigil before finally the fighter slips quietly away. A peaceful death after so violent an injury. Kim remained alive, technically speaking, for five days. His mother gave permission for her son's still-excellent organs to be used for transplant purposes. Shortly after Duk-Koo Kim's funeral in Korea, his mother committed suicide.

For many boxing fans I knew, that fight was the last one they would watch, or watch with a fan's passion. In many cases an emotional involvement in that fight had made people feel vaguely like accessories to a crime. People who had believed professional boxing to be an uncivilized, exploitive, and destructive activity moved for its abolition. The fight had been a brutal one; a perfectly healthy young man had died. For the championship match

Duk-Koo Kim received $20,000. There ought to have been re-
vulsion.

At roughly the same time it was disclosed that Muhammad Ali
was suffering from a disorder of the central nervous system. It
didn't particularly matter that doctors at New York Presbyterian
Hospital eventually settled on Parkinson's "syndrome" as their
diagnosis and would not definitively attribute it to the blows received over a twenty-year professional career. What mattered was
the way he appeared on television. In his early forties, Ali quivered
like an octogenarian when he was not medicated; his once vibrant
and boastful tenor was a dull mockery of itself, the comic's punch-
drunk fighter become reality. You'd have thought young Cassius
had signed a pact with the Devil in 1960 that allowed him to
become great in the world's eyes; now Beelzebub was claiming his
part of the bargain.

It will be hard to convince future generations how superb a
fighter Ali had been purely on the basis of films of his fights. The
three Frazier fights are famous for their fury and bravery, but as
you watch replays of the matches with Norton, Spinks, Foreman,
Holmes, and various others, especially toward the end of his career, you're amazed by how often and how cleanly Ali was caught
in the head. History's visual record will treat Ray Leonard far
better. Ali will probably be as well remembered for his jaw and
his courage as for his youthful speed and braggadocio. What was
most amazing about Ali, I realized after reviewing most of his
fights, was the great number of ring wars he managed to survive.

Ali had more tough fights than most fighters of the modern
era. Still, he continued, managing to find a way to win most of
the time, often when it seemed entirely unlikely. Joe Frazier, by
contrast, a younger man and known for being indomitable in the
ring, had nothing left after his three wars with Ali and knew
enough to leave the hard business with his money and most of
his sense shortly thereafter. Ali chose to stay and paid more dearly.
Duk-Koo Kim did not have such a choice.

For defenders of the blood sport, the single most powerful
argument against it is its intent to injure. When critics say "It is
the only sport where the sole objective is to render your opponent

unconscious" there's no legitimate way to refute them. You might parry with the despicable "get the quarterback" strategy in football, the cowardly, "beanball" tactic in baseball, and the intimidating goons who "police" the ice in hockey. But those are evasions; the sports are not at all comparable. Boxing is a blood sport in its essence and intent; death hovers over it always.

Should a civilized society—or at least one that aspires to be such—continue to tolerate so brutal a blood sport? Could the death of Kim, or any of the half dozen unseen, no-name fighters who died that same year, possibly justify its existence? At the time of Kim's death the answer was undeniably "No," but for me it was a "No" that formed reluctantly on my lips.

Not wanting to lose something I loved simply because it was dead wrong, I searched among my friends who were fight fans for reasons that might allow me to justify the blood drama. Most of them were in the same boat. None could either shrug off Kim's death or justify it. Nor did they wish to say they'd never watch another boxing match again.

Pete Bonventre, the *Newsweek* and *Inside Sports* writer who had moved on to TV as an Emmy Award-winning producer for Howard Cosell's *SportsBeat* show on ABC, was also struggling to justify his appreciation of the old blood drama. We met in a Midtown restaurant to discuss our futures as boxing fans. "No, I really can't defend boxing anymore, especially after fighters are killed like that. God, it's morbid." It surprised me then when he suddenly said, "But I still can tell you what's good about it." Clearly Bonventre wanted to be allowed to continue loving something he ought not love.

Soon he was talking about Ali and Leonard, whose fights he had covered over the past decade, with a sense of awe that no other sporting events had ever evoked in him. Nothing could match them as spectacle or as personal experience. He could measure his life in great championship fights, and it was hard to tear yourself away from your own history, especially such gaudy, exciting history.

He told me about driving deep into the jungle in Zaire after a rainstorm at 5 A.M. to discover Ali sitting on the steps of a porch performing magic tricks for a dozen saucer-eyed kids. No one else around. Just hours earlier Ali had miraculously and valiantly knocked out George Foreman and regained his championship for the third time. "Do you believe Ali could have become the best-known, most charismatic figure in the world through any other sport but heavyweight boxing? If he weren't the heavyweight champion of the world, would he have left his mark on America the way he did?" Of course not. "Still," Bonventre added quickly, "none of that could honestly justify the human toll boxing takes." But Bonventre had not been justifying or even weighing debits and credits: He had only been reminiscing about a love object.

Significantly, Ali, painful as it is to see him these days, especially for his admirers, adamantly accepts his present state without regret, and certainly without self-pity. For him the issue has always been choice. It was choice when he adopted a Muslim name. It was choice when he refused to step forward in that Selective Service office in 1967. It was choice when he opted to linger on the ropes and take Foreman's blows in Zaire until his powerful opponent had punched himself empty and was ready to be taken. Without risk, without the possibility of significant loss, choice is a sham, a rationalization at best.

Critics argue that young men who become professional boxers don't truly choose to do so, but are usually driven to it by difficult personal or economic conditions. The typical picture is of a tough, uneducated, and, as a result, ignorant kid who simply doesn't know what he's getting himself into. The picture is accurate enough as far as a kid's false expectations of financial reward are concerned. Surely the business of boxing has to be torn apart and reconstructed. But for most young fighters the choice of a boxing life is as individual and as much a true choice as Andre Watts choosing to play the piano.

The piano is a good analogy. Millions of kids take piano lessons; a small percentage stick with the lessons; a smaller percentage still become real players. Those points of transition are the moments of true choice. Lots of kids box on various amateur levels; most of them quit after a glove with a little steam behind it is stuck in their faces. By the time the small percentage that persists turns pro, most of those guys know what's at stake far better than their social critics. Of course some of them have deluded themselves badly about their ability, but they'll soon learn the hard way. Even in this, it seems to me, society cannot legislate against self-delusion. These, however, are not generally the sorts of fighters who are severely damaged: It's the fighter with just enough skill and too much heart, like Kim, or even Mancini, who has to be protected from himself.

There is not a fighter I know who does not understand that he is in a life-risking profession and who does not choose it anew each time he steps into a ring. If society owes him anything, it is to protect him from unscrupulous promoters and managers and to ensure the safest possible working conditions. That is not an impossible task, given the will to accomplish it.

Another fundamental misconception about professional boxing is that money alone is the fighter's driving force. That one is fueled by the exaggerated purses a few fighters can command and the rags-to-riches copy they make on the sports page. "Most of the guys I know," says Eddie Davis, a man who fought twice for the light-heavyweight title and banked most of his boxing income, "would still be fighters even if there was no money. I would. When you get in there, in the middle of a fight, other things develop, even if they weren't on your mind when you began, things like glory, the respect of your peers . . . and, well, other things." It's a good thing there is some financial reward for the risk, but overwhelmingly men who have chosen to be and to remain professional fighters would fight, just as Andre Watts would take on Scriabin for nothing, even if no one came to hear him do it.

A ghetto kid who would be a fighter knows perfectly well that he's putting his central nervous system at risk. These kids may not be very well educated but they're not particularly stupid either. The risks become painfully clear after a few tough fights; the pleasures of boxing are less easy to express, but they're present as well. So we come back to the essential issue of choice. Is Ali not to be believed when he says he is happy with his choices, that the rewards have been more than worth the cost? And who, finally, is the best judge of individual choices?

In all the years I've taught Homer's *Iliad* to college students, there has never been a single one who would deny Achilles what mythology tells us was his choice of Fates—a short, heroic life or a long, uneventful one. Achilles chooses flaming brevity over enduring anonymity—that's what makes him Achilles in the first place. It is a choice—and a tragic Fate—better understood by the blood, by the passions, than by the prudent, reasoning mind. Ali is in many important ways the Achilles of his age.

The prudent life, the careful day-to-day experience of commuting to work and making monthly mortgage payments, of saving for yearly vacations and college tuitions, of condo retirement in the sun financed by carefully anticipated and nurtured investments—is such a life intrinsically superior to the life of physical risk just because so many more opt for it? And is even the "safe" life really without its costs? Don't the years of compromise and conformity take their slow, grinding toll too? The suppressed anger, the quiet desperation, the petty hypocrisies, that nagging perception of impotence—aren't these often the surcharges for a lifetime of prudence? There are indeed hidden costs even when the central nervous system takes no deliberate physical blows.

Bonventre's love of boxing, I was not too surprised to learn when our desserts arrived, was also entwined with his love for his old man. "I can't help but think my appreciation of fighting was shaped by something my father did when I was a kid," he explained. "There was this crank who lived in the neighborhood, a guy named Nulty—it's amazing how this has stuck with me after all these years—a big guy. One day our ball went on his lawn. The other kids were all scared, I was too, this guy was a real crank. But we needed the ball so I went up to get it. Nulty had it, and when I kept asking him to give it back to me, he finally pushed me away. I don't know how my father heard about it, probably one of the other kids told him. He went running out of the house over to Nulty's ready to take him apart. My father was a small guy. It didn't matter though—someone had laid a hand on his son, and my father was going to teach Nulty a lesson. He'd have done it too, but a neighbor intervened. He really kept my father from killing Nulty."

Bonventre was, as I always am when recalling my old man bobbing and weaving inside the circle of men on a Brooklyn street, transported back to a critical and proud moment in a boy's education. "My father, you should know," Bonventre explained, "was a surgeon, but that didn't matter. He was a man of honor. Maybe it was his Sicilian roots. Someone had laid a hand on his kid and something inside him just snapped. Who knows? All I know is that I was proud as hell of him that day."

There was a broader, deeper point to the story. "I believe there are certain things in life you ought to respond to that way. Not indiscriminantly, of course, but there are times when our passions ought to be let loose. I've seen women insulted and the guys they're with turn away rather than popping the wise guy one. If it were only the impulse to punch out a bully that was involved, it would be no big deal. But I believe other instincts come from that same core of feelings, things that just well up in us sometimes. Things like generosity, the instinct to give, to help someone out of a jam. That isn't learned; it just springs out. I know lots of people who have the means to be generous but not the impulse. If you have to think carefully about giving or lending your money, you'll probably find reasons not to. I even think our basic goodness is an elemental impulse. If we learn anything in life, unfortunately, it's usually to control that impulse."

There was not only good feeling but great good sense in what Bonventre had said. Blood knowledge tapped not only our savage natures but our best natures as well. And maybe the two couldn't be separated at the core. It was distinctly possible that the denial or rational control of any part of that core of instincts diminished the whole. That helped explain why at the end of a tough match fighters usually embrace and love one another to the same degree that they had tested each other and themselves. Afterward the mind speaks of respect and skillfulness, but at the final bell there is an emotional bond between fighters that defies their own language—they say things like, "Good fight, man" and "Yeah, you, too, man."

For me, an embrace, no matter how brief, was essential at the end of the fight ritual. I hadn't quite known why. I think I do now. First, it is a sign of respect; both fighters are on their feet at the end, and that fact should be acknowledged and appreciated. More important, the embrace indicates that the bond between anger and love—for self as well as for the opponent—is still intact. When Roberto Duran rejected and then mocked Ray Leonard at

the end of their first fight, he refused to allow any tenderness—
if he had any—to be revealed. It was a sign of incredible weakness.
He was obviously incomplete as a human being, a deficiency Leonard exploited masterfully in the rematch.

Bonventre did not for a moment argue that professional boxing could be justified purely on the basis of courage. There had
to be more to life—and to boxing—than "my old man can lick
your old man." What was best about boxing, he thought, was that
even in its elemental ferocity it tapped that basic and profoundly
mysterious core of what, for better or worse, we still are essentially
as a species. If that core was not always "good," it was at least
"true" when it was allowed to be. Whether that justified boxing
or not in light of the inevitability of ring deaths, he couldn't say.
He wanted to think about it for a long while. I did too.

Whatever its benefits, technology creates dependency. That,
in turn, can lead to a sense of individual weakness and frustration.
At the same time, modern technology raises human expectations
to an unrealistic level that it does not and cannot meet for large
numbers of people or for the deepest self of almost anyone. I
notice the dependency and frustration most dramatically while
attending sporting events, especially at football and hockey games.

The players are packaged in helmets, protective equipment,
and uniforms that even from up fairly close render them difficult
to recognize and differentiate as individual human beings. They
are mostly a blur of color and a number. The fans thrill vicariously
at moments of pure violence and rely on a huge screen in the
stadium that brings plays closer, enlarged and slowed down so
they can be further dissected and appreciated. The screen also
shows the fans to themselves much of the time, and as many people
enjoy seeing themselves magnified as they do the live action.

Made reliant on distant and abstract powers greater than individual will, many of us develop a sense of personal helplessness
that enfeebles us physically, psychologically, and morally. In such
a state we are easily put out of touch with our own bodies and
psyches at an enormous, if subtle, personal cost. The fitness craze
may be understood as an effort to counteract those debilitating
forces; body building, an attempt to make men and women at

least appear powerful in the contemporary world. An irony here is that most working featherweights could knock an iron pumper senseless.

Powerlessness also tends to make people mean-spirited, and you see this venom rise in the acceptable rage that seems to come out of thousands of anonymous fans at the so-called civilized sporting events. A great many complex forces contribute to fan violence, verbal and physical, but the lack of control people feel outside the arena is one reason they vent such rage when they blend into the mass inside the arena. These days it is not "conscience" that "does make cowards of us all." It's the lack of it.

If I could not justify boxing deaths or the exploitation of fighters, I could at least see boxing's comparative virtues. In the ring you see two men, unpackaged, damn near naked, in fact. The species itself, unadorned. You see their fists do the damage directly and intentionally; you see their bodies and their heads take the blows, the raw punishment. Primitive, yes; savage, of course; but so direct, so honest, so pure. The balance between mind and body in the "advanced" societies has tipped heavily toward self-justifying mind, and the imbalance diminishes us terribly. Boxing, if it does nothing else, at least restores the blood to its place of importance.

Men who fight are not like other men. Their activity requires a continuous, strenuous dedication unknown in other sports. Because most fighters are in constant touch with that core of deepest emotions, they tend to confront themselves as few athletes—or people, for that matter—ever do. Blood sports simply make demands other athletes could not comprehend. Fortunately, fighters expend so much of their anxiety and frustration in violent activity, even while in training, that they tend to be unusually calm, straightforward men outside the ring. They get their anger out of their systems on the heavy bag and with sparring mates. There are, of course, notable exceptions, but generally the demanding and dangerous nature of what they do as their livelihood makes fighters wise.

Even if the fight racket were completely fumigated tomorrow, damage and death would not stop. Boxing would remain the blood sport. With serious reform, however, there would be fewer deaths and far less serious damage. Most reformers believe in the establishment of a federal boxing commission. Every time there is another ring death, the federal commission idea gets lots of media play, hearings in Congress, and the promise of legislation. Nothing happens.

Boxing operates as it does because its essential structure is feudal and unregulated. Various dukedoms and duchies protected by state lines and overseen by pathetic commissions allow, and in some cases create, its corruption. I have observed a medical exam in Texas that took twenty-five seconds. I've seen the boxing commissioner of Indiana higher than a kite in the dressing room of a boxer about to leave for the ring. I know of a fighter who fought in three states during a two-week period, knocked out each time under a different name.

"What do you expect?" says the pragmatic and cynical Mike Trainer. "How many guys in Congress do you think have ever boxed, or even really care about boxing or boxers? Fighters don't have any real constituency. So those guys have no reason to produce any legislation for them. And if they ever did, what guarantee is there it'll be any good?"

Ever the realist, Trainer nevertheless believes the boxing business has no other choice but to wash itself cleaner. "Four states at the present time are really the mainstays of boxing—New York, New Jersey, Nevada, California. More and more it's in their interests to take the lead, to get together and set the tone for reform to bring the sport into general respectability. That, of course, is precisely what Sugar Ray was doing until . . . but that's water under the bridge."

The major obstacles to cleaning up boxing don't seem at all insurmountable. Fighters would have to be individually and readily identifiable; a national system of identity cards seems feasible given the centralized information systems of government agencies. Rigorous standardized medical exams before matches should be required with ophthalmologist-administered eye tests, mandatory brain scans, and EKGs after a predetermined number of rounds fought and certainly after each fight in which a fighter has been knocked down or given a standing-eight. After a knockout, six weeks enforced inactivity and the most complete neurological tests. With a relatively small percentage of every television purse allocated for protective purposes, not only could medical safeguards be financed, but a disability and retirement fund could be started as well.

Even under the best conditions a human blood sport will take a human toll. That's precisely why the American Medical Association adopted a resolution in 1984 to ban amateur and professional boxing. For decades any serious reform would have been welcomed by the AMA, but it never came and now it was too late. Most Scandinavian countries have already abolished professional boxing, and there is pressure in the British Isles and Canada to do the same. In a few other countries, like France and Germany, it is simply being allowed to atrophy, and boxing is obliging.

In this country, Howard Cosell, who ironically made much of his national reputation by a close identification with boxing stars, now makes the most dramatic antiboxing arguments. It is George Vecsey, however, who makes the best. Vecsey, *The New York Times* sports columnist and an old friend, had begun backing away from boxing in print before Kim died. Kim's death gave him the issue and the will to break completely, also the inspiration to make the most powerful case against the blood sport. I knew his antiboxing articles were good—I never wanted to read them.

When we finally got around to talking about the sensitive subject, George surprised and disarmed me by offering, in anecdotal form, what he believed was the best single argument anyone could make in favor of prizefighting. One night Vecsey found himself sharing a dais with José Torres, the former light-heavyweight champion and present head of the New York State Athletic Commission, which oversees boxing in the state. "I had strong beliefs and had written repeatedly that professional boxing ought to be banned. Torres knew my position, and I thought it might make him uncomfortable if I sat next to him. He was very gracious, though. We talked a while. Finally he said, 'You know, I don't want my kid to become a fighter. I want him to go to medical school. But *I* never had that option. For me growing up, fighting was the only way out.'"

The economic necessity argument has some validity, sure. But I'd always believed that the choice to box was more individual than ethnic, since only the tiniest handful of kids from any specific underclass ever stuck with boxing as a way out and up.

Vecsey admitted he was bothered while talking to Torres. Who was he, after all, to tell kids like the young José Torres they shouldn't be permitted to fight? It troubled him also that the overwhelming majority of people who were actively campaigning against the blood sport were educated and white while the fighters were mostly black and Latino school dropouts. It was not an easy position for a fair-minded person to hold. Finally, Vecsey recalled telling Torres, "I respect a kid's right to try to earn his living in the ring. But the personal risk is so great. I just wish there were some way they didn't have to do it in gyms and arenas. Maybe if, somehow, someone could devise a way to determine on computers who was tougher, who was more skillful . . ."

The understandable human desire to make personal pain and social injustice disappear in some abstract fashion is often the motive behind any decent reformer's impulse, I'd always felt. Until I came to understand it as an impulse that usually deceived the reformer, that more readily became an evasion of life rather than a true engagement, a deception that dismisses the wisdom that pulses through our veins.

The blood still has a human function more profound than the computer and all the other gadgets that distract the modern mind. As does pain and suffering, frailty and forgiveness, loyalty and love. Fortunately. What makes it so hard to be a *mensch* (my old man's word for "human being") these days is that we each must live a double life—part wisely civilized, part noble savage—and know just when to apply each part. The delusion that we improve our human lot by denying the savage is more dangerous than the fear of our savage past reemerging with destructive force. The missile game, after all, is played by coldly "intelligent" men on both sides with batteries of computers at their fingertips.

In the end I chose to stay in love with my own small savagery—and with boxing. Forty years after my old man stung that stiff jab in my face and made my eyes water and my tooth come loose, I can still vividly recall the fury and frustration I felt. I can see clearly my wild swings, his laughter, a few more jabs, my tears, and then my flailing rage. My body has its own memories; it knows important things; it feels loss and an abiding love. You couldn't put those punches in a computer any more than you could quantify your passions.

And believe it or not there are indications that boxing, at least in Vegas, is beginning to clean up its act. The example is a morbid one but nevertheless a positive sign to those of us who wish to keep the distinction between brutality and slaughter. One night last March, Richie Sandoval, the WBA bantamweight champ, was defending his 118-pound title against Gaby Canizales in a prelim on a big closed-circuit card anchored by Hearns–Shuler, Hagler –Mugabi.

In the seventh round Sandoval was downed three times, giving Canizales the title on the three-knockdown rule. The last knockdown blow was a shocking overhand right to the temple; Sandoval's head bounced sharply on the canvas. Referee Carlos Padilla should have stopped the bout after the second knockdown in the seventh because Sandoval was defenseless and had been knocked down also in the first and fifth rounds. He didn't.

After the fifth-round knockdown Sandoval fought back bravely. That's what made me worry. I said to the fellow sitting alongside, "I don't like this. Sandoval could get killed. Literally." He had looked sluggish from the start, having lost too much weight in the two weeks before the fight. As he lay deathly still with only seconds left in the seventh round, I was certain my hateful prediction had come true. Later one ringside physician claimed Sandoval had stopped breathing for over a minute. He was unconscious for at least fifteen minutes. It was a scene I'd seen played out too often.

But the Nevada State Athletic Commission had three doctors at ringside, one, importantly, a neurologist, and an ambulance at easy access. The unconscious fighter was wrapped warmly, placed on a stretcher, and on his way to Valley Hospital without a moment's hesitation. He regained consciousness in the hospital. His critical condition was downgraded the following day. A CAT scan proved negative.

Boxing was no less brutal that night, but it had put a little money in protection, and quality medical care on the spot had saved a fighter's life.

If fighters are willing to risk, I applaud their courage; their choice is beyond my judgment. When a fighter's death could have been prevented, the boxing business stinks all the more and simply has to be restructured. When a death really couldn't have been prevented, it demonstrates how slender is the thread of our mortality, fighter and nonfighter. It demonstrates also the only real choice the Fates offer us: How do you want it—fast or slow?

In spite of the ring deaths and the damage to brain and body—and in some perversely ennobling way, *because* of such high human stakes—I embraced boxing again. Most of us taste human loss prudently in small ways, by incremental degrees over a lifetime. Fighters rush out of their corners to meet their fates with rage, with courage and fear, with the taste of their own blood in their mouths. With the body's wisdom.

Sugar's Secret

If you ask the operator at the New York Hilton for Ray Leonard's room, you'll wait awhile. "Sorry, no one of that name is listed, sir."

"Please check again, Operator. Sugar Ray Leonard."

"Oh, *Sugar* Ray. Is he in the hotel?"

"I believe so."

No wait. "Yes he is. I'll put you through." It's the "Sugar" they remember. The Sugar Ray of the little screen who has become and remains, even in retirement, larger than life.

Ray is in New York to participate in *Sports Illustrated's* "Sportsman of the Year" presentation. This time it's Kareem Abdul-Jabbar; back in '81 it was Sugar Ray. Ray is going to introduce Marvin Hagler, without doubt the most dominant fighter still active. There'll be the usual wisecracks about how much this Leonard–Hagler get-together would be worth if it were taking place at Madison Square Garden, just a few blocks away. The award presentation will be shown on HBO, the cable outfit Sugar Ray does his boxing color commentary for.

Given the crop of fighters around these days and the post-Ali, post-Leonard pall that seems to have fallen on the sport, a boxer as "Sportsman of the Year" figures to be light-years away, if it ever comes around again at all. But, of course, that's what they said after Ali, and *voilà*, the kid from Palmer Park burst on the scene.

Ray's suite at the Hilton is luxurious, far from garish. Like the man he's become, elegant in a casual, American style. Slacks, shirt, sweater are in deepening shades of brown. His long, tapered fingers grip a hand with only moderate pressure. A bottle of champagne sits iced in a bucket on the table. Ray nods toward a sheet of paper alongside. "I'm working on my introduction for Hagler. It's important to say just the right thing. I want to say how maybe he's not the most artistic fighter but he gets the job done, and that's what's really important." The left-handed compliment to the left-handed fighter makes it clear that Sugar Ray is still proudly combative.

The ability of the man to put an interviewer completely at ease, or more probably my first glass of champagne, causes me to forget momentarily my purpose for being there—I want Sugar Ray to tell me what's good about boxing. Instead, we start talking about the young fighters who might possibly emerge from the pack and capture the public's imagination. "This might sound very strange, Sam, but if he could learn to watch his mouth," Ray opines, "this 'Macho' Comacho might be the fighter to do it."

I'm dumbfounded. Maybe Sugar Ray knows something I don't know. Comacho can fight. He's undefeated and seems willing to fight all challengers to his lightweight title. But boxing's savior has to appeal to a broader sporting public than just hard-core boxing fans; for that to happen either charm or class, ideally both, have to flow out of that cathode tube. Comacho can fight, but he cuts a villainous figure. He seems to want to make it as the bad guy.

"Oh, I know he's got a lot to learn, but the talent seems to be there. That's the important thing." A lot to learn is putting it very mildly: In a nationally televised postfight interview after a particularly impressive knockout of a fine challenger, Comacho challenged "any nigger" out there to try to take his title. Later he explained he had used the term only in its "street sense." Sugar

Ray says, "I told him those thirty seconds after the fight probably cost him half a million bucks." So much for "Macho" as savior.

Donald Curry is another story. A superb, proven fighter who unified the diverse titles in the welterweight class with a second-round knockout of previously undefeated Milt McCrory, Curry might fill the bill. At twenty-four, Curry is undefeated and seems to be working himself toward larger opponents—and purses—in the middleweight division. The timetable has him on track for Marvelous Marvin Hagler in early 1987, if Hagler chooses to hang around and is still "getting the job done." But Curry, intelligent and articulate enough, is on the shy side; somewhere along the way pizzazz lessons might be in order.

Fortunately, I remember that I'm there, sipping more of this man's champagne and nibbling on ladyfingers, to get him to discuss two things above all. I want to know how, since he did not come from a truly deprived background, he developed the hunger normally associated with those men who have something in the depth of their souls to prove to the world. And I want the man who beat the system to tell me what's good about a sport in which he's virtually the sole exception to the rule of exploitation. The dark eyes say, *How much time you got?* Ray Charles Leonard takes a deep breath.

"Well, I do believe that boxing is a realistic alternative for a ghetto kid who wants to take it. And believe me, when we lived in Northwest D.C. we were poor. Poor. Even when we moved to Palmer Park, the pocketbook got a little better, but life was still rough—except for the weekends when my father would pile us in the LTD and we'd go down to the shore and eat crabs. Monday to Friday, though, were the pits. But I always knew I could get out. I could sing. I was a terrific gymnast, could do a backward somersault off a second-story roof. And I found boxing, but it was just a means to an end, a way to make people respect who I was. Even when I was a teenager, fighting in the amateurs, boxing enabled me to travel all over the world. Poland. Russia. Imagine that, a poor kid doing those things. I understood concentration camps, dictatorships—the whole world. It gave me an understanding of things in reality that kids who read about them in books don't get."

It wasn't very clear which of my questions Sugar Ray was answering, and it didn't matter. He wasn't losing any steam either. "I remember sitting on my stool after the fifth round, I believe it was, of the Hearns fight. My advisers were talking, telling me what to do, but I didn't really hear them. My left eye was just about closed, and Hearns was giving me a pretty good beating. I just looked across the ring and said to myself, 'This guy's trying to take everything I've fought for all these years. I ain't gonna let anybody do that.' I knew I had to find a way. People think boxing's a barbarian sport. They get that from those *Rocky* movies. But you really don't win fights against good fighters with brute force. You win fights with your mind, by finding the angles that'll let you hit a guy, even a monster like Hearns. And that's the part I love about boxing, the one-on-one, how each guy makes the fight for the other, trying to solve the problem of different styles."

It's all good to hear firsthand, but I realize there's nothing really new in what Sugar Ray is telling me. No scoops. Just the good old economic necessity argument in combination with the blood-thrill of extreme individual risk and skillfulness. Maybe there's nothing new to be said about what men have been doing for millennia.

"So, tell me, Ray, if the sport is so satisfying, why were you retiring all the time?"

"*All the time?* I only retired twice. When I found out about my eye problem. And after my comeback fight against Kevin Howard."

"Are you kidding? I counted five or six times."

"Ha, those others were just speculation. The last one is the one that matters. After that Howard fight, I was really down. I knew I could have gotten sharper and with a few more fights have gotten to a level where I could have fought Hagler. Could have made $12 million for forty-five minutes. Quitting right then, though, was my most satisfying moment in boxing. Because I was finally doing it for myself. I could walk away from it even then, without having to go out on top."

I understood, then, the complex love-hate relationship boxers have with boxing. It becomes a need, a compulsion, the very thing that defines and controls them. Throughout his career, even as an amateur, this young man sensed that confusion; that was why he had always been on the verge of walking away from it. Ray

Charles Leonard's pride refused to let him be mastered by anything, even by the activity that offered him fame and wealth. Ray Leonard would not allow himself to be dominated by the means of self-expression he believed he had chosen, not the one that chose him. The open option to leave proved to him that boxing was indeed a matter of choice. His inclination from the beginning had been to use boxing for his purposes—he sensed also from the beginning that the only alternative was to be used by it.

"It didn't have to be boxing for me. There were other ways to express myself. I chose boxing because I saw I had the talent. When I first lost back in the Olympic Trials of '72, that's when I knew I wanted to prove I was the best. I was gratified and proud to be able to show the world what I was made of. At first, when people saw me in the ring they thought I was a copy, just someone flashy, not authentic. But I knew I was unique. When you saw me in the ring, you really saw three people. You saw me. You saw my mother's grace and her fire. You also saw my father's determination to overcome terrific odds."

I might have known that at least partly, in one way or another, it came back to his old man.

For a while there's been sports-page gossip that Sugar Ray was thinking comeback. The speculation made some sense. Ray has never taken a real pasting: his brain hasn't been scrambled; his eyes have recovered perfectly. He's in excellent gym condition because he spars often with Shawn O'Sullivan, Mike Trainer's white-wish welterweight from Canada. It was those sparring sessions, in fact, that prompted the comeback talk and got Ray to thinking.

Then, in May of 1986, two years after the Kevin Howard debacle, Ray Charles Leonard, true to his pattern of quitting and unquitting just as abruptly, announced to the world that he'd be quite willing to come out of retirement for one fight and one fight only—the long-delayed showdown with Marvin Hagler.

The news was received with shrugs and stifled yawns for the most part. Boxing comeback stories have come to hold about as much excitement as a Liz Taylor wedding announcement, and for pretty much the same reasons: they're usually very cynical affairs. The aging fighter and the aging actress miss the spotlight terribly, and the paydays that go with it. In Ray's case, however, money was not a motivator: he's far more solvent than the federal government.

Although he'd kept himself busy as a boxing analyst on cable and network TV, and was still considered a desirable guest on a talk show, Ray was really yesterday's news on the sports pages. So the prospect of a comeback fight with Hagler was dismissed by most experts as the deluded longings of a diminished star. Once again, true to the pattern of misjudgment and misunderstanding that had dogged his entire career, Ray Leonard's thinking and motives were typically undervalued. Of course he welcomed the ink, his name once again on people's lips, but he had something quite different in mind, something that harked back to an ancient past. It was nothing less than to become godlike, to accomplish a feat no mere human had ever before achieved and thereby attain an historic serving of immortality. Nowadays such naked arrogance is called egomania.

The Greeks knew it as hubris. That mad urge to go beyond limits, to attempt the unthinkable, was the source of downfall for the would-be heroes of Greek drama and myth and was intended as a severe object lesson to the audience. Tempt the fates and pay the price, the moral went, and be assured you've brought it all on yourself with an error in judgment caused by that extremely inflated ego. Sugar Ray knows all this, not through training in the classics but by having learned the hard lessons of personal limits in the prize ring, the toughest school there is.

The other side of this cosmic egotism, however, is the rare chance it offers a daring individual to go beyond all previous limits, to push the envelope back as no others have before. It was precisely such daring even the prudent Greeks couldn't help admiring. Prometheus stole fire from the gods and made us all a little more godlike in the process. Of course, he paid for his indiscretion with torture eternal.

If the fight with Hagler comes off, Ray, who will not be competition-sharp after only one fight in four and a half years, could quite conceivably look bad against Hagler, a Hell of a Fighter seemingly at the peak of his skills and confidence. Fears about Ray's reinjuring his eyes and of facing possible blindness, which will certainly be part of the prefight hype, are unfounded. The retinas have healed completely; Ray is as likely to tear his Achilles tendon as he is the lining of his eyeball. Even his reputation, his place in boxing history, would not be particularly sullied. Worst that could happen for Ray is that boxing gospel, which establishes unequivocally that no fighter can work off ring rust in a gym, will once again prove itself infallible.

But if . . . If Sugar Ray Leonard can somehow manage to be 90 percent of the fighter he was in Duran II or with Thomas Hearns, when and if he steps in with Hagler, fans would be very foolish not to give him a decent chance. Styles make fights, as we've learned if we've been paying attention to Dundee's wisdom and the lessons on the previous pages. In a classic slugfest, Hagler knocked out Hearns in three; Hearns, the same fighter who gave Ray the fight of his life. But a shopworn Roberto Duran took Hagler to a close decision. The only fighters who've made Hagler look un-Marvelous, in fact, have stayed on top of him, cut down on his punching room, and refused to be bulled off. A competent Ray Leonard would be able to master whatever style is called for to neutralize Hagler's brawn. Be reminded also that the old Sugar has always surprised folks with his ability to take a punch.

Age favors Leonard also. It is rare that the comeback fighter is considerably younger than the champion. Ray Charles Leonard was thirty in May 1986. Marvin Hagler is anywhere from three to five years older: his true age is one of boxing's best-kept secrets. In a recent fight against John "The Beast" Mugabi, an untutored slugger, Hagler took substantial punishment and showed some signs of wear. He, and not Leonard, may in fact be the fighter on the brink of ring senility.

Great as he was in his salad days, Sugar Ray Leonard has always been underestimated and undervalued by many boxing critics. So it is not surprising for them to see his challenge to Hagler as nothing more than bravado. There is no way to prove it isn't unless the match is made. If and when it is, fists and minds and hearts —not posturing, not the words or theories of experts—will determine whether or not Narcissus falls head first into the pool and drowns or Prometheus steals the fire.

I, for one, always root for the fire stealers. I love their daring, the recklessness, indeed the arrogance that challenges all limits, all restrictions. Yes, almost always hubris gets slapped down, put in its place, and the conventional I-told-you-so explanations of the chalk-players are handed down as great profundity. Ah, but every once in a great while . . .